The State
of War

The State of War

Essays on the Theory and Practice of International Politics

Stanley Hoffmann

FREDERICK A. PRAEGER, *Publishers*

New York · Washington · London

FREDERICK A. PRAEGER, PUBLISHERS
111 Fourth Avenue, New York 3, N.Y., U.S.A.
77–79 Charlotte Street, London W. 1, England

Published in the United States of America in 1965
by Frederick A. Praeger, Inc., *Publishers*

Library of Congress Catalog Card Number: 65–24942

Printed in the United States of America

TO
RAYMOND ARON

FOREWORD

THE ESSAYS THAT comprise this book were written during the last four years. Many of them have been published, in somewhat different form, elsewhere; some of them were written and published in French. I have thought it useful to translate the latter and to collect them along with the pieces written in English. My reason for submitting these essays to the reader is my stubborn belief in both the relevance of the main themes and their interdependence.

My basic concern, throughout these essays, is to elaborate a certain kind of theoretical approach to international relations. For the reasons summed up in the first chapter, I want this approach to be closely tied first to history and secondly to the teachings and insights of political philosophy.

To move from method to substance; the central conception in these essays is one that Hobbes and Rousseau developed and that the whole record of history suggests. International politics is "a state of war"—a competition of units in the kind of state of nature that knows no restraints other than those which the changing necessities of the game and the shallow conveniences of the players impose. Obviously, there are oases of real peace and periods in which the competition is less fierce, but, as I have tried to suggest in Chapters 2 and 3, the "state of war" is the aspect of international relations that dominates. It is with this aspect alone that the essays collected here are concerned; I have not included my various studies of the two types of attempts to alleviate or overcome the "state of war"—i.e., international organization, or the institutionalized effort to organize restraints, and transnational integration (especially in the European and North Atlantic areas). So far (unfortunately?), we have not made much progress in moving "beyond the nation-state." Thus, it is with the rivalries of nation-states, and with the traditional *ultima ratio* of those rivalries —war—that I am concerned here.

The central concept of the "state of war" stresses the fundamental difference between domestic politics and foreign policy. I am aware of the criticisms hurled by scholars against this distinction, which is a distinction of "ideal-types"; but their objections strike me as based on either (a) marginal cases, in which the distinction breaks down—cases whose existence I would not at all deny but which I continue to see as exceptions to the rule; (b) the fact that in a revolutionary era of world politics, the boundary between the two realms is generally violated—which often contributes to making domestic politics like the ideal-type of international relations, but not at all to turning international relations into the ideal-type of domestic politics; or (c) wishful thinking.

I have also tried to show how such an approach to world politics could help to reintegrate the study of international law into that of international relations and provide the basis for a sociology of international law. International organization and transnational integration are recent phenomena, but international law is the oldest attempt to make the "state of war" less antisocial and to make war itself less necessary, less savage, or less possible. The growing gap between students of international relations and specialists of international law is damaging to both groups.

No problem today is more important for the scholar and the citizen than that of knowing to what extent the invention of nuclear weapons opened a totally new phase in history—of knowing whether the "state of war" was drastically transformed (for better or worse) or whether, on the contrary, the traditional competition persists, although at a higher level of risk and with new rules that allow the players to keep playing despite the change in stakes. Is war still the "continuation of politics by other means"? If it is, does this kind of a continuation make sense, when it may put an end to the "state of war" once and for all? If not, what substitutes for war will the competitors invent, or will the atrophy of war itself lead to a withering away of the "state of war"? Or is the situation more ambiguous, and are only certain kinds of wars obviously senseless? In that case, can and will a firm barrier between them and the others be erected? Needless to say, we have no final answers, but the study of both the unique and familiar features of the present international system, of both the factors of stability and the forces of disruption in our world, is of theoretical and practical importance.

Any student of the restless "state of war" who tries to find patterns in the historical record, who observes both the constraints that weigh upon the competitors and the boundless variety of their initiatives and ambitions, is faced again and again with one problem: how much freedom of action does the actor really have? It would take a full systematic treatise to give, not *an* answer, but an organized and foolproof *set* of answers, for the actor's freedom depends on the international system, on his own position within it, on his perceptions of his own position and of the situation of the others, on the internal political system, etc. The "game" of international politics is not a mere schematic game that can be usefully described in abstract terms as if the players were *x, y, z*; it is a game in which the players are located in time and in space and are neither geographically nor sociologically interchangeable. Two of the essays in this book are attempts to discuss the problem— one in the concrete case of the contemporary United States, and one in more general terms.

I want to thank the following journals and publishers for having permitted the material originally published with them, now considerably revised, to appear here:

Mr. Jean Touchard and the *Revue française de science politique*, in which "Theory and International Relations" first appeared (June, 1961), as well as part of "Terror in Theory and Practice" (under the title "Terreur et terrier," December, 1961).

Mr. Jean Piel and *Critique*, in which "Minerve et Janus" was published in January and February, 1963.

Professor Harvey Mansfield and the *American Political Science Review*, in which "Rousseau on War and Peace" appeared in June, 1963.

Professor Klaus Knorr and the Princeton University Press, for "International Systems and International Law," originally published in *The International System* (Klaus Knorr and Sidney Verba, editors, 1961).

Mr. H. C. L. Merillat and the American Society of International Law, in whose 1963 *Proceedings* "The Study of International Law and the Theory of International Relations" first was published.

Mr. Stephen Graubard and *Dædalus*, where "Restraints and Choices in American Foreign Policy" appeared in the Fall, 1962, issue.

Mr. Jean-Marie Domenach and *Esprit*, where "Roulette in the Cellar" appeared in January, 1965.

Finally, I want to thank three persons who have helped me in my efforts to understand the problems discussed throughout this book: my former teacher Madame Suzanne Bastid, to whom I owe a most tenacious interest in international law and organization; my former teacher and esteemed friend McGeorge Bundy, who first guided me in the labyrinth of American foreign policy; my friend and intellectual mentor Raymond Aron, to whom this book is dedicated and whose imprint on the ideas expressed in it is not difficult to discern.

S. H.

Cambridge, Massachusetts
April, 1965

CONTENTS

The State
of War

THEORY AND INTERNATIONAL RELATIONS

T HE THEORY OF international relations is both very old and very young. It is old in the sense that, with the end of the medieval dream of a Christian Community, political philosophers very soon began to reflect on the "state of nature" in which states found themselves. These philosophers presented on the one hand interpretations of past and present relations among states; the question from which their interpretations flowed was whether these relations were such as to assure a minimum of order and peace (or under which conditions and thanks to which practices this minimum would obtain) or whether, on the contrary, the division of the world into discrete units condemned mankind to virtually permanent war. They looked for the causes of conflicts, as a recent book reminds us,[1] in human nature, in the nature of political or economic regimes, or in the very structure of the international milieu. On the other hand, these philosophers reflected on the future of relations among states either as philosophers of history certain of the direction history would take, or as reformers con-

[1] Kenneth Waltz, *Man, the State and War* (New York, 1959).

vinced that there were institutions, methods, and ideas which could ensure that harmony prevailed among nations and whose triumph it was necessary to insure.

But the theory of international relations is new, if one takes it in the sense of a systematic study of observable phenomena that tries to discover the principal variables, to explain the behavior, and to reveal the characteristic types of relations among national units. Such efforts of empirical theory, as opposed to philosophical theory, really began only after the Second World War. Why did they come so late? Why are they so important?

They came so late for a number of reasons, among them the fact that the study of international relations only recently began to free itself from the disciplines of history and law. For a long time, the systematic analysis of world politics had been smothered by the history of international relations and by the study of the legal norms which attempt to order these relations but which, both insofar as they succeed and insofar as they fail, ought themselves to be included in a properly political study of international relations. Secondly, empirical theory developed in reaction to the ideologies that flourished before the Second World War, when the liberal vision of democratic and reconciled nationalities, the social-ist vision of peoples finally united after the proletarian revolution, and the myth of international order—not to speak of ideologies forged by fascism and national socialism—all coexisted with and competed against each other. These ideologies were based on some of the philosophies I have already mentioned; they were well stocked with predictions and recommendations; they bolstered prejudices, they inspired statesmen, they were instruments for action as well as objects of belief. The reaction against them, when it came, naturally was to debunk them; understandably, it began in countries where ideologies had wreaked most damage in men's minds but where the social sciences were free to carry out their task to disclose and disenchant, and at a time when the differ-ences between favorite utopias and international reality could no longer be reconciled: *i.e.*, in the England of E. H. Carr and the United States of Spykman and Morgenthau. It was also normal that an empirical theory of international relations should have de-veloped most rapidly in the country where the grip of history and law on the social sciences was weakest—that is, where political science had long enjoyed academic autonomy—*i.e.*, in the United States.

As to the scope and significance of the effort, it is easily explained. First, in every discipline, empirical research and theoretical elaboration go hand in hand. Any good empirical study is no mere conglomeration of facts but is the verification of an implicit or explicit hypothesis, or at least it is the answer to a preliminary question and contributes to the construction of a hypothesis. In traditional political science, the relation of research to theory has always been close: thus, Aristotle's study of the political life of his time is mixed with a typology of regimes that is both a theory of forms of government and a theory of the relations between the social structure and the political system; in Tocqueville, we find both a detailed study of the United States and a theory of democracy.

Secondly, in the study of international relations itself, a certain haste in theoretical formulation can be accounted for both by the subject matter and by the country in which these formulations have been attempted. So many disciplines—law and sociology, geography and cybernetics, history and demography—impinge upon the study of international relations that priorities are indispensable; even if one considers political science as a science of synthesis rather than as an autonomous discipline, one must acknowledge that there is a basic difference between synthesis and juxtaposition, science and chaos. Each discipline tries to answer a different series of questions, and these questions and answers are not of the same kind: they differ in subject matter (man as a biological unit, or relations among men or goods, or geographical factors) and in aim (description, or explanation, or philosophy). To achieve synthesis, there must be a common denominator, a currency unit into which one can change the currencies of all the other disciplines. In the study of international relations, this standard is the *theory* of international relations, a body of statements aimed at elucidating phenomena that are studied in political science or in other relevant disciplines. In the United States, the theory of international relations has developed apace partly because the contemporary orientation of *all* political science is theoretical, due to its reaction to earlier "hyperfactualism," and also because of the influence of the physical sciences, sociology, and the new communications sciences.

At present, one can classify the main theoretical attempts as follows:

1. *According to degree of elaboration.* Some "theories" consist only of methodological *questions* for the study of international relations. On a more complex level, we find *hypotheses* meant to guide research. The last stage is that of *laws* that purport to ex-

plain phenomena and that are thus answers to questions or definitive hypotheses.

2. *According to scope.* In each of the preceding three categories, we can distinguish efforts to develop *partial theories* and attempts at a *general theory.* The respective advantages and disadvantages here are the same as in sociology or domestic political science. Some theories of foreign policy, such as those on "decision-making," are partial, elementary theories; theories of strategy are partial, middle-range theories.

3. *According to object.* Here we find on the one hand *empirical theory,* oriented to the study of concrete phenomena, and on the other hand *philosophical theory,* which is oriented to the realization of an ideal, or which judges reality according to certain values, or which provides a description of reality based on *a priori* concepts of the nature of man or of various institutions. A third category is created by the "policy sciences," that is, action-oriented theory, the study of reality not for the pure pleasure of understanding but in order to act on it through power.

Among these empirical theories—whether partial or total; questions, hypotheses, or laws—we can make further distinctions: (a) *according to method*: the contrast here is between the deductive method, which tries to build abstract models from a small number of postulates so as to discover the rules of rational conduct in different situations; and the inductive method, which tries rather to start from concrete reality and to identify its significant features so as to make it intelligible; (b) *according to focus*[2]: certain theories are above all conceptualizations; their aim is to analyze and refine the main concepts used in the effort to understand relations among states. These conceptualizations provide the material for the two other types of theories: schematizations, which try to define the characteristic rules of conduct and the different types of relations from which these rules follow; and those concerned with determining factors, with a systematic analysis of the forces that account for events occurring as they do, for certain types of international relations emerging when they do, or for the actors behaving as they do.

These distinctions apply, of course, to all theory in the social sciences; the problems they pose (Can and should one concentrate first on such-and-such a category? Can and should one combine

---

[2] Here, I am borrowing a very important distinction from Raymond Aron. See *Paix et guerre entre les nations* (Paris, 1962), "Introduction." (To be published in 1966 in New York under the title *Peace and War Among Nations.*)

different types? What is the best method? *Et cetera*) are in particular common to theory in political science. Nevertheless, the theory of international relations is in certain ways deeply original; the general problems of the social sciences are raised in it in special ways and with special sharpness.

II

This is not the place for a history or detailed critique of the principal attempts to formulate a theory of international relations.[3] Briefly stated, *general* theories—or theories that attempt to be general—have appeared in two forms. On the one hand, there is the work of Hans Morgenthau, which is presented as at the same time empirical *and* philosophical, as a conceptualization, a schematization, a study of determining factors, *and* a series of laws. On the other hand, there are the apparently more modest theories, growing out of conceptual frameworks designed to identify the main variables and provide the organizational scheme for research —the theme of "decision-making," the theory of equilibrium, the notions of international systems or of "calculated control." As for *partial* theories, some of the most interesting of them focus on international integration (which owes a great debt to communications theory) and on strategy (based on game theory). These attempts raise, it seems to me, a number of logical problems.

1. Conceptualization is often not rigorous enough. A basic concept is sometimes troublesome because the analysis has not been fully carried out. Thus, the basic concept of power, dear to Morgenthau, suffers from multiple confusions: not only does the author fail to distinguish among different forms of power, but he confuses the quest for power which is the consequence of a human instinct common to all men in all societies, and the quest for power which is directly attributable to the structure of the international milieu. He also confuses power as the object or goal of politics and power as the means used to achieve a whole range of goals (of which power may or may not be one). Similarly, the concept of the international system—a useful concept, now very much in vogue—has not yet been sufficiently worked out, perhaps be-

[3] I take the liberty to refer the reader to the second part of Hoffmann, *Contemporary Theory in International Relations* (New York, 1960), as well as to my article "Vers l'étude systématique des mouvements d'intégration internationale" in *Revue française de science politique* (June, 1958), and to my review of books by John Herz and Morton Kaplan (*Op. cit.*, December, 1959).

cause the author who has carried it furthest, Morton Kaplan, has proceeded deductively without paying too much attention to concrete phenomena. Three issues in particular need to be investigated here: the temporal limits to international systems (the criteria of historical definitions and determinations), spatial limits, and, finally, the exact nature of the relations between the international system and the actors in it; one of the dangers of the concept as it is now formulated is that it makes one believe that the system tyrannically determines the policy of national units within it, thus underestimating the autonomy of nations and the diversity of their actions at any given moment.

At other times, a basic concept is not useful because it is based on an unjustified generalization of an idea that is valid for a limited historical period only: such is the case with the concept of national interest, developed by Hans Morgenthau and Kenneth Thompson. This concept, if it is to be useful at all, presupposes a period of stability in international relations, limited objectives, national regimes that are similar enough to have roughly similar goals, and foreign policies that can be and are free from domestic passions and pressures.

Lastly, a basic concept may be faulty because it was taken from another discipline where it has a precise meaning and put into the framework of international relations where it is hardly more than an evocative metaphor: this is the problem with the concept of equilibrium, whose meaning is uncertain when the phenomena to which it is applied are not measurable and are as disparate as, for instance, military potential, relations between social classes, structures of international organizations, and a state's international commitments. Detailed empirical analysis of the "balance of power" reveals a multiplicity of practices that can hardly be subsumed under this single heading. In the same way, the notion of message, used so much in theories of "decision-making" and integration, suffers from a formalism that makes it difficult to apply to the complexities of international life.

2. A second problem, that of the level of abstraction of the schematizations, is raised by the widespread resort to deductive models. True, any schematization tends toward abstract models; examples from economic theory are often given in order to show how useful they can be. But, as Jean Meynaud has said, there is an essential difference between models that differ from reality only by a few degrees of abstraction and those whose divergence from

reality amounts to a difference in kind.[4] The difference is one only of degree when the model deals with a measurable reality whose elements—goods or services—can be expressed in monetary terms, and with a relatively simple form of behavior expressed in monetary terms—such as maximization of the national product when one focuses on the over-all community, or the maximization of profit if one speaks of individual enterprises.[5] There is a difference in kind when the model attributes questionable objectives to the actors—the maximization of power or maintenance of the system —and above all when it eliminates variables that are extremely important but difficult to measure—the role of institutions, the decisions of political leaders, the ideologies that so often determine the choice of objectives (that is, the hierarchy of values which the gross national product, the nation's power, and its actions within the international system are meant to serve)—in other words, everything that distinguishes political phenomena from other processes of communication, political systems from other systems. The usefulness of a method that requires a reintroduction of essential variables when one wants to pass from the model to reality is very dubious.

This is why the use of deductive models has been important until now in only one area: in the study of strategy, where the analogy between the behavior of nations in conflict and firms in competition may be fruitful. Many writers see game theory as another systematization of strategies that is valuable both for theoretical understanding and for action. But there are two limitations. In the first place, game theory has still not progressed much beyond situations in which the antagonists are completely opposed, in contrast to conflicts where the partners are interdependent in certain ways, which is much closer to reality.[6] Secondly, all of international life can not be studied as a single strategy of conflict: it is made up of a series of competitions, and the stakes are too varied to be reduced to a common measure; cooperation and

---

[4] *Introduction à la science politique* (Paris, 1959), p. 285, *à propos* the model of Anthony Downs. It may also happen that an apparently deductive model merely describes in abstract terms the main features of a concrete situation or system but does not really reach the situation's or system's essence; thus, it is not a real schematization. Mr. Kaplan's first two models are of this kind.

[5] On this point, see the excellent remarks of Charles P. Kindleberger in William T. R. Fox (ed.), *Theoretical Aspects of International Relations* (South Bend, Ind., 1959), chap. 5, pp. 78 ff.

[6] See Thomas C. Schelling's important work *The Strategy of Conflict* (Cambridge, Mass., 1960), in particular, chaps. 1, 3, 4, 9, and 10.

conflict, coordination and bargaining are mixed in many and diverse ways; the prevailing uncertainty requires that the actors make a complex choice of means to attain whatever range of goals they have selected.

3. A third problem concerns the search for determining factors. Some of the theories that attempt to be at the same time schematizations and analyses of determining factors in international affairs stress one special factor. An interesting and little-known theory advanced by Panayis Papaligouras[7] posits an extremely strong tie between the behavior of states toward one another and the degree to which their political structures are similar or different. The international system is homogeneous when they are similar and stable (that is, when all the states comprising it have strong institutions, an effective legal order, and a generally accepted moral code); otherwise, the system is heterogeneous. More recently, George Modelski has emphasized the economic and social order by constructing two models of international systems, agrarian and industrial, which differ in size, composition, from the viewpoint of the division of labor, their stratification, and the methods used in each to assure order.[8] Both these theories tend to attribute to one determining factor consequences that could equally well be due to other factors and effects that can occur only when additional other conditions are present.

Inversely, theories such as those of Kaplan, which try to formulate the logic of national conduct without indicating which correlations are the most significant and which variables the main ones, remain in some way incomplete. This flaw is related to the tendency mentioned above of turning the international system into a kind of closed and rigorously deterministic society that dictates its laws to the states that make it up.

4. Some theoreticians (particularly those concerned with strategy, but also some writing on international law or integration) raise the cardinal issue of the relation between empirical theory and the so-called policy sciences. Research oriented to action requires both an analysis of reality and a definite choice of values. Unfortunately, these values are not always made as explicit as they should be. The theory may be based on the postulate that men should act according to the author's own ideals, or that the foreign policy of the nation for which he writes should adopt as its goal the achievement of these ideals—whether the maximization of

[7] *Théorie de la société internationale* (Geneva, 1941).
[8] See his essay in Klaus Knorr and Sidney Verba, eds., *The International System* (Princeton, N.J., 1961), pp. 118–43.

power according to the criterion of greatest efficiency, or the growing integration of the Atlantic Community.[9] If, on the other hand, the values are made explicit, the orientation of the study raises another problem: were the Author to adopt the Prince's values and goals, he would become a professional apologist and an official propagandist; were he to start by defining his own values but subsequently shift to the study of how they could be achieved by his country's leaders and institutions, he might stumble into an even more dangerous nationalist perversion, trying to prove that the measures taken by the Prince actually do serve those values or that the triumph of those values would serve the national interest.

5. There is also the acute problem of the relation of empirical to philosophical theory. Some writers have denounced in "modern" (i.e., empirical) political theory a perversion of "classical" political theory that replaces comprehension of the essential nature of things with perception of process and of causal laws that allegedly determine man's behavior; the result, according to these critics, is to depreciate the value of prudence and to emphasize a utilitarian approach to research; it encourages a mushrooming of hypotheses that assume man's infinite malleability, a simplified view of power, and the abstraction of man from the polity.[10] Some of these critics would be more convincing if they were less indiscriminate, if they did not virtually condemn the very idea of empirical theory. And their views would be most respectable if they told us how philosophical theory all by itself penetrates to the "essence" of things, and what the order established in and by nature is. Unfortunately, we are only told that we have been "corrupted" so completely by modern theory and modern philosophy that we no longer have any way of finding out!

A second approach, not much more helpful, is provided by Morgenthau. His work does not exclude one theory to the benefit of the other but suffers from a confusion of the two. An *a priori* concept of human nature leads him to find, always and everywhere, forms of behavior whose permanence he states rather than proves. As a result, he confuses the present form of competition among rival units (the contest among nation-states) with a permanence of such competition in history; he considers as the chief techniques for accommodation and international order practices whose effi-

9 See, for instance, Henry Kissinger, *Nuclear Weapons and Foreign Policy* (New York, 1957), and Karl Deutsch *et al.*, *Political Community and the North Atlantic Area* (Princeton, N.J., 1957).

10 See Richard Cox, "The Role of Political Philosophy in the Theory of International Relations," *Social Research* (Autumn, 1962), pp. 261–92.

ciency is neither complete nor everlasting. Any theory based on a belief in eternal truths of human nature brings us back to Bossuet's providential reading of history; it tends to find in concrete investigation only the evidence for those truths which had been smuggled in at the start. Neither philosophy nor science makes headway thereby: science ought not to be the mere demonstration of philosophical presuppositions; philosophy should not be satisfied with the assertions that all human actions are ambiguous and vitiated by original sin and that "moral absolutism" in inter-state relations therefore should be avoided. For, when incompatible values are locked in battle, an invitation to universal tolerance, to pure relativism, or to abstention is of little philosophical or practical help.[11]

However, the kind of empirical theory that tries to cut itself off from political philosophy completely and aims at total objectivity and neutrality is that which falls most readily into the previously mentioned errors—imitating the physical sciences, postulating a closed society, and tending to consider what is as what must be, since the international system it advances is ruled by laws that dictate their values and objectives to the units. Conversely, an insufficient analysis of reality has led a whole series of normative theorists—international jurists who follow Hans Kelsen or Georges Scelle—into the opposite mistake, that of believing that what ought to be already exists.

Thus, the radical divorce between the two kinds of research results in confusions between "is" and "ought" which are as serious as their deliberate mixture.

6. Most theories of international relations rest on an insufficiently developed study of the notion of rational behavior in international affairs. They all try to describe the rules of rational behavior—Hans Morgenthau even states that this is in fact the ultimate aim. But the difficulty is to know what kind of rationality one is talking about. Some theorists (including strategic theorists) simply describe what would be rational conduct if the objectives they postulated were actually those of the nations under discussion —the quest for power, the achievement of the national interest, or the maintenance of the present international system. But do those nations really resemble these models? If they have different goals, or especially if the priorities of those goals have not been coherently and clearly set out, or if the goals are incompatible,

[11] This is Kenneth Thompson's tendency, under the influence of Hans Morgenthau and Reinhold Niebuhr. See *Political Realism and the Crisis of World Politics* (Princeton, N.J., 1960).

the model of rational behavior loses much of its usefulness. This is why Morgenthau's and Kaplan's theories are most appropriate for stable systems with virtually fixed national objectives, when rational conduct consists almost entirely in the choice of the best means. In other periods, the first problem is the choice of goals: in such cases, one is no longer necessarily within the realm of rationality; values matter then, and they are often irrational—or unreasonable. Only if the system determines the goals which states must pursue even in such periods will we have a more or less satisfactory yardstick for judging rational behavior. Decision-making theory, on the other hand, presents a model of a rational decision-maker but without any reference to national goals and without asking whether the model conforms to the real world, in which many leaders often lack the information they need to make a wise choice of rational means after the goals have been set, and where decisions determining both ends and means are made collectively and are not always coherent.

There is another difficulty. The theorist tries to explain the behavior of the actors. But the system he analyzes, the logic of which seems unimpeachable to him, is to a certain extent his own artificial (if heuristic) construct: the actors themselves live in the daily uncertainty of competition; they perceive the rules but dimly; and they have the power to affect, indeed change, the conflicts. The theorist tends to set forth what would be the most rational behavior for the actor given the laws of the system; the actor tries to set his course according to his own goals, which are only partially determined by the system and which also derive from all sorts of domestic forces. What is rational to the theorist may not be rational to the actor, for their frames of reference are not identical. Theorists, thus, at times consider as rational (hence, commendable) moves which presuppose that the nations recognize their common interests in the framework of the system—whereas the nations, involved as they are in international conflict, try to make gains at each other's expense and define their interests in terms of these contests.

These are the main difficulties. What kinds of research, accomplished in what way, could overcome them?

III

The starting point of any valid theory of international relations is the recognition of the radical difference between the domestic and the international milieu. There are circumstances where this difference tends to vanish—in nations whose cohesiveness is so weak that relations among its social or political groups resemble international relations. Also, at certain points in history, the two milieus are interlocked: at the present time, international politics borrows various institutions from domestic politics (parliamentarism, pressure groups, parties, unions); domestic politics is often subordinated to and, in some cases, even determined by international competition. However, a discipline must be based on a kind of ideal-type, a representation of the essence of the phenomena that are studied and of the essential difference between these and other phenomena. This does not exclude a subsequent analysis of instances in which the difference is blurred, but we find such an ideal-type at the starting point of any theory. "Domestic" political science and sociology are based on the model of the integrated society—a Community (a basic, if imprecise, consensus among the members, a fairly elaborate division of labor, and belief in a common good that is more or less broadly and clearly defined) endowed with Power (a monopoly of the legitimate use of force which the state exerts directly on the citizens). The model from which a theory of international relations must start is that of a decentralized milieu divided into separate units. It is not a Community, but at best it is a society with limited and conditional cooperation among its members, whose primary allegiance is to the constituent parts and not to the body formed by their sum total; at worst, it is a battlefield. It has no central Power—hence, resort to violence by each unit is legitimate, and the institutions established among the units have no direct authority over individuals within the units.

Only if one starts from this point can one understand not merely (and obviously) the characteristic processes or institutions of international relations—war and diplomacy—but also the *internationales* of political parties and labor unions, or the legal and institutional efforts to rule out the use of force by nations. For the differences between *internationales* and domestic parties or unions, and the many failures of international juristic efforts, can be explained only if the difference between the two kinds of milieus is kept at the center of one's study.

From this starting point, it follows that:

1. The theory of international relations, since it asks questions common to all political science but in a unique framework, cannot simply transpose into this framework the hypotheses or laws of "domestic" political science. For there is an essential difference

between the science of Power (or of "authority structures") and the science of the absence of Power (or of the multiplicity of powers, which amounts to the same thing). The decline of so-called idealist theories is due to their neglect of this distinction.

2. The theory of international relations—understood as a body of organizing principles allowing one to select from the contributions of the many disciplines dealing with relations among separate units and to use those contributions wisely—is a political rather than economic or sociological theory. Economic or sociological theory could provide the study of international relations with organizing principles only if a well-developed international community existed; at present, economic phenomena among nations and trans-national relations among individuals and social groups of different countries clearly reveal the latter's separation and rivalries. In some sociological theories of industrial society (especially Parsons'), there is little room for the political sector; certainly, political life is not at the center of the theory. While this may be valid for some national societies (certainly not for all), one cannot conceive a theory of international relations that did not place in a central position the political phenomena deriving from the fragmentation of the world into separate units.[12]

Where does one go from there? Three possibilities occur almost at once. The first concerns the very purpose of theoretical research: it is essential that its first objective be understanding rather than action; pure theory must precede applied theory. Of course, the theorist should not lock himself in an ivory tower. The questions he asks in order to elucidate international relations are often provided by current events—indeed, each generation tends to study the events occurring about it in order to find answers to the pressing questions of the day—and the conclusions he reaches will probably, if they are correct, be useful for action. But if action becomes his goal, his research may be entirely distorted. To advise the Prince presupposes adequate empirical knowledge and a discussion of values. "Policy scientists" tend to skip over the latter and to be premature about the former. Moreover, there is a wide gap between the intellectual solution of a problem—i.e., a conclusion that allows us to understand the nature, origins, development, and effects of a problem—and its political solution. Theory tries to rise above events; action must take the events into account. From a

---

12 Hence the flaws of theories that try to find in the economic structure of society the clue to international relations—for instance, the theory of imperialism and the theories of peace through trade or industrialization.

given theory, multiple actions can be deduced; its main usefulness is negative—it shows what cannot be done. To move from empirical theory to action requires the re-introduction of events and values.

A second choice, related to the first, concerns the scope of theory. Should one begin with limited theories or with general theory? The former can be misleading, if they somewhat arbitrarily isolate one sector amidst all the phenomena of world politics and reach erroneous conclusions due to the neglect or distortion of the bonds that link this sector to the rest; policy scientists have not always been careful enough in this respect. Moreover, general theory is never built up from a mere sum total of more limited theories— scientific discovery usually proceeds the other way around—and the accumulation of partial theories raises the same problem of "convertibility" as the accumulation of disciplines. But we do not have any general theory, in the sense of a set of hypotheses covering all the data or in the sense of validated laws—far from it. We ought, then, to begin with a more modest general theory—a framework of concepts and questions dealing with all the phenomena and capable of orienting research by placing partial sectors in the context of the whole. From this point, efforts to produce well worked-out partial theories and efforts to refine the general theory by filling the framework with increasingly precise hypotheses could be made side by side.

A third choice concerns method. There are two schools of thought here, as we know. On one side, we find deductive theorists eager to provide us with a few highly general abstract propositions, from which predictions could be derived. They consider theory meaningful only if it makes prediction possible, and they regard theory's main function to discover regularities. On the other side, there are theorists who are concerned at least as much with differences as with similarities, and who do not believe that in the social sciences the bond between understanding and prediction or prescription is very close.[13] What they try to construct is a theory that distinguishes different categories or types of foreign policies and international relations and shows both the regularities—the rules—within each such category or type and the specific features that distinguish one from another. This kind of theory can, of

---

[13] The difference can be formulated as follows: for the first school, the more we understand, the better we should be able to predict; for the second, the more we understand, the clearer we should be about the limits and uncertainties of prediction.

course, at a high level of abstraction, use deductive models, but only in those areas where the difference between the model and reality is one of degree; in other words, at the level of general theory, these theorists prefer to take history as their point of departure. Of course, the concepts they apply may be both abstract and very general, but the schematizations they aim for and the hypotheses they try to verify will be much nearer reality than models of the first type. I, for one, prefer the second approach; its fruitfulness has been well demonstrated by Raymond Aron.

What can, indeed, be accomplished by this kind of general theory, aimed at understanding rather than action? Three tasks ought to be performed by empirical theory:

To sharpen concepts. It is necessary, not to revise our vocabulary or invent a new one, but to analyze, indeed to dissect, the phenomena covered by terms such as power, interest, system, war, peace, alliance, equilibrium, international law. These efforts should lead to typologies as precise as it is possible to make them. None is needed more than the typology of national aims pursued in international relations: as we have seen, it is the absence of any classification of such aims that falsifies the concepts of power, of interest, and of rational conduct. There could be distinguished, I believe, the goals pursued by units in competition, and the tasks (or functions) accomplished through the process of international relations —the latter either a consequence of national drives to attain certain objectives or independent of such policies (trade and commerce, the diffusion of ideas and political systems, economic development).

To prune and sort out. An enormous number of models and hypotheses have accumulated over the years. Political philosophers and philosophers of history have provided us with models of international relations. Other social scientists have worked out theories that are filled with assumptions about world politics, usually with respect to the influence that a given variable (geography, population, or economic systems) exerts on world politics. The great ideologies that claim to make clear the present and future of inter-state relations and that continue to affect the actions of political leaders are another rich source of materials. A serious theory of international relations must filter out these explanations and predictions, determine the amount of truth in them, explain their flaws, and draw from all this hypotheses about the relations among different variables which can be tested by methodical research.

To study international systems. The idea of systems is probably the most fruitful of all the conceptual frameworks. It makes it possible to separate the theory of international relations from foreign-policy analysis, and yet it allows both to advance. Relations among states are not merely the peaceful or bellicose convergence of separate foreign policies. Important elements of the system—the structure of the world (the nature of the basic units, the distribution of power), supranational or transnational forces—may be neglected if one focuses exclusively on the competing units. Furthermore, the units' policies are themselves conditioned by the system—to what extent is a question to be reassessed with each new case. The comparative study of international systems should also allow one to define the main kinds of typical national behavior and the relative importance of the determining factors, as well as how the influence of each factor on national policy and consequently on the international system combines with the influence of other factors. Finally, the study of systems raises the problem of change from one system to another. Each element of an international system is in constant motion; one must, therefore, distinguish changes within the system from changes of systems. To do so requires a rigorous selection of criteria—that is, of the essential features selected to define each system,[14] a problem analogous to the characterization of types of political regimes in Aristotle or Montesquieu.

The theory of the contemporary international system also remains to be worked out. Here, we find some very original features —a revolutionary transformation in military technology; heterogeneous political regimes and economic systems; a change in the role of the state, which has practically ceased to be a unit of military defense; a dual evolution toward the formation of blocs and toward an increasing fragmentation into independent units; the coexistence of different ages of world politics; the presence of an international organization in which disparities are supposed to fade and the unity of the world is intended to emerge.

IV

These are the most urgent tasks of a general empirical theory of international relations, but there remains the important problem

[14] Richard Rosecrance's *Action and Reaction in World Politics* (Boston, 1963) suffers from the author's neglect of the problems of delimitation between systems. See below, Chapter 4.

of the relations between empirical and philosophical theory. As we have seen, confusion between the two is as bad as their total separation. I would like to emphasize how grave the latter error is for empirical theory. It makes neither neutrality possible nor objectivity certain. As many writers have shown, the choice of concepts, the selection of data, the interpretation of reality are always partly subjective. Reality is susceptible to multiple "readings"; each reading reflects the reader's personality and his more or less explicit philosophy. If total neutrality is beyond reach, the theorist must be saved from the antinomies which tore Max Weber between the universe of science—with its neutrality, its rationality, and its devotion to truth—and the world outside, a battlefield given over to conflicts of the gods, laid waste by prophets and demagogues, a terrain where one must choose between undemonstrable values. Such dichotomies tend to impel the scholar, outside his work, to nihilism, and even to let chaos creep into his research in the social sciences; for understanding, which gives pride of place to some of the correlations research has produced, implies a choice among the possible interpretations of reality; since reality does not entirely dictate this choice, irrationality can insinuate itself.[15] The more generalized the research becomes, the more the choice risks being arbitrary.

The formula I would suggest as a way out of this vicious circle is the permanent and reciprocal warning by each kind of theory against the other. General empirical theory provides a first resort against the risk of arbitrariness, against the tendency to phophecy and political bias within empirical research itself: "The road to objectivity passes through theory,"[16] through the rigorous and systematic examination of the whole, through the construction of a framework in which even very general hypotheses can be submitted to a critical test. Empirical theory has its own laws, which require that biases be restrained and that taboos erected by society be ignored or destroyed. The point is to keep our prejudices from becoming obstacles to the search for truth, but this does not mean the values we believe in should not serve as our guide. The usefulness of philosophical theory for the empirical theorist is precisely that it helps him to make explicit the preferences subsumed in the categories he uses and the relationships he stresses, to reveal to him

---

15 See Raymond Aron's introduction to Max Weber, *Le Savant et le politique* (Paris, 1959).

16 Aron, "Science et conscience de la société," *European Journal of Sociology*, I, No. 1 (1960).

the postulates about the nature of man, of society, of the state, or of relations among states that are deeply rooted in him and that cannot but affect his work. A genuine understanding of philosophical theory will therefore operate as a methodological warning system. Moreover, since political philosophers have been concerned primarily with issues at the heart of international relations—order, peace, the effects of the absence of power—the empirical theorist will find models for study and comparison in their works.

Conversely, the philosophical theorist ought to know and accept the results which empirical theorists reach, for, if there is a chasm between "is" and "ought," the theoretician of "is" nevertheless can suggest to the philosopher what is and is not possible, what follows from our desires, and what actual contradictions are hidden in them. Philosophy that ignores this advice ends up floating in a vacuum or becoming an escape from the political world (*cf.* various philosophies of international law), or its concluding tenets are unacceptable—excessively idealistic, or overly resigned to violence or to the ambiguity of all action—precisely because it oversimplified reality.

Does this mean that the empirical theorist should become a philosopher? If he is capable of it, why not? "The conclusions reached by scientific understanding lead spontaneously to wisdom."[17] Furthermore, the political philosophy of international relations is in such a lamentable state that help is sorely needed. In the past, the great theorists of international law were also philosophers of inter-state relations; today, at the very time that the theory of international relations takes as its basic assumption the difference between domestic affairs and relations among states, prevailing theorists tend to ignore this contrast, either because they belong to the natural-law tradition or because they proclaim the unity of all law and reduce the state to a mere reference point of legal norms. The gap that has thus been opened can be filled only by integrating political philosophy to the issues of world order instead of to the problems of national foreign policies on which it focused under the influence of so-called realism.

Faced with the problem of order in a fragmented world, political philosophy must not ignore the difficulties which the very uniqueness of the international milieu poses and which frustrate the three conditions any political order tries to fulfill: security, satisfaction, and flexibility. The history of international relations

[17] *Ibid.*

is a graveyard of theoretical and practical attempts to establish order despite the psychological, moral, and legal problems that render inoperable so many of the solutions worked out within nations. But the very values that any serious empirical theorist accepts and tries to promote in his work—respect for truth, freedom to investigate and to criticize, belief that mankind's history is not mere sound and fury (a belief without which there can be no social science)—guide him toward a certain kind of philosophy: if the multiplicity of gods and beliefs cannot be denied, yet how can the theorist refuse to embrace those values that make it possible to produce his work and that give it meaning? To opt for theory is to choose in favor of the universal, of reason, and of freedom against "carnivorous idols." Since universal imperatives are always threatened by excessive formalism, it is essential for political philosophy to discover how, within what limits, and at what cost these imperatives can be introduced into the world as it is: such philosophy must therefore both judge and condemn any solution that would restrict human freedom or increase violence in the world, and it must also recognize that whatever ignores the limitations the world imposes on rational action to promote these values works against the very ideal whose victory is sought. Political philosophy must be, therefore, both the quest for an ideal that corresponds to the values which inspire it, and constant awareness of the limitations.

To refer to the limits of action is to evoke Albert Camus—a man concerned with justice, with the dialogue between nations as well as within them, and concerned about limits, precisely because he saw nihilism threatening any artist or any philosopher who neglected either such imperatives or such modesty. Indeed, is the situation of the empirical or philosophical theorist so different from that of the artist which Camus so eloquently described in his essays and in his Nobel Prize speech at Stockholm? The theorist and the artist are both witnesses to man's longing for liberty and for order; both are torn between the need to isolate themselves from other men in order to create and the conviction that their work will contribute to that liberation of others which any effort guided by the "most humble and the most universal truth" will foster; both cannot fail to be aware of their own weaknesses; neither can become the servant of those who make history; nor can they abandon the right to proclaim that the men who make history do not always serve the values to which artistic or scientific research thus understood are dedicated.

MINERVA AND JANUS

P EACE AND WAR AMONG NATIONS, Raymond Aron's great treatise on international relations, is a *discours de la méthode* for the new discipline of international relations, a rigorous and scholarly attempt to apply this method to the whole field, a learned meditation on the past, present, and future (or possible futures) of the "adventure" of man, who has made history consubstantial with war and yet continues to long for peace.

I

The problem of war and peace has been at the very heart of political thought for a long time. The quest for the ideal social order and the search for conditions of peace were twin philosophical concerns, especially for Hobbes, Locke, Rousseau, and Kant. But in the nineteenth and twentieth centuries, a dangerous division occurred. On the one hand, empirical studies and theories proliferated; on the other, traditional political philosophies were replaced by ideologies which, as Aron has shown,[1] purported to solve

[1] Aron, *Dimensions de la conscience historique* (Paris, 1960).

the conflict between "eternal values" and historical relativism by discovering or inventing so-called laws of human development. Aron's essential merit is to have worked out a doctrine of historical sociology and to have drawn its normative implications in the light of his own values without resorting to the method and resources of classical philosophies (starting from an *a priori* concept of human nature and society, reasoning about "the essence of things rather than events"[2]) and yet without stumbling into ideology. In one of his courses at the Sorbonne, Aron notes that the major sociological doctrines of the past entailed an analysis of human action, an interpretation of the present, and a vision of long-range historical development,[3] but that these elements have been dissociated by contemporary writers. As heir to the great sociologists of the past, Aron thinks that such a dissociation is undesirable: why should sociology be reduced to a cacophony of abstract theories and small-scale investigations? His preference for historical sociology, which aspires to global interpretations and general propositions yet begins with the history of society rather than abstract models, explains his own procedure.

Within historical sociology, Aron's preference is for doctrines that abstain from ideology, whose interpretations and propositions are not merely derived from the comparative study of societies but also verified and validated by scientific methods, even at the cost of reducing their scope. Aron's masters are Montesquieu and Weber, not Comte or Marx: science is an endless quest, not a source of dogma. Weber's concept of science excluded value judgments; Aron, who is much closer to Montesquieu in this respect, thinks that Weber's very conception allowed him to make value judgments even while it obliged him to stress their limitations.[4]

Aron's book is an implicit warning against a sociology so abstract that it would no longer understand the historical diversity of human behavior. It is a warning against an empiricism so petty as to forget that a work of science is only interesting when the questions it tries to answer are important. It is a warning against a concept

[2] Jean-Jacques Rousseau, *Fragment sur la guerre,* in C. E. Vaughan, ed., *The Political Writings of J. J. Rousseau* (Cambridge, Eng., 1915).
[3] *Les Grandes Doctrines de sociologie historique,* II (mimeo.; Paris, 1962), pp. 259–60.
[4] See, on this point, *Le Savant et le politique* and "Science et conscience de la société." It is here that Aron is furthest from the concepts he expounded in *Introduction à la philosophie de l'histoire* (Paris, 1938), written before the Second World War.

which, on the grounds that scientific research inevitably leads to suggestions and prescriptions, makes of theory a mere auxiliary of philosophy. And it is a warning against a conception of science which, conversely, purports to keep the scholar from showing to what extent his values could be realized in the light of the propositions worked out by theory. Aron's work brilliantly demonstrates that it is possible not only to avoid all these dangers but also to make a major contribution to scientific knowledge and to political thought —by raising the most crucial of all problems.

Aron's attempt at synthesis can be considered from two other viewpoints. First, it is an impressive discussion of other writers' ideas. One of the attractions of *Peace and War Among Nations* lies in its many close investigations of earlier writings. There are few important theses Aron does not challenge or test. Among the classical writers, there are Hobbes and Locke on the state of nature, Hume on the balance of power, Clausewitz on strategy, Proudhon's book on war and peace, Treitschke's doctrine of power politics, Bergson's philosophy of open and closed societies, various economic theories of war, and, particularly, Lenin's theory of imperialism; among modern writers, there are the contemporary philosophers of history, John Paul Scott and Konrad Lorenz on aggression, the American students of international relations (Hans Morgenthau, Morton Kaplan, George Kennan, and John Herz), the geopoliticians, the theoreticians of nuclear war (Herman Kahn, the game theorists, General Pierre Gallois), the *doctrinaires* of disarmament: all these are discussed, and yet the book is never a mere history of doctrines.

Peace and War Among Nations is also a synthesis of Aron's thought. To borrow terms from his vocabulary, it is at the confluence of three series: one is a prolonged reflection on sociology and on the nature of research in the social sciences, which Aron began in his introduction to the philosophy of history and his book on contemporary German sociology (he returned to it in his introduction to Max Weber, his courses at the Sorbonne, and his essays on history); the second is made up of his articles on methods in the study of international relations as a discipline[5]; the third consists of his writings on the postwar world and war in the atomic age (*On War* and *War and Industrial Society* are the main steps here).

But above all, *Peace and War* provides a new concept of socio-

---

[5] Especially a chapter in a book published by UNESCO, *La Nature des conflits* (Paris, 1957), and two articles in the *Revue française de science politique* (March, 1953; June, 1954).

logical theory. Only if we define this concept will we be able to assess Aron's contribution to science and philosophy.

II

As a scientific discipline, the study of international relations is of recent origin. Most of the attempts to define its limits and work out its theory have been made in the United States.[6] To accomplish these tasks is Aron's fundamental objective as well; whereas historians describe or narrate, he tries "to understand the implicit logic of relations among organized communities."

To grasp the originality of this concept, one must begin with Aron's idea of what the social sciences are. For him, as for Weber and Montesquieu, sociology is the "science of understanding social action." The sociologist must try to distinguish types of action and, in order to comprehend the "intelligible structure of behavior," must make reference to the meaning that the agent gives to his behavior. In this regard Aron differs from Weber: he does not think that sociological understanding is *limited* to the discovery of the subjective meanings of behavior (or to the formulation and clarification of subjective meanings only dimly perceived by the agents); however, what matters here is Aron's rejection of any science that gives to the forms of behavior it studies explanations *contrary* to or *divorced* from the meaning understood by the participants. On this point, his theory differs from practically all American theories of international relations,[7] which start either from general concepts ill adapted to the meaning of foreign-policy behavior or else from deductive models that are not only abstract but dissociated from political reality.

What is action in international relations? One must begin with the characteristic agents and forms of behavior. Aron finds two typical agents, the diplomat and the soldier. From these two, we understand what is special about social action in international affairs and where the limits of the field are, the originality of the discipline and the criteria of its scope. "International relations entail, in essence, the alternatives of war and peace"; the study of international relations concerns "relationships of political units, each of which claims the right to self-help and the right to be sole master of the decision whether to fight or not to fight," relations

---

6 See above, Chapter 1, pp. 4–5.
7 And of a good number of contemporary theorists of international law (Kelsen, Scelle).

among those units, and their birth and death. There is no clear demarcation between conflicts that take place among states and conflicts that take place within them; despite its variability and lack of precision, the distinction nevertheless exists. Therefore, the theory of international relations must be specific. The behavior with which it is concerned Aron calls *diplomatico-strategic behavior*. Aron's restriction of international relations to this one field eliminates two types of theories, which he discusses carefully.

First, diplomatic-strategic action is not to be confused with domestic political action. The study of international relations is a separate chapter within the general science of politics; there are essential differences between domestic politics and foreign policy.[8] Domestic politics has no clear *essence*: it is equivocal, and can be analyzed in terms of either competition, a quest for an ideal order, or peace at any cost (Hobbes), and so on. That is why specialists in comparative politics find it so difficult to agree on a single scheme of analysis (unless it be purely formalistic) and why the search for so-called laws of political development is likely to be disappointing. One cannot reconstruct *the* logic of domestic political behavior. Moreover, the existence of a consensus and of central power within the domestic framework drastically transforms the role of power. If by "power politics" one means politics as the clash of wills and confrontation of commands, then the range of power politics in a fairly coherent polity is quite restricted. For one thing, its scope is narrow. The arena in which wills clash covers only part of the political system—much of a system's political energy is either channeled through legal norms, which originally emerged from a confrontation of commands but which are now endowed with a kind of "de-powered" life of their own, or else concerned with carrying out commands (for instance, in the sphere of administration) but not with determining the outcome of a conflict. And not even the realm in which this conflict of wills prevails can be analyzed in terms of a pure and simple competition of demands and commands. Among parties or pressure groups, for instance, it often occurs merely in the interstices or over the details of implementing a consensus. Secondly, domestic means of power politics are limited: there are always restrictions on the players' options.

8 Even though he insists on the difference in kind between foreign policy and domestic politics, Aron often points to the close links between domestic and international violence. Thus, he rightly sees in the weakness of the social consensus within many nations today one of the chief obstacles to disarmament: now, as in the past, too many governments need armed forces to maintain domestic order.

Non-coercive means usually prevail over coercive ones; among coercive means, the use of force is reserved to one actor alone—the state, or the rulers.

International politics, on the contrary, owes its existence to the division of mankind into groups that feel themselves different from one another and that obey no common power: it therefore operates under the permanent threat of violence. The "Hobbesian situation" must be our starting point. In international relations, there is an *essence* of political behavior, what philosophers have called the "state of war," a competition without any restraints other than those that this state itself ceaselessly creates and destroys. It is therefore possible to reconstruct the logic of foreign-policy actions, to work out a theory of international politics. The range of power politics here is broad enough to explain why "power politics" and "international politics" are often used interchangeably: it is the fragmentation of consensus and power that turns international politics into power politics.

To begin with, the scope of international power politics is potentially total; zones from which not only the confrontation but even the presence of national wills is removed (many of the so-called functional areas, for instance) can always be reclaimed by the competing units. And, wherever the conflict rages, it can be analyzed in terms of a competition of wills. The pace of world affairs, hence the priorities of foreign policy, are set by the "relationship(s) of major tension": there is a prevalence of conflict over consensus, or over cooperation; even in the areas of relative consensus, such as in alliances, there are elements of conflict—i.e., the conflict continues even in situations of relative consensus. Secondly, the means for such conflicts are unlimited: the tone of international affairs is set by coercive means, whether they are used directly or are merely there as a brooding omnipresence behind the non-coercive means that are actually employed. Among the coercive means is numbered the possible resort to war by any of the competing units.

Thus, to say that all politics is power politics is both banal and confusing, since the phrase can be used to describe two fundamentally different kinds of behavior, which would remain different even if the foreign-policy option to resort to war were to become atrophied, as long as the other differences in the range of power politics persisted in the otherwise untransformed international state of nature. It is the essential competitiveness of this state of nature that obliges each contestant to calculate the forces it may have to use or against which it may have to defend itself.

Since it starts from one basic problem—the risk of war—and since it entails the calculation of means (i.e., power) necessarily following from this risk, does not diplomatico-strategic action resemble economic action, and cannot the theory of international relations find inspiration in the theory of economic action? Aron's reply, a most Weberian one, is negative.

Once more, Aron begins with the meaning of the action involved. Economic action is instrumental, economics is a science of means: foreign-policy action is both instrumental and value-oriented, the study of international relations is the science of ends as well as means. To be sure, one could argue that in both cases there is one basic problem and multiple solutions: in economics, there is the problem of scarcity and the many choices for overcoming it; in foreign policy, there is the risk of war and the various means to insure survival. But the resemblance does not go further, for, whatever individual preferences may be, the existence of currency injects both a rigorous instrument for measuring the *means* and the possibility of replacing the chaos of individual preferences with one relatively precise *end*: maximization of monetary satisfactions. As an instrument that is both measurable and indispensable, money makes it possible for economic theory to subsume the ends under the necessary means; it does not have to take the ultimate ends into account and can consider the acquisition of the means that all must use as the first necessary objective. The theoretical *homo oeconomicus* differs from the concrete economic agent only to a degree. Since economic theory is the theory of a competitive action with a relatively clear-cut objective and (due to the interdependence of economic variables) rigorous rules, it is possible to define the rational behavior of an agent. (Aron shows, nevertheless, that this possibility becomes much more dubious if one shifts attention from the individual to the collective interest, if one looks at the interest *of* the community instead of the maximum interest *for* the community, if one reintroduces the time dimension, and if one stops considering the economic system as intangible.)

Diplomatico-strategic action is of a completely different sort. There is no central problem to which everything can be attributed and from which everything can be derived. The risk of war is certainly a basic feature, yet not only is the maximization of power hardly the necessary and universal recipe for overcoming the risk (whereas the maximization of monetary resources is the solution to scarcity), but the avoidance of this risk is not a universal objective. Thus, the multiplicity of the participants' goals is irreducible.

There is also no measuring instrument. First, as Aron shows in considerable detail, power cannot be measured: there is no proportionality between the measurable components of power (material capabilities, instruments of force) and the non-measurable elements (spiritual capabilities, capacity of collective action—i.e., of domestic mobilization and external enforcement). Secondly, power is not the measure of foreign policy: the calculation of forces is necessary, yet it is "neither the first nor the last word of behavior." On the one hand, maximization of power—assuming it could be measured—is a legitimate primary aim only when the actor has *certain* ultimate objectives, not at all when he has other kinds of ultimate objectives such as the preservation of the balance of power, which a quest for maximum power on his part would disrupt. On the other hand, even when his ultimate political goals require this maximization of power, the hazards of international competition may still frustrate him: for instance, the increase of his force may decrease his security and bring about a coalition of other units against him. Thus, since the means—power—are not necessarily appropriate to the end, the means cannot be kept as a yardstick. It is from the ultimate goals that we must start: they can in no way "be deduced from power relations"; on the contrary, the forms and elements of power depend on the historical goals of and relations among the actors.

This critique of theories that use concepts such as power, survival, or the national interest as themes for the study of international relations[9] allows us to establish a crucial fact: diplomatico-strategic action is a competitive action with multiple and ambiguous ends and with unsettled rules; the calculation of power is never easy or sufficient, power and the national interest must be defined in relation to what goes on both within and without the unit, and, finally the characteristic feature of international relations —resort to force—entails incalculable hazards. Diplomatico-strategic behavior is undetermined: hence two important consequences for the sociologist.

1. He cannot define what "rational behavior" for a government is and thus cannot prescribe it. In a final note in which Aron

[9] Aron's main target is Morgenthau's theory as it appears in the first two editions of *Politics Among Nations* (New York, 1948 and 1954). In a chapter written with characteristic irony, Aron shows how close the "crusader of realism" comes to Treitschke's idealism. The labels change, the goods do not. Adding insult to irony, Aron shows that the German idealist was more realistic than the American realist because he was more aware of the differences between domestic politics and foreign policy.

briefly and incisively criticizes the application of game theory to international relations, he shows that international relations are a mixture of game and struggle that allows for no mathematical solution which would tell us what rational behavior ought to be. The game has no clear-cut beginning and no clear-cut end, no finite number of moves, no stakes that can be either measured or ranked; the value of the stakes changes during the game, cannot be separated from the over-all conflict, and can never be known in advance. Game theory cannot be *the* theory of international relations any more than Morgenthau's theory of power. International political action is risk-taking, and it looks more like a series of gambles than a chain of rigorous calculations.[10]

To be sure, foreign-policy decisions are based on an assessment of the relative value of a stake compared with the level of risk entailed by pursuing this stake, but both evaluations are highly subjective and hardly quantifiable. Consequently, the notion of rationality is open to a number of attacks. It is clear only if it concerns the choice of means to ends that are beyond discussion (*Zweckrational* action).

Now, first, evaluation in foreign policy of the means' adequacy is always fraught with the danger of miscalculation, because of the actor's lack of control (insufficient information, incidental or unintended results of an unexpected nature, etc.). Secondly, foreign-policy conduct cannot be evaluated apart from the ends. To judge the "rationality" of ends, one must try to answer a set of extremely difficult questions dealing with both the political and moral components of the choice: are the ends consonant with the means? —a question that gets us into circularity and uncertainty, since a skillful leader can reach the chosen ends even if his initial means are scant. Are they compatible with the system? —a question that all too easily suggests the policy is doomed if they are not, whereas in reality it may be the system that is doomed. Are they ethically rational? —a question to which there may be as many answers as there are moral codes. Thirdly, the ends-means dichotomy itself is open to challenge. If by means one understands (as Arnold Wolfers does) only power—i.e., the fuel for the policy-makers' car—then the category of ends becomes too unwieldy; one would have to distinguish different components of the ends, such as the state's (or leaders') vision, its objectives, its policies; if one includes

---

[10] The Cuban crisis of October, 1962, confirmed Aron's analysis. The Soviet Union's move was not irrational, but the game has shown that the gamble on which this move was based was relatively unreasonable.

within the category of means all the policies (animated by and utilizing power) at the service of basic goals, then the difficulty is that anything can be either end or means. Foreign-policy action, being political action, is a continuum. At any point in time, its rationality is hard to judge, so long as the game is not over.

2. Since the behavior it tries to understand is undetermined, the theory of international relations cannot "reconstitute a closed system," as economic theory does. This does not mean that there can be no theory. One of Morgenthau's mistakes has been to want to retain only the rational elements of inter-state relations in the construction of a theory. Aron, who here again continues Montesquieu and Weber, believes that the "intelligible structure" of behavior can be grasped even if it is not logical behavior in Pareto's sense. Intelligibility and rationality are two different notions; Aron thinks that foreign-policy actions can be more or less reasonable, but reasonable and rational are not synonymous. The definition of what is reasonable entails value judgments in addition to the calculation of forces (necessary because of the competitive nature of foreign-policy behavior, even if it is never precise or sufficient). Hence, a theory of undetermined behavior will never be able to blossom into a global theory, a complete network of general laws that make prediction possible. Aristotle's rule remains essential: one should introduce into each subject matter no greater measure of precision than it can bear. If foreign-policy behavior is risky, any theory that tried to reduce it to a system of laws would be equally risky. Throughout his book, Aron restates what he wrote in an essay on Thucydides—that political action can be based only on probability, for history, in which such action unfolds, is both a field of deep forces about which general propositions (which are not synonymous with global and necessary laws) can be hazarded and a theater of unpredictable events. Whoever has lived through an international crisis—in other words, all of us, be it Sarajevo, the Rhineland crisis of 1936, or the Cuban crisis of 1962—knows one truth instinctively: only after the event do events appear to have been "inevitable," only the benefit of hindsight puts them in that light.

The question this raises is, what kind of theory of international relations remains conceivable?

In any science of social action, according to Aron, one can distinguish four levels of conceptualization. The four parts of his book correspond to those levels:

1. *Theory*, in the narrow sense, tries to define the basic concepts

of the special order with which it deals and to describe this order's typical situations—such as, in the case of international relations, models of systems formed by the units, types of wars and of peace. At this level, the indeterminacy of behavior imposes the sharpest limits on the theorist, for, if his aim is to "bring to light the intelligible texture of a social order," he must beware of falsifying reality by presenting, for instance, diplomatic constellations as if they were closed systems that dictate their laws to component parts.[11]

2. *Sociology* takes as its starting point the schemes and types analyzed by theory and examines the material and sociological determinants that shape them. Thus, physical and social causes must be submitted to empirical—i.e., historical—research, so that scholars become able to work out propositions formulated not as categorical laws but as probabilities, as chances or risks, or as partial relations between sectors of reality—according, once again, to Weber's method, the merits of which were demonstrated earlier by Montesquieu and Tocqueville.

3. *History* tries on the one hand to apply the "rationalizing theory" and the "sociological theory" and on the other hand to describe the unique features of situations and to explain events.

4. *Praxiology*—i.e., normative theory—aims at putting into question the very meaning of the social action under study. It raises the philosophical problems to which theoretical, sociological, and historical analyses lead; it therefore offers advice and prescriptions. In the political realm, the indeterminacy of behavior (because of the plurality of goals and uncertainties of means, and because of the multiplicity of determining factors) acts as a goad to, and a lesson of humility for, both the philosopher and the Prince's adviser: the participant's margin of freedom justifies prescriptive reflection, but the basic uncertainty of action, the impossibility of predicting the future, the intertwining of the factors through which the actor must work his way incite both the thinker and reformer to modesty.

As one can see, each aspect of research depends on the results achieved at the previous level; they are parts of the same undertaking and the same conception. But each one activates different qualities of the mind, requires different forms of reasoning or methods of verification. At every level, the research is inseparable

---

[11] As Aron puts it, "It is possible neither to predict diplomatic events on the basis of the study of a typical system, nor to prescribe a form of behavior to princes on that basis."

from history, but the role of history is not the same in all four cases. At the level of theory in the narrow sense, it is the primary raw material, and the concepts and types defined by theory are drawn from the systematic comparative study of concrete data. At the second level, where hypotheses about material and moral causes are filtered through historical analysis, history is the touchstone. At the third level, it is an object of direct investigation. At the level of philosophy, history is being judged.

III

In *Peace and War Among Nations,* Aron applies this fourfold method in its virtual entirety—the only exception being the limitation of historical material to the global system of the thermonuclear age, i.e., to the present. The monument he has built has two sides, like the temple of Janus. On one side, it is the greatest effort ever made by one man alone to embrace the whole discipline of international relations; on the other, the most extensive knowledge serves to prove the limits of knowledge. Since Montesquieu and Weber (always these two), there had been no such attempt to analyze the "conditions of historical choices" in all their diversity, without giving up systematization thereby; but, since Montaigne and Descartes, doubt had not been built up to such an extent as the method and conclusion. We must, therefore, expect all those who ask from theory in the social sciences (especially political science) more than it can honestly give to denounce the monument as a mirage, to say that its analyses are juxtaposed but do not add up, to complain that Aron's arguments destroy but do not replace, and to lament that the inexhaustible subtleties of his critical powers have only accumulated distinctions that preclude any general proposition and question-marks that dispel any certainty. But whoever considers Aron's conception of the social sciences as the only valid one will admit that his anti-theory is the most thorough and systematic of all legitimate theories. It is not a synthesis centered on a major demonstration or flowing from major hypotheses—neither the subject matter nor the method lend themselves to such treatment; it is a mosaic construction of partial analyses often filled with doubt and negation. But I say mosaic and not motley, for there is a unity provided by Aron's very conception of his purpose: to understand in *all* its aspects the logic of *one* specific form of behavior; the work is therefore much more coherent than Montesquieu's. Aron's originality as a sociologist lies both in this over-all conception and in the piecemeal conclusions; it is an originality of combination rather than of invention or of general conclusions.

Every one of the problems Aron raises can be analyzed *more in detail*: after all, this scientific *summa* is barely eight hundred pages long, which is rather short if one thinks of all it includes. But on practically none of these problems can one go any *further in depth* without being misled by one's neglect of indeterminacy. A gigantic literature about power, the causes of war (especially economic causes), international law and organizations says little more than a few dozen pages in *Peace and War*. The union of historical knowledge and understanding of diplomatico-strategic behavior allows Aron to go to the heart of the matter.

It is not possible here to analyze Aron's work in detail. Leaving temporarily aside the philosophy that emerges from the first three parts of the book and that is spelled out in the fourth, it will be enough to point out a few features.

First, the reader who might otherwise flounder in the midst of this or that argument ought not to lose sight of the book's over-all design. Even in the social sciences, there is no great work that is not in some way a work of art. Not only is there nothing artificial about the book's division into four parts of six chapters each, but the composition of the whole and of each part reveals how inseparable method and substance are. The risk of war, the distinctive characteristic of international relations, provides the starting point for the book; that the risk persists is Aron's conclusion in his final note. In the first two parts, Aron asks, in a variety of ways, what has war been in history? The first chapter, in accordance with the method which requires that one start with the meaning of the activity under study, opens with quotations from Clausewitz about the phenomenon that makes this particular activity unique—war; from this beginning, Aron demonstrates the unity of foreign policy, of which war is one of the expressions; at the end of his journey through history, in the last chapter of the second part, he tries to discover the "roots of the institution of war." In the second half of the book, again in a variety of ways, Aron asks whether war is still a reasonable expression of foreign policy, and discusses the conditions under which the institution of war could be overcome.

In *Peace and War*, Aron undertakes two tasks the accomplishment of which are obviously essential to any progress in the discipline of international relations. On the one hand, a much more advanced *conceptualization* is needed than the one that has been at our disposal. Every one of the concepts used by historians, lawyers, or sociologists must be refined, subdivided, and broken down so as to account for the many different realities that are all too often lumped together. In this respect, *Peace and War* is a triumph of the art of meaningful distinctions. Here are the main ones: distinctions among types of strategy (to win *vs.* not to lose); the distinction between force and power; analysis of the ingredients of power (milieu, resources, collective action); distinctions among the different ways of using power (in peace or in war); scrutiny of national goals and of the historical factors that account for changes in goals; analysis of the many meanings of the concepts "offense" and "defense" (in the initiation of war, in the consequences of victory, in the strategy followed during the conflict); study of the criteria of membership in a system; the distinction between homogeneous and heterogeneous systems and between bi-polar and multi-polar systems; typologies of war and peace (with reference to types of political units, to stakes, to kinds of weapons); distinctions among the roles played by geography in international politics (space as milieu, arena of conflict, or stake); distinctions among the roles played by resources or among the situations described in the single, confusing term "overpopulation"; distinctions among the social orders that are often but not necessarily included in a nation (political order, military order, cultural order); study of the elements of a military or economic regime; discussion of the meanings of the word "nature"; discussion of the sociological types of wars and of forms of pacifism.

In Aron's analysis of the contemporary system, his main conceptual distinctions concern the following: the system and its subsystems; the various asymmetries of the two blocs (in relations between the super-power and "its" lesser powers, in economic and political regimes, in techniques of influence, in geography, ideology, and objectives); types of neutralities, conceivable types of nuclear war, and three models of deterrence with drastically different political effects (the model of the "two gangsters," the model in which crime and punishment are even, the intermediate model in which crime and punishment are not proportionate). By contrast with the purely abstract classifications that are so frequent in contemporary American sociology and so hard to apply to concrete situations, all of Aron's distinctions help one to understand reality better, either because they lead to a more rigorous causal analysis or because they give one a better grasp of the logic of behavior.

The second task to which Aron addressed himself was to clear

up and sort out the types and models provided by previous philosophers, theorists, and sociologists. Aron has done this by putting
under investigation all the writers listed earlier, subjecting them to
two tests: (1) Are their postulates, their schemes, their propositions in accordance with the logic of foreign-policy behavior? (2)
Are they validated by a study of history? In the frequent case
where the answers are negative or when one finds not merely a mistake or a distortion of reality but a genuine mythology, Aron has
also examined the historical circumstances that explain the genesis
or success of such myths.[12] The test of the logic of foreign-policy
action confounds not only Morgenthau's theory of power and the
national interest but also Morton Kaplan's elaboration of the rules
of multi-polar systems,[13] Kelsen's theory of international law, and
all theories of peace through law. The test of empirical research is
fatal to Bouthoul's doctrine of "demographic relaxation,"[14] *Lebens-
raum* geopolitics, Lenin's theory of imperialism, Comte's proph-
ecy of industrial peace, the theories that make of the nation the
cause of wars, Toynbee's and Spengler's philosophies of history,
and John Herz's thesis about the decline of the nation-state.[15] The
requirement that the two tests be passed eliminates both the
theory of the single origin of war and the hopes of those who
believe that peace will be automatically insured either by disarmament or by terror; it also damages the enthusiasm shown by champions of European supranational integration and by apostles of
"clandestine federalism," who forget all too easily the tough and
resilient autonomy of politics.

Do these sweeping dismissals mean that Aron's work is purely
destructive? This is not the case, for he tries, in the three chapters
devoted to concepts in international affairs, to demonstrate the
true relation between goals and means; in the three chapters devoted to systems, he tries to define the decisive determinants
(distribution of power, homogeneity or heterogeneity of ideas or
political systems) as well as the types of characteristic foreign-
policy action. In his analysis of material causes (Part 2 of the

---

[12] This historical explanation of myths, in which Aron unleashes the full
force of his irony, is particularly devastating when he analyzes Lenin's theory
of imperialism ("the imperialism of the late nineteenth century was not the
last phase of capitalism but the last phase of an imperialism that was thou-
sands of years old") and theories of international law.

[13] Morton Kaplan, *System and Process in International Politics* (New York,
1957).

[14] Gaston Bouthoul, *Les Guerres* (Paris, 1951).

[15] John Herz, *International Politics in the Atomic Age* (New York, 1959).

book), he tries to show to what extent, when, and through what intermediary factors geography, demography, and economics influence foreign policy. In his study of social factors, he tries to indicate what is valid in the theories stressing the influence of political systems, national character, military organization, or the biological and social roots of violence. In his analysis of the present international system (Part 3), he demonstrates with considerable subtlety the complexity of deterrence. In his analysis of the relations among super-powers, their respective allies, and other nations, and of the forces making for hostility and solidarity between the two "enemy brothers" of East and West, he intertwines diplomacy and strategy more skillfully than any other analyst of contemporary international relations.

The main conclusion reached in almost all those demonstrations, however, is *uncertainty.* The answer to the questions raised either is negative or else it is a question-mark. In the details of Aron's study, one finds again the two kinds of uncertainties that stem from the very nature of the social activity under investigation. Some reveal merely various aspects of the indeterminacy of diplomatico-strategic behavior—this is the case with uncertainties in measuring power (in earlier as well as today's attempts to calculate deterrence), with uncertainties of national interest and survival, and with uncertainties in the quest for security (yesterday, through the balance of power, as well as today, through mutual deterrence). It is also the case with the main uncertainties of the atomic age: those of "the double commitment" to vital stakes such as Berlin, which makes the outbreak of a crisis less likely and the risk of escalation, if the crisis does break, more serious; or the related uncertainties of deterrence when thermonuclear forces become more and more invulnerable. It makes less and less sense for the super-powers to threaten nuclear war in order to deter each other from provocation, but to discard an increasingly "irrational" strategy may multiply the possibilities of non-nuclear war, thus raising the problem of escalation and inciting lesser powers to try to protect themselves through their own means. For those lesser powers, the many military weaknesses of the theory of graduated deterrence, which Aron so often underlines, are nevertheless not sufficient to deprive it of all political charm. Security is not their only goal.

Other uncertainties in Aron's analysis derive from the nature of causality in social action. Thus, it is "sociological" rather than "logical" indeterminacy that characterizes the influence of the geographic milieu; of military and economic systems ("none makes

war inevitable, none removes all opportunities for war"); of national character; or of a surplus of men ("I do not mean to say
that wars would disappear if one could eliminate the surplus of
men nor do I mean that wars have been determined by the number
of idle men"). Sociological indeterminacy also marks the relation
between moral and material factors. Similarly, the discussion of
qualitative or quantitative hypotheses about the bellicosity of civilizations or historic periods ends in failure: "historical comparisons
lead to one's understanding events that will never occur again."

Uncertainty thus springs from the diversity of determining
factors and from the risky nature of foreign policy. But even
though the sociologist finds uncertainty at the end of every road,
his mission is to discover the limits and the causes of this uncertainty, which are always in flux. Although it is impossible to define
the rules of a system or to generalize about any one determining
factor for all times and all places, it is necessary to state to what
extent and how a given system limits an actor's freedom of choice:
indeterminacy prevails in essence, but with varying attributes.
Similarly, it is possible to analyze how the impact of a given cause
changes over time and space. Aron, following Weber, recognizes
that the social sciences are constantly and legitimately renewed "by
reference to the questions we ask," which do indeed change with
almost every generation. It is not surprising that the question
dominating *Peace and War* is: how far do the conclusions reached
by past theory and sociology remain valid in the present? In other
words, to what extent do the *specific features of the contemporary
system* invalidate past theory and sociology?

In the first part of the book, Aron studies the three original
aspects of today's "war-like peace"—deterrence, persuasion, subversion—and the "dialectic of antagonism" that results from the
use both super-powers make, more or less symmetrically, of those
techniques. The sociological part of the book contains an analysis
of "space in the scientific age" (when the importance of the land-
sea dichotomy is replaced by "the law of air and fire") as well as a
discriminating study of the relation between population and resources in the new countries and in the Western nations. In Part
3, where Aron examines the present international system, he refers
to three new data: the extension of the diplomatic field to the
whole world, which accounts, in part, for the end of sanctuaries;
the disappearance of economic interest in domination—i.e., the
divorce between conquest and gain; and the advent of thermonuclear weapons in a bi-polar world, which reverses the ordinary

hierarchy between the strong and the weak and drastically separates the balance of deterrence from the ratio of over-all forces (the former is decisive; thus, to acquire allies in order to restore a deteriorating balance is no longer useful). Another consequence of the last factor is a new aspect of the age-old policy of deterrence: at present, carrying out the threat of nuclear war would be disastrous; thus, the threat becomes "the less convincing as its execution is more clearly contrary to the interests of those who make it"; it is precisely the effort *not* to carry out the threat that transforms the diplomatic game. But when we come to evaluate the real impact of those changes, we are dealing with both history and praxiology. Insofar as the latter challenges the very meaning of diplomatico-strategic action, it cannot be divorced from the scientific study of an age that raises the question, is not the traditional meaning of behavior made obsolete by new phenomena?

IV

The normative section of *Peace and War* is not mixed into the empirical theorizing—if it were, we would fall back into mythology or ideology—but it does depend on the empirical analysis; the two are separate but complementary. Faithful to Weber, here as elsewhere, Aron knows that social science can neither predict the future nor tell the Prince what to do. While he is eager to overcome Weber's relativism by taking a stand, Aron insists that the moral judgments he wants to make are grounded in reality: the philosopher must take social science into account—in order to find out what is impossible, or in order to discover the narrow limits within which his ideals have a chance of being realized, or in order to assess the uncertain or damaging social consequences of choices that would be blameless in the realm of values alone.

Theory and sociology teach the philosopher that war has always been an essential, inseparable part of the history of mankind. Action in international affairs has always implied war; both the study of historical events and the scrutiny of subjective meanings reveal this:

> Statesmen, citizens, and philosophers have always recognized that there is a *difference in kind* between the domestic order of states and order among states. . . . It is as impossible to reconstruct a history in which men would not have killed each other as it is to imagine literature if men and women had come together out of chance desire only and had not known love.

Aron explains this permanence of violence in a key chapter on the roots of the institution of war. Socialization multiplies the opportunities for conflicts—particularly modern, i.e., competitive, socialization. In domestic affairs, forces that derive either from the consensus or from the existence of a central power generally but not always prevent conflicts from erupting into political violence. These forces are missing on the world scene, however: hence war —especially since it is always the domestic political order, whatever it may be, with which individuals identify. It is through wars (civil and imperial) that the great historical transformations have taken place; it is through general wars that international systems have been enlarged.

"Inseparable from man's historical destiny," war cannot, however, be called inevitable. What seems to go against the nature of societies is the end of conflict altogether; but "it is not proven that conflicts must *perforce develop* into the institution of war": the only conclusive evidence for this would be a demonstration of a human instinct of aggressiveness, which biologists either deny or describe as eminently flexible, adaptable, and capable of sublimation.[16] War has been a constant expression of human pugnaciousness, but not a necessary one. In other words, the impossibility of peace is not demonstrated. Aron's sociological analysis confirms Kant's reasoning.

Is one allowed, therefore, to believe that the terrifying originality of the contemporary international system will put a favorable end to war-like history? Aron's deliberately neutral analysis (in Part 3 of *Peace and War*)—a remarkable example of how even a morally committed theorist can reach, if not the total neutrality about which some writers continue to dream, at least objectivity, by rigorously refraining from confusing preferences and possibilities— leads to a conclusion that is just as ambiguous and therefore just as disquieting as the conclusions of the first two parts. Yesterday, war was not necessary, but it was constant. Today, war is not inevitable, but it remains possible. To be sure, a game with the inherent danger that the players may be destroyed strikes one as unreasonable, but the players are prisoners, and an intelligent analysis of the present system shows that in spite of new weapons, war remains in *certain* circumstances a *reasonable* instrument. The international system today is extraordinarily heterogeneous in

---

[16] Konrad Lorenz, in his book *Das Sogennante Böse* (Munich, 1963), argues along these lines. His argument, which takes off from his biological studies, is remarkably close to Freud's.

many respects; the hostility of "enemy brothers" is both a situational antagonism and an ideological conflict.

Moreover, none of the forces that might theoretically be capable of preventing the conflict from erupting into violence is really decisive. The United Nations is not decisive, for it is an epiphenomenon with a limited role and no general will. The "Third World" of the underdeveloped countries is not decisive, for it is incapable of acting collectively or as an umpire. Not even thermonuclear deterrence is decisive, because of the very uncertainties of the "delicate balance of terror." The "potentially immeasurable cost of the highly unlikely event," which is the essence of thermonuclear deterrence, has led the super-powers to act so as to avoid the unbearable choice between massive attack or retaliation and inaction. They have increased the size and weight of their military panoplies; the possibility of limited wars in which new weapons will not necessarily be used has therefore also increased. Furthermore, the game is more historical and psychological than ever: the boundless consequences of resort to thermonuclear weapons—either deliberately, by escalation, by misunderstanding, or by accident—have made this game even less quantifiable than it was in the past and ever more like a pure test of wills. Aron's pessimism here confirms in politico-military analysis Herman Kahn's celebrated conclusions.[17]

Nevertheless, Aron notices a tendency, not to peace, but to the limitation of the volume of violence. The great powers' armament policies have moved in the direction of more diversification (although this has produced a somewhat opposite effect upon the states that rank just behind the super-powers—hence an additional uncertainty). Moreover, there has been a "tendency toward a decreasing resort to organized force, to regular armies." In various circumstances, the two super-powers have shown a common will to restraint—sometimes at the expense of their own respective allies: America's reluctance to resort to force and the caution that moderates the Soviet Union's offensive strategy have contributed to this limitation. Aron's analysis is entirely confirmed by the Cuban crisis of October, 1962: "The immoderation of technology brings war back to its essence—the test of wills—either through the substitution of threats for acts or because the mutual impotence of the super-powers makes direct conflicts impossible."

Unfortunately, as long as the three main causes of the cold war

[17] See Kahn's *On Thermonuclear War* (Princeton, 1960), *Thinking About the Unthinkable* (New York, 1962), and *On Escalation* (New York, 1965).

persist—the division of Europe, the fate of the Third World, and the arms race—the chances of subversive wars and the risk of wars pure and simple will also persist. From the viewpoint of the logic of action, from the viewpoint of sociological analysis, war still has meaning. Peace is humanly possible, but it is not guaranteed by the international system. It is between these limits that praxiology must struggle.

The steps Aron takes in the last part of his book must be carefully traced; he discusses praxiological problems that spring from the very essence of international relations. Diplomatic-strategic action is both social and asocial: asocial insofar as it involves the use of force; social insofar as the actors calculate their mutual reactions, try to convince each other as much as fight each other, and try to justify themselves when they fight. Whoever "lives" international politics is torn between his longing for peace and his solidarity with the unit to which he belongs. (Aron defends this solidarity with special eloquence, as he once again rejects any sociology or philosophy that would clash with the meaning men give to their lives: "How could the individual be obligated toward the whole of mankind without being obligated toward the nation that makes him what he is?") It is this ambiguity of action, this heartrending dilemma (so deeply felt by Rousseau) that raises the two problems Aron calls Machiavellian and Kantian: the problem of legitimate means, and the problem of universal peace. Aron discusses them in the following terms: what are the values I would like to promote? What are the forms and opportunities that I see for them in the modern world?

Previously, Aron had defined atheistic humanism as that which "accepts the limits of human existence."[18] The values he cherishes are those both of a *modest* liberal and of a *consistent* sociologist. Throughout *Peace and War*, as in his other works, we find an ideal of *moderation*, which explains and is made explicit by the quotation from Montesquieu on the title page: "International law is naturally based on this principle: that the various nations must, in peace, do to each other as much good, and in war as little harm, as possible, without harming their true interests." What Montesquieu called "relations of equity prior to positive law"—relations of justice and reciprocity, a conception of freedom in which the sense of legality and the rejection of arbitrariness are dominant—obviously hold pride of place in Aron's philosophy. The values of science—respect for truth, dedication to the universal—require him

[18] *Polémiques* (Paris, 1955), p. 195.

to reject ideology, even liberal ideology, inasmuch as any ideology distorts the truth and tends to fanaticism or opportunism. At the same time, these values provide him with a criterion according to which he can discriminate among political systems. The first section of Chapter 23, which shows that the values of the West deserve being defended despite all Western imperfections, is an exemplary demonstration. Aron's analysis develops "by reference to the values that *both* camps proclaim as their own": the sociological analysis itself shows that under the test of the values allegedly common to both camps, the two blocs appear to "differ as much as negative differs from positive." Consequently, those who claim these values as their own cannot use the argument that the two camps share a so-called community of values in order to justify a refusal to choose between them. The rejection of Communism is a rejection of "the imposed lie." The intellectual who calls himself "faithful to the essential values" but selects the Soviet camp Aron deems to "suffer from a perversion of the moral sense."

The sociologist, even if he considers that all values are not equivalent, also knows that "relativism is the true experience of political man." This imposes a double duty: on the one hand, he must not judge events "in the future perfect tense," not draw his values from the "meaning of history," not justify a present regime or policy by putting himself "in the place of those who will judge as history the events we now live through." Those who absolve today's totalitarianism by invoking its future "thaw," look for "an alibi for cowardice or abstention"; the sociologist who makes such a mistake has unconsciously abandoned respect for the meaning of human action, for a mythology, or for a philosophy of history. On the other hand, the philosopher-sociologist must not exchange moral "historicism" for moral absolutism. If his ethics are those of pure conviction (to go back, along with Aron, to Weber's distinction), then the only judgment he can pass on political activity is condemnation. If the statesman and the citizen are to be judged with due respect for the meaning they give to their acts (respect not being synonymous with approval), the ethics of responsibility imposes itself. "To sum up, ethical judgments of diplomatico-strategic action are inseparable from historical judgments of the actor's goals and the consequences of their success or failure." Aron's position is a subtle one: he rejects the philosophical relativism that treats all value judgments as equally undemonstrable and all value conflicts as inexpiable, the kind of nihilism that consists of "imagining that one has already reached the end of the story," and the absolutism of an ethics of conviction.

What, then, is left? —The duty to fight for the "essential values," but with no illusion as to the possibility of achieving them in full or forever. The degree to which they can be achieved varies according to the field of social action. Even if the values one supports are universal, moral conduct must yield, so to speak, to the special circumstances of each field of behavior. In the case of international relations, given what their essence is and their pathos, the position of the philosopher is especially uncomfortable: the antinomies of action threaten to nail him to the very dilemma he wishes to overcome. For, as Aron shows in a chapter devoted to realism and idealism, the requirements of "modest thinking," to use Camus' expression, condemn the ethics of international action to equivocation as long as international society is equivocal. The moralist can choose neither the ethics of combat, which are always on the verge of "degenerating into the ethics of gangsterism," nor the ethics of law. The latter tends, in its abstract version, to overlook the actors' need to calculate their forces and the competitive nature of foreign-policy action.[19] In its concrete version—international law—it ignores the fundamental weakness of a body of rules that shares all the uncertainties of the international state of nature.

Thus, only the ethics of wisdom is left, and it is an ethics of compromise. For Aron, this raises two questions: what can such an ethics *be?* What can it *accomplish* in the thermonuclear age?

One must start with the world as it is. Does the ethics of wisdom still have any meaning in a world in which war, which is still possible, may destroy everything? Traditionally, wisdom was synonymous with caution; it meant giving oneself concrete goals and limiting the volume of violence.[20] Aron examines the possibilities and limitations of caution in the present system. Using his distinctions between types of possible wars, he concludes that not every thermonuclear war would be tantamount to genetic destruction; therefore, the search for a limitation of violence remains possible: the interest of the Machiavellian and the interest of the Kantian coincide. The moral problem of war has not been transformed:

[19] The state that wants to play the angel all alone will play the beast or will be food for beasts.

[20] Aron remarks that caution does not necessarily mean concessions, negotiation, unconcern for the political regime. It depends on the system; such techniques can be highly incautious in a heterogeneous system (Anglo-French diplomacy in the 1930's).

"the originality of thermonuclear weapons is qualitative only because of a quantitative change. If one could eliminate the impact of this quantitative change through an appropriate strategy, the originality of the moral problem would disappear."[21] Therefore, the "unilateralist" arguments of those who hope that the West will give up their new weapons, so as to eliminate the risk of total war even at the cost of a triumph of the other camp, either come out of an ethics of conviction, or else—if they are held by people who profess an ethics of responsibility—they are due to stupidity.

Aron, who thus destroys *en passant* the confusions for which Lord Russell and Sir Charles Snow are responsible, examines next the ways and means of a policy of limiting violence. He dismisses "peace through fear," disarmament, and negotiated arms control— the latter with extraordinarily skillful arguments in which he demonstrates to the highest degree the art of distinguishing hope from reality: the hope is for the very limitation of violence that theorists of arms control seek; the reality is a heterogeneous and asymmetrical system in which the dynamic logic of antagonism rules out explicit agreements between the super-powers, even in the area of their common interest in preventing total war, except over matters of very little significance. And yet this common interest exists: the narrow way through which it (together with the imperative of moderation) can pass is that of tacit bargaining, represented by an arms policy that each camp may adopt *for itself* to keep an eventual war from inevitable escalation.[22] Insofar as the risk of war persists, a policy that relies on the threat of destruction alone to avert war subjects the states to complete and absurd annihilation if it fails. The threat's increasing lack of credibility ought to incite states to provide themselves with the means to give up such a policy altogether. Of course, the risk of limited war increases by the same token, but limitation of the volume of violence has never been proportionate to infrequency of wars. Today, the attempt to limit war could thus lead to the apparent paradox of higher military budgets and diversified arsenals of available weapons. Wisdom suggests not that war be retained in all its horror so as to prevent its outbreak, but that mankind be saved from a certain kind of war even if this favors other kinds. Such wisdom is narrow

[21] Aron agrees in this respect with most of the theologians who try to adapt the theory of the just war. See Paul Ramsey, *War and the Christian Conscience* (Durham, N.C., 1961); John Courtney Murray, *We Hold These Truths* (New York, 1960), etc.

[22] This convergence of separate arms policies has actually occurred in the budgetary decisions made by the super-powers.

and fragile: converging policies are not enough if one wants to stabilize deterrence; only technology could do so.

At least, there is a possibility of taking advantage of the trend toward moderation that the existence of the new weapons creates. Moreover, according to Aron, there is also a possibility of concretely limiting the objectives. The chapter he devotes to this is a perfect example of his method: after having shown, with the arguments I have outlined, the importance of the values at stake, he nevertheless demonstrates the lack of symmetry of Eastern and Western objectives (the limitations of the latter are due to the very meaning of Western action, to the very essence of the West), and the fact that the limitation of Western objectives meets all the requirements of prudence.

In the first place, he emphasizes (*a*) the differences between the Soviet strategic objective—the death of the *West*, and the West's objective—the death of Soviet *ideology* but not of the Soviet Union. What characterizes the West, as Aron has shown earlier, is its lack of ideology. By its very nature, the West would "cease to consider the Soviet regime as its foe as soon as this regime ceased to deny the right of the West to exist." (*b*) The differences between the cold war and earlier great historical competitions. Here, it is impossible to contemplate either a lasting coexistence (the present blocs are too precarious) or a death struggle, which would be meaningless precisely because the present rivalry is one between an ideological *imperium* and a camp that challenges not its foe's *imperium* but only its messianism. Aron's targets here are the adversaries of Bertrand Russell—the American champions of "forward strategy" and "roll-back."

Secondly, Aron still has to prove that so modest a strategy will be adequate from the viewpoint of prudence. Prudence requires on the one hand the maintenance of a balance of over-all military forces and on the other hand the limitation of violence. The strategy of Cato would violate the latter imperative. A defensive strategy is required that gives priority to military considerations, especially since only this priority would allow the West to find a middle ground between capitulation (wholesale or piecemeal) and annihilation. Once again, Machiavellian precepts and Kantian ethics meet. To choose survival and peace as one's objectives is both an act of wisdom and a contribution to the moral victory of the West, for the West would "win" as soon as its rival gave up the thought of destroying it. Such a strategy implies that the main battlefields for the West are in the arms race and in Europe, but not in the uncommitted world. The West could thus renounce the Third World as the most important stake and deal with problems of development independently of the cold war. The strategy also implies that in all the areas where the two blocs clash frontally, the West should both continue to moderate its own "roll-back" impulses and learn to meet the foe on the most likely battleground, that of subversion. Finally, priority for weapons and for Europe implies a strengthening of the ties between the Atlantic nations.

The aims are modest, the perils persist—the perils of war, and the perils of a gradual choking of the West, should subversion spread. Only if those dangers are overcome will the West's survival and victory coincide. Meanwhile, power politics will continue, with its physical dangers and its moral dilemmas; even afterward, can one envisage without horror mankind freed from ideological poisons but still divided into rival groups and still armed with nuclear weapons? In the past, lovers of peace could feel assured by wisdom, because of their very concern for "responsibility," their awareness of the fundamental antinomies, their rejection of utopias. But the scope of wisdom today is so narrow, the consequences of its failure so great, that it may not be enough. Would it not be wise to recognize that if *at present* the only prudent policy is that which has just been described, *in the long run* a reasonable mind requires not merely this moderation of the antinomies of action but their *elimination* through "a historic conversion of nations and of international relations"? In order to answer this question, Aron examines what could eliminate war and what the chances are for universal peace.

A mere disappearance of traditional stakes (such as economic ones) in a world otherwise unchanged is not likely, nor is it sufficient. As long as the situation persists that makes war possible—i.e., the fragmentation of social groups and of power—perpetually renewed and concrete stakes will be involved. The hope of peace through law—the subordination of all units to a common law even while the groups remain divided and power splintered—founders on the same obstacles: Aron's sharp analysis of the evolution of international law shows that it is unlikely, and international law is fundamentally imperfect. For a "society of nations" to function, there would have to be a homogeneous system of constitutional states that had bid farewell to arms, as Kant foresaw. But there will be no such farewell until the very structure of international action is changed, until there are no more states capable of using arms.

Thus, we come to the last hypothesis: "peace through empire," through the universal state, whether a world-wide federation or an imposed empire. As regards a federation, Aron, repeating an essential point he has often raised, stresses that talk of a gradual "federalization" of mankind confuses a change in the form of "tribal conscience" with a transformation of mankind. A federation (or federations) in a divided world is a "change of scale within one history whose nature remains the same"; *the* federation of the entire world "would mean a transformation of history." The political chances of achieving this last are small; as for the question whether such a voluntary pacification is philosophically conceivable, whether a world in which all conflicts occurred without violence is imaginable—it cannot be answered categorically since there has been no such experience. A positive answer would be "a wager on the conversion of mankind"; a negative answer would condemn the world *a priori* either to war or to an imposed empire.

It is to the latter than Aron comes at last. Here again, his conclusion is ambiguous: at present, empire does not pay and a war to impose it would pay even less; in the long run, the competition of nations with growing populations for resources and space could make empire "rational" again—for the master.

A sociologist who "confesses that it is impossible to know the future" and who "condemns the vain pretense of drawing models of an ideal society" cannot but end on a note of uncertainty. Once again, the humanist and the sociologist meet in "ideological skepticism." "Doubt about the very possibility of an exemplary order," bred by science, keeps moral exigencies modest. "There can be no unconditional faith where the preferred order is not certain and where the goal cannot be perfect." To state that mankind must convert itself now to peace implies that mankind is able to do so, but we do not know this. The end of antinomies is neither historically likely nor philosophically guaranteed. At the end of the fourth part of Aron's book, just as at the end of the second, we know that war and history have not yet come to a parting of the ways, and if one cannot demonstrate that war is necessary, one cannot demonstrate that peace is philosophically possible. The duty of peace-loving men, therefore, consists, as before, in struggling for peace not with a complacent expectation of utopia, but "in the world as it is." "It is our knowledge that reveals to us the limits of our power and suggests that we improve little by little what exists, instead of starting from scratch after having destroyed the accomplishments of centuries." In philosophy as in empirical theory, one must adhere to the degree of precision the subject matter allows. According to Aron, the philosopher can determine what should be the domestic social order required by moral conscience today, but this is not feasible in international relations. Neither the modern means of war nor "the germ of a (single) human conscience that is both moral and pragmatic" demonstrates the emergence of a new phase of mankind on whose behalf the philosopher might speak. "Tribal conscience" is still the stronger. Since the antinomies of action have not been overcome, we cannot predict the outcome of man's adventure nor act as if we did not have "two duties, not always compatible, toward our people and toward all people, the duty to take part in the conflicts that are the warp and woof of history and the duty to work for peace." Aron's last sentence is an expression both of moral hope and of pragmatic doubt: one must "hope and act with the firm intention to prolong the absence of war until the day when peace becomes possible, supposing peace ever becomes possible."

v

The myth of our time is the myth of Sisyphus. Only those who think that the rock will stop rolling down the slope if one merely wants it to, will indict Aron for what they might call inability to come to a conclusion or excessive moral shyness. Aron's actual conclusion is that he who wants peace is most likely to contribute to it if he has freed himself of illusions about a world of undetermined behavior, in which "nothing will be accomplished as long as there remains something to accomplish." The philosopher would be able to overcome the antinomies of diplomatico-strategic action only if mankind were in the process of overcoming them too. "We cannot know it, we must want it, we are entitled to hope for it."

Some of Aron's critics, "with a gift for illusion," will reproach him for having put himself where, in fact, he wanted to be: at the very heart of the logic of competition. It is certain that all those who deem today's international competition senseless will be exasperated by the profoundly conservative nature of a reasoning that aims to save (certain forms of) war rather than to establish universal peace, that suggests that states increase their defense budgets, and that likes to underline the resilience of traditional behavior, the essential weakness of transnational society, and the illusions of federalism. A somewhat ironic rehabilitation of Treitschke, the praise lavished on Kennan, the judicious commentary on Proudhon's assertion of the right of might will undoubtedly suggest to some critics that Aron finds it hard to escape from the framework of the *Staatslehre*; they may apply to him the charge he makes against Morgenthau—that he mistakes a certain kind of politics for eternal politics. These objections strike me as of little value. Throughout *Peace and War*, Aron demonstrates the shifts in forms, the diversity of historical situations, the impossibility of defining once and for all the substance of prudence, *and* the permanence of a behavior whose logic corresponds to the very essence of the phenomena. As long as this essence persists, "changes of scale" are of only relative importance; the study of history shows that most of them have been achieved through war; it does not permit us to believe that the risk of thermonuclear war will of itself bring about a genuine "conversion." Our guiding rule must be not to speak today as if the future we ask for were already here. For we live in daily peril, and the danger will not be eliminated by still unbuilt defenses.

A genuine discussion of Aron's ideas requires that we argue from within, not without, his own positions, just as it is from within that he examines and challenges international relations. On this point, three remarks are in order. Owing to his concern for systematization (a system exists only among political units linked by regular relations) and because his knowledge of history is less universal than Toynbee's or Weber's (everything is relative!), Aron deals almost exclusively with relations among units of the Western world endowed with clear territorial boundaries: the Greek city-states, the Roman Empire, the European states after the Middle Ages. His references to periods and areas of diffused sovereignty, as well as to states and empires in Asia, are more scarce.[23] It is not clear that more references to those areas or regions would have changed his analysis in any way, but it is certain that his very concept of international relations—a scientific enterprise of *rationalization* whose starting point is the behavior of the diplomat and soldier and whose frame of reference is the calculation of forces— leaves outside of the field of research large chunks of material that Toynbee or Spengler did not disdain: the history of times and places where the specific activities that a student of international relations wants to investigate fade away.

Secondly, there are three questions to be raised about Aron's empirical analysis of the *present* and the *possible*. To begin with,

[23] See Adda B. Bozeman, *Politics and Culture in International History* (Princeton, 1960).

it is possible that the gate that opens into wisdom is even narrower than Aron thinks—he is, perhaps, too "reasonable." On the one hand, his preference for a strategy that resorts as little as possible to an ever less credible threat of annihilation (even if this strategy brings about a return to limited wars) represents a wager on reason. It is based on the assumption that there will be no unreasonable risk of escalation if war should break out, unless the stake is vital, and, in such a case, the very existence of the risk should be enough to stop the troublemaker provoking his rival. But Aron recognizes how hazardous a crisis is once violence has started; when the stake is vital, how can one convince the troublemaker that the risk is enormous, without resorting to an ominous threat? On the other hand, while the basic difference is clear to us between asking for an end to Communist proselytism and calling for the *death* of the sinner, in terms of the meaning the participants give their actions, will not the sinner, insofar as his life finds its meaning in his ideology, see the Western goal as anything but moderate; will he not see it as amounting to the destruction of the Communist camp and its moral surrender? It is, of course, a more moderate goal than physical annihilation through war (which is not the present Communist objective either), but Aron reminds us that physical survival is not the only goal of a great power. Finally, if we look to the future, Aron, without indulging in risky predictions, could perhaps have discussed at greater length not the utopias of salvation (peace through law or unity) but the forces for change at work in the world today. His analysis of the imperatives of wisdom is based on a pattern of forces and ideas which the historian of the period 1945–1960 can see, but will this pattern be the same in the 1970's, even if there is no war and quite apart from any move the two super-powers make in areas where they clash directly or quite apart from their defense budgets? Aron mentions the dangers of nuclear proliferation; he recognizes that a system in which many states had invulnerable nuclear forces and thus the power of life and death over each other and over all mankind would oblige the human race "to abandon either the diplomatico-strategic game or its life" ("without any possibility of predicting what the choice would be"!). The super-powers, he argues, would probably not permit the establishment of such a system, but he warns against the illusion that it will be easy to prevent third powers from acquiring nuclear weapons. He states, moreover, that China's development of nuclear weapons would affect the situation considerably. To what extent will these probable or already accomplished changes affect, not the policy of states (to pronounce on this would be to hazard pure guesses), but the substance and chances of wisdom?[24]

Thirdly, in the difficult and painful definition of what is *desirable*, I wonder whether the imperative of peace must really be limited to the effort of introducing the greatest possible amount of traditional wisdom in a world condemned to the antinomies of action. It is not easy to do more and the temptation of utopia is constant, but would one "escape from a war-like history" if one wanted to go beyond an indispensable but somewhat short-sighted wisdom so that history would stop being war-like? Traditional wisdom has two shortcomings. Its eventual success would only result in making war-like history less synonymous with the end of history (and of mankind); moreover, the states' "game," also traditional in many respects, now entails a radically new element—the infinite risk—the game's capacity to destroy itself. It is certain the antinomies cannot easily be overcome; that one cannot philosophically or sociologically prove they can be overcome must not mean there is no duty to *try* to overcome them, especially since one cannot prove they are invincible. It is certain that a change in scale is not a conversion; but it does not follow that one should not work for the two concepts to come closer to each other; it does not follow that changes of scale are necessarily negligible or secondary; and it does not follow that there is no Machiavellian and moral interest in encouraging some such changes.

Aron's conclusion, half sociological and half praxiological, is "politics as usual but with a much greater dose of caution." Insofar as the world is increasingly nuclear, insofar as dependence on the postulate that possession of nuclear weapons is the best inoculation against the folly of war is but a risky gamble, I wonder whether the formula ought not to be amended for both the philosopher and statesman: "Act so that traditional politics, the necessary framework of and starting point for action, bring about through prudence the coming of the postwar age—supposing this age ever were possible." The imperative is to move from the vicious circle to the spiral. To do all that can be done in order to make the world of antinomies bearable is necessary, but *perhaps* not sufficient; what *perhaps* might be sufficient, the end of antinomies, is *perhaps* not possible. Is this a reason not to try? Does not salutary

---

[24] To what extent would those changes also affect the possibilities for and effects of an imposed empire—the last hypothesis Aron deals with in his last chapter (in a way that struck me as unclear)?

ideological skepticism otherwise risk lapsing into moral skepticism? After all, the purpose of praxiology is to "challenge the initial hypotheses"; while diplomatico-stategic action still has meaning for the players, the need to take its meaning into account cannot be the last item on the sociologist's quest, especially since the participants themselves tend more or less deliberately to act as if the prevention of all-out war had become "an objective as obvious" for them "as the defense of purely national interests." It is the evolution of the game that challenges the meaning of the players' behavior and, therefore, the antinomies of action.

These remarks do no more than add a nuance to Aron's conclusion, and Aron will find that in practice the nuance does not amount to much, but he has always asserted that men make their own history and that ideals have effect.

It is paradoxical to feel impelled to add further questions to those Aron has already accumulated. But have not his scientific method and his prudent, anxious philosophy turned each of his books into the triumph of the question-mark over the full-stop? A monument of scholarship in the service of doubt, *Peace and War* gives letters of nobility as well as a masterwork to the discipline of international relations. It also gives the example of a mind that always knows how to understand without justifying, to explain without ceasing to judge, to make lucidity prevail without becoming the twin of cynicism. Undeniably, the ideological skepticism that informs it is the prerequisite to the establishment of any social science and the yardstick of its progress; it is also an essential condition for progress toward peace. For the future of sociology and for our own future, let us hope that the modest ethics of wisdom will be followed and will be enough. Is it only at the dusk of mankind that the owl of Minerva will enter the temple of Janus?

THREE

ROUSSEAU ON WAR AND PEACE

FOR MANY REASONS, Rousseau's writings on international relations should interest students of Rousseau and, more generally, of international relations. The former have recently celebrated the two-hundredth anniversary of *Emile* and *The Social Contract*. Those works, and the *Discourse on the Origin and Bases of Inequality Among Men*, have been analyzed *ad infinitum* and well. But Rousseau's ideas on war and peace, dispersed in various books and fragments, some of which are lost,[1] have had only occasional attention and then often of the hit-and-miss variety.[2] Incomplete as his own treatment of relations among states was, the frequency and intensity of his references indicate the depth of his concern.

Students in search of theories of international politics will also find Rousseau's views useful in the interconnected areas of empirical or causal theory and of normative theory. In the quest for

[1] See the strange story of Rousseau's manuscript on federations, in J. L. Windenberger, *La République confédérative des petits États* (Paris, 1899), chap. 2.

[2] A recent discussion, however, although incidental to a general analysis of Rousseau's politics, is admirable: Iring Fetscher, *Rousseaus politische Philosophie* (Neuwied, 1960), chap. 4.

54

models of state behavior or in the analysis of the nature and cause of war, social scientists could do (and often have done) worse than take and test Rousseau's formulations: in Arnold Wolfers' words, they were "far removed from amateurish guesswork" and "cannot fail to be valuable to anyone seeking to understand what makes the clock tick in international relations."[3] Significantly, Rousseau's remarks point to the same conclusions as those in Raymond Aron's exhaustive and systematic study *Peace and War*. For today's revolutionary system of international politics confirms the sharp and gloomy analysis of Rousseau, whose pessimism was all too easily discounted in the moderate system that died at Sarajevo.

More specifically, the normative aspect of Rousseau's writings is relevant today because of his awareness of a dilemma that also dominated Kant's thought and that has become vital in any consideration of world politics in the nuclear age. We can no longer afford to be preoccupied only with the issue to which political philosophers used to give most of their attention—the "conditions of a just peace" in domestic society, the search for the good state, for the legitimate political regime. We are also (perhaps primarily) concerned with conditions of peace in international society, because the very institution of the state—celebrated as the source of order, liberty, and morality for citizens—has also turned out to be a source of international chaos and consequently of physical danger and moral agony. How to be both a good citizen of a nation and a good citizen of the world; how to prevent the state from oppressing its subjects or from obliging them to behave immorally toward outsiders, under the pressure of international competition, without meanwhile destroying the bond of loyalty and sense of identity that link each citizen to his compatriots—these have become the major issues for political thinkers today. Rousseau considered those issues at some length and thought he could resolve the dilemma: the formula he devised, in *The Social Contract*, to rescue man from the fall into which the passing of the state of nature had plunged him, was also supposed to put an end to international disorder. However, the philosopher who was the sharpest critic of man's plight in society (both domestic and international) provides only an escape from the international jungle he had so brilliantly described, not a solution.

[3] Arnold Wolfers and Laurence W. Martin, eds., *The Anglo-American Tradition in Foreign Affairs* (New Haven, 1956), p. xiii.

I

Kenneth Waltz's admirable book *Man, The State and War* has helped the understanding of world politics by distinguishing three "images" of international competition. But I am not so sure he has similarly served some of the authors with whom he deals—Hobbes, Rousseau, and Kant in particular. With each, any sharp separation between conceptions of human nature, of the state, and of the international milieu destroys the unity of his philosophy. At the risk of covering very familiar ground, therefore, it needs to be shown first how Rousseau's trenchant critique of world politics and his "model" or image of states in conflict derive from his most fundamental notions about man and society.

For that purpose, compare Rousseau's picture with that of Hobbes, whom he constantly invokes and attacks. Rousseau's point of departure is just as individualistic or atomistic as Hobbes's: they begin neither with God or society, nor with man as a social and moral being; Rousseau made it clear that there was at the outset no such thing as a general society of mankind.[4] Both begin with man, an atom in the state of nature—neither moral nor immoral, neither good nor bad. But Rousseau's concept of the *state of nature* is not like Hobbes's; his owes much to Montesquieu's happier version.[5] Hobbes's men in a state of nature led miserable lives:

[4] First draft of *The Social Contract*, in C. E. Vaughan, *The Political Writings of J. J. Rousseau* (Cambridge, Eng., 1915), I, 447 ff. Vaughan's edition is the most useful to date of Rousseau's many, often fragmentary, political writings. Many of my references are to untitled fragments that are assembled in this book, in which case I have simply cited the pages on which they appear in the Vaughan edition, since this is how they can be most easily identified.

[5] See *L'Esprit des Lois*, Book I. For a searching analysis of Montesquieu's concept of the state of nature and of laws of reason prior to positive laws, see Raymond Aron, *Les Grandes Doctrines de sociologie politique* (mimeo.; Paris, 1960), pp. 42–55. Two important differences distinguish Rousseau's and Montesquieu's state of nature: (1) in Montesquieu's state of nature, laws of reason, which he calls "relations of justice prior to positive laws" and which are moral standards and goals for men, already exist—in addition to the "natural law" derived from man's nature in the state of nature (self-preservation, sociability, etc.). In Rousseau's state of nature, only the latter exist (self-preservation and compassion). In this respect, Montesquieu is closer to Locke, Rousseau to Hobbes. (2) For Montesquieu, the state of nature is just an early stage of man's development; for Rousseau, it represents a state of liberty and happiness that makes society appear as the cause of man's fall and that can only be recaptured under the thoroughly new guise of moral autonomy and good citizenship. (Hobbes's state of nature, in contrast, expresses an

they were strong enough to kill each other, too weak to be safe, and driven into deadly competition for scarce goods by an infinity of desires and an unlimited passion for getting what they wanted —an unlimited quest for power. Quite the opposite, Rousseau's state of nature was characterized by men who were graced by a generous nature that provided them with more goods than they needed; there was enough space between and among them to prevent their desires exceeding their needs.[6] Consequently, if, by accident, two men should happen to clash over the same food, the most likely result would be flight, not fight; if they fought at all, it would be a minor brawl.[7] Independence, indifference, abundance, *amour de soi* (a healthy concern with self-preservation, limited to the fulfillment of basic needs), compassion—such are the key features of the idyll.[8] Man's life on earth may be solitary and brutish, but it is pleasant precisely because of these qualities.

Rousseau shares Montesquieu's concept of a state of nature that is peaceful and unperturbed by inequality, Montesquieu's belief that trouble began when the state of nature faded, and Montesquieu's distinction of three stages in man's development—an original state of nature, a state of *de facto* society that is a "fallen" state of nature, and a state of civil society—and he charges Hobbes with having mistakenly confused the first two stages. Nevertheless, Rousseau's idea of the genesis of civil society is very different from Montesquieu's. The latter, quite traditionally, saw man as a social animal, society as the outcome of a natural human drive[9]: even though its first effects are inequality, competition, and war, these are only temporary nuisances that the establishment of political communities endowed with laws is intended to eliminate. (In this respect, Montesquieu's analysis does not differ from Locke's.) Rousseau, however, believes that *de facto* society resulted not from man's sociability[10] (in itself a notion he discards), but

---

analysis of human nature that remains valid in civil society, the latter entailing neither moral progress nor moral disgrace, but merely physical safety.)

[6] *Discourse on Inequality*, Vaughan, I, 159 ff., 203 ff.

[7] *Ibid.*, p. 203; and *Economie Politique*, Vaughan, I, 293–94.

[8] *Ibid.*, pp. 305–6.

[9] *L'Esprit des Lois*, Book I, end of chap. 2. Consequently, and paradoxically, the establishment of civil society is treated as beneficial both by Montesquieu and by Hobbes: the former sees it as the outcome of man's social inclinations and the remedy of early society's defects (*cf.* Locke); the latter sees it as man's chance for salvation from violent death. Rousseau, on the other hand, sees in most civil societies a perpetuation of man's fall.

[10] Vaughan, I, 138.

from a combination of accidents and physical necessities. It is the human "situation," not human nature, that is responsible; nature's tricks and the growing needs of a growing population, not man's natural desires, bring men together.[11] And he sees *de facto* society not as a mere nuisance but as a genuine fall that affects mankind after settlements have appeared, as communications and contacts develop, property spreads, and inequality sets in.[12] Thus, his analysis of man in *de facto* society comes close to Hobbes' image of man in the state of nature—a picture of fear, waste, want, and war; in both instances, the springs of conflict are defined as competition, diffidence, and glory. Thus, a close, if superficial, resemblance marks Hobbes' and Rousseau's accounts of the establishment of civil society: the former sees in it a necessary escape from general war, a liberation from fear and want; the latter concedes that this was indeed the purpose of the enterprise.[13]

Here, however, the resemblance ends. Rousseau's judgment of the effects of civil society differs from Hobbes'; their similar descriptions of man's predicament before the appearance of the state conceal conflicting notions on the origins of this predicament and totally different emphases on what is evil about it. Hobbes finds the causes of conflict in man's nature; those causes will remain, latent and repressed, in man-under-laws; the only thing that can be ruled out (at least, within the state) is violence. Hobbes's concern and supreme value is safety; consequently, civil society, which makes safety possible, is a blessing. His obsession is with the use of force, which can be managed, whereas its causes cannot. Thus, civil society does not change man's nature but merely transforms his possibilities of action: it suppresses some and, as a result, increases and protects others.

Rousseau's analysis is very different. He is concerned more with the roots of violence than with its manifestations, not because he does not care for peace, but because he denies that these roots are in man's nature and because his supreme concern is man's freedom, conscience, and virtue, which require that the roots of violence be torn out. To him, *de facto* society is evil not just because it is a state of war but because it is a state of moral contradiction and disgrace which corrupts man's peaceful nature and of which

---

[11] *Discourse on Inequality*, Vaughan, I, 173 ff. See also Rousseau's *Essai sur l'origine des langues* (*Oeuvres Complètes*, Paris, 1905, Vol. I).

[12] This, again, is very close to Montesquieu. See *L'Esprit des Lois*, Book I, chap. 3.

[13] *Discourse on Inequality*, Vaughan, I, 179 ff.

violence is merely the outcome. Entry into society effects a mutation in Rousseau's man. On the one hand, through contacts with other human beings, he gains a moral sense and becomes able dimly to conceive the ideal of force at the service of a law that would be his own—the idea of a positively defined freedom, consisting not merely in the absence of hindrances to action (as in Hobbes' and also in Rousseau's state of nature) but in the capacity to be one's own master. On the other hand, man has lost his original independence and innocence; his condition is the worst of all possible worlds, for he enjoys neither the old, negative freedom which is lost forever, nor the new, positive one to which he can aspire. He is capable of moral understanding but not of moral fulfillment. The old "natural law," based on the instincts of self-preservation and compassion, is dying; but the very forces that killed it prevent the new natural law, understood as the moral dictates of reason, from acquiring sufficient strength.[14] The passions bred by inequality, the inflation of desires fostered by society, gradually starve out compassion and submerge *l'amour de soi* in *l'amour-propre*—a concern for oneself that comes not from the natural desire for self-preservation, but from an artificial reaction to other people's judgments, opinions, attitudes, and actions toward oneself. Thus, what makes of man in *de facto* society so miserable a being is not merely the violence to which he is exposed: it is what triggers the violence, an insecurity that did not exist in the state of nature, which stems not from man's real nature but from his cupidity[15]—not so much a physical as a psychological need to compare oneself to others, a fall from *être* to *paraître* and from original indolence to social restlessness—and that is evil even if it does not lead to the actual use of force.

Thus, Rousseau and Hobbes agree here on one point only: civil society rules out violence among citizens. However, whereas Hobbes' ideal state is the Leviathan in which man submits to the force that protects his life, removes external hindrances to his action, and leaves him free to indulge in all the drives and desires that motivate and move him (as long as he does so peaceably), a civil society based exclusively on self-preservation is an absurd one for Rousseau. For, in it, all the vices that marred *de facto* society

---

[14] First draft of *The Social Contract*, Vaughan, I, 448–49.

[15] *Ibid.*, p. 447. Property, which Rousseau singles out in the second *Discourse* as a crucial factor in inequality and consequently in violence, should not be seen as a *cause* of war but as a *consequence* of the "cupidity" and insecurity that dominate men once their original isolation comes to an end.

would be perpetuated—except one, violence among the citizens—with the addition of two new, and huge, evils: international wars, and tyranny. If civil society, which replaces man's natural independence with its network of conventions, makes man the permanent pawn of others, it is a curse. Only the society that makes man autonomous is good. In other words, the philosopher's quest cannot stop with the elimination of violence, it must be pursued until the origins of conflict themselves have been eliminated. The absence of violence is not the supreme good: violence is a symptom; its causes must be cured—and they can be, since, in Rousseau's view, they do not lie in human nature. *The Social Contract* provides the formula through which a civil society can be established, in which not only violence but the "evil propensities" of man-in-society will be purged, in which his inevitable passions will be turned to the common good, and "rational natural law" can flourish, thanks to the civil laws decreed by the general will.

The differences between Hobbes and Rousseau on the subject of world politics are as serious, and rather paradoxical. Hobbes has little to say on the subject, but what he does say is that the international state of nature is less intolerable than the "individual" state of nature. To be sure, both are marked by the same quest for power, and for the same reasons.[16] Both show insecurity and conflict; states, consequently, have to be armed and prepared. Both show the same deficiency of law: in the absence of superior power, the "laws of nature" are mere precepts of self-interest whose application depends on their perpetually uncertain observance by others. However, while Hobbes explains how insecurity incites men to crawl out of their state of nature to set up the Leviathan, he does not invite the Leviathans to follow suit. Here is the key of the paradox: in the international competition, it is the state itself that serves as a cushion. Even though international politics, in the absence of constraining power, is not a state of peace, even though it is a condition in which the nasty features of human nature (repressed, within civil society, by the setting up of the Leviathan) can, so to speak, re-emerge at their worst, nevertheless the international state of war is *bearable*. It is the *intolerable* aspect of the "individual" state of war that drives men to sacrifice their "right of nature" so as to preserve their existence.

There are two reasons why the international state of nature is less atrocious. First, states are stronger than men in the state of nature: their "security dilemma," their fear of annihilation, is less

[16] Hobbes, *Leviathan*, chaps. 13, 17.

pressing.[17] Secondly, the very existence of the state is a guarantee for the security of the citizens: no man is safe in the state of nature, whereas inter-state war does not affect the daily lives of all men. Consequently, "laws of nature" *à la* Hobbes have a greater chance of being observed in the international state of nature: since there is greater force behind the partners to an inter-state compact than there is behind individual signatories of a contract, the risk of violation will be less; the idea of reciprocity of interests, on which the solidity of international law depends, emerges here. Moreover, each state has an essentially domestic interest in self-restraint, since, should it implicate its population in all-out wars of extermination, the subjects' duty of obedience to it would disappear.

Thus, surprisingly enough, Hobbes ends by differing not too much from Montesquieu, who thought that just as the establishment of the state restored peace among men, the development of international law among states would allow them to live under conditions of merely troubled peace, not permanent war.[18] We can see in Hobbes the father of utilitarian theories of international law and relations, and we can extrapolate from his theories, for policy guidance, the notion of the balance of power: by definition, it is fragile, but it is a relatively efficient technique for enforcing the "laws of nature," since it corresponds to the interests all participants have in keeping the competition moderate. Should the "security dilemma" worsen, should the competition become more intense, should the risk of total destruction, affecting all citizens, become intolerable, we could also surmise that Hobbes's relative complacency would lose its justification; the same arguments he used to justify the Leviathan would have to be applied to the establishment of a world-wide one.

Rousseau's views are far less reassuring. With Hobbes, he recognizes that the criterion that distinguishes world politics from politics of a civil society is the ever-present possibility of violence which he, like Hobbes, terms a "state of war" (whether war is actually in progress or not)[19]; it is also clear that, for both, the fragmentation of power in the international system is the immediate cause of the state of war. To use Waltz's useful classification, both Rousseau and Hobbes are "third-image" writers to this ex-

---

[17] *Ibid.*, chap. 13.
[18] Montesquieu, *op. cit.*, chap. 3.
[19] See Vaughan, I, 300; *Leviathan*, chap. 13.

tent. However, their agreement stops here. On four main points, they are in conflict.

First, they differ in their judgments on the nature of international violence. For Hobbes, violence is an expression of human nature, whenever it is not repressed by a Leviathan; international war remains inevitable because man is an asocial animal, even after the establishment of civil societies. For Rousseau, war is *not* a human necessity or drive, because man is not social by nature. "One kills in order to win; no man is so ferocious that he tries to win in order to kill."[20] War is a social institution: hence Rousseau's famous insistence on the idea that wars are, by nature, contests between states (i.e., artificial bodies) but not between individuals and consequently ought to be waged as such. This idea was directly inspired by Montesquieu's writings,[21] but Rousseau formulated it more categorically, so as to make clear that man, *dénaturé* by bad social institutions, is alienated, his acts springing not from his true self but from a distorted self which society has manufactured and for which society alone is responsible. Since nothing in human nature forces one man to kill another, the aims of wars are always far removed from citizens' lives: the stakes of war are not man's needs, but the frills and fancies grafted on those needs by society.[22]

Second, Rousseau does not share Hobbes' belief that the state is a mitigating force in international conflict. The same reasons that made man miserable in *de facto* society (or make him so in inadequate civil societies) are at work among nations. He singles out two factors of insecurity especially. One is mutual dependence: insecurity among men grows because each one is at the mercy of others' services or opinions; relations among states are also plagued by such entanglements. In both cases, he denounces economic dependence most acidly, as if it were the serpent's apple. It is one of Rousseau's deepest insights, one that shatters a large part of the liberal vision of world affairs—that interdependence breeds not accommodation and harmony but suspicion and incompatibility.[23] Another cause of insecurity is inequality, that *inégalité de combinaison* which results from division of labor and multiplies the effects of natural inequality[24]; similarly, the unevenness of states

---

[20] Vaughan, I, 313.
[21] Montesquieu, *op. cit.*, chap. 3, and Book X, chaps. 2, 3.
[22] Vaughan, I, 312–13.
[23] *Discourse on Inequality*, Vaughan, I, 203 ff.; first draft of *The Social Contract*, Vaughan, I, 447 ff., and *Project for Corsica*, Vaughan, II, 308 ff.
[24] *Discourse on Inequality*, Vaughan, I, 178.

is the fuel of world conflict.[25] Hobbes had stressed natural equality as the main incentive to competition, and assumed that all men (and all states) were equally driven by their nature toward power and conflict. Rousseau remarks instead that (just as it is enough that one man say, "this is mine," for property claims to mushroom) the emergence of one state is enough to force all other human settlements to choose between annihilation or resistance—which means other states are established in a kind of chain reaction. Once again, very rightly, the blame must be put on the dynamics of the situation: even if most states wanted to live in peace, they could not do so as long as a few major delinquents made trouble.

Moreover, international quarrels are in many respects far worse than the competition among men before the establishment of civil society. States, far from dampening violence, amplify it.

(*a*) There is a difference in the scope of violence. Rousseau makes a fundamental distinction between kinds of violent conflicts: only organized violence among consolidated groups deserves to be called war. War is "a permanent condition that requires constant relations." Throughout most of the period that precedes civil society, relations among men were too unsettled for genuine wars to develop: insecurity resulted merely in "fights" and "murders."[26] Only after the appearance of states, in which laws are made that delimit the rights and duties of the nation, and that often promote close relations with other nations, can real wars break out—not, of course, among the citizens, but among states. One may object that, just before the emergence of civil society, according to Rousseau himself, human settlement had become sufficiently stable (and the growth of human greed, dependence, and inequality sufficiently disastrous) for a real "state of war" to break out among men.[27] Also, Rousseau himself defines war as arising from "links between things rather than between men."[28] Specifically, contests over "things" (such as possessions) had already developed in *de facto* societies. This is true, but violence

[25] *Ibid.*, and Vaughan, I, 297. Strangely enough, Proudhon, who spent so much time attacking Rousseau, follows Rousseau very closely in Volume II of his book *La Guerre et La Paix*: it is the same attack on greed, property, and inequality as in Rousseau's second *Discourse*; war is seen as the result of disputes over wealth, due to the end of primeval abundance and to the "somber rapacity" that grips societies when man's original temperance fades away.

[26] *Discourse on Inequality*, Vaughan, I, 180, and Vaughan, I, 294; II, 29.

[27] *Discourse on Inequality*, Vaughan, I, 180.

[28] Vaughan, II, 29.

within and among these societies remained less devastating than wars among states. The roots of the older kind of war were individual greed—the rapacity of the rich, the envy of the poor—in other words, inequality among men (even if those men were beginning to be organized, for instance, in "gangs of bandits"); the root of inter-state war is inequality among nations; and the inequality of men has sharper limits than the inequality of states. The size of a state is always relative: "it is forced to compare itself in order to know itself"; its "absolute size" is meaningless, for its rank depends on what other states are, plan, and do. Thus, by definition, each state is always totally dependent on all the others.[29] Its security dilemma affords no escape: if it is strong, its power makes it a danger to peace; if it is weak, it becomes a tempting pawn. Restlessness is at its worst on the world scene.

(*b*) A difference in the stakes also makes war among states far worse than war among men. In *de facto* society, the stakes of fighting remained essentially individualistic and therefore limited. As against hit-and-run raids to steal land or goods, inter-state war offers clashes over territory, resources, and manpower on a grand scale.

(*c*) Another difference is in the intensity of war. The Leviathan, in accordance with Hobbes' mechanistic conception of society, was made of the sum total of the citizens. This Rousseau denies; he points out that the state is always weaker than the sum total of the citizens' "particular forces."[30] Paradoxically, whereas Hobbes nevertheless believed that the impact of war on the citizens would be limited, Rousseau came to the opposite conclusion. For he saw that the state must try to compensate for its deficiency in collective force with passion—the one element Hobbes had left out. Prophetically, Rousseau warned that the body politic was moved not by cold *raison d'état* but by passions: hence the ferocity of wars. The passions that had pitted man against man before the appearance of civil society remained somehow dampened by what was left of human compassion, while the passions that states mobilized against one another ignored such restraint. Here we find another deep insight: what makes of states, in Nietzsche's terms, the coldest of cold monsters, is not reason of state, but the horrible fact that their passions are untouched (or unrelieved) by commiseration.

(*d*) Consequently, the effects of international conflict are far more nefarious than those of conflicts among men. States being

[29] *L'État de Guerre*, Vaughan, I, 297–98.
[30] *Ibid.*, pp. 298–99.

more powerful than individual men (even though each state's strength may be less than the cumulative total strength of its citizens), their antagonisms produce greater upheavals than the clashes of individuals. There are more murders in one day of battle than there had been for centuries in the state of nature.[31]

A third major area of difference between Hobbes' and Rousseau's approaches to world politics concerns ethics in international relations. In Hobbes, the problem of ethical action in politics can hardly be called important; it is a pure matter of definition, since human nature does not change after man's entry into society. Moral action in the Leviathan consists simply of obeying the sovereign's law. In international politics, there is no such law, and consequently one is left with the clash or occasional convergence of different national moralities. Rousseau could not be satisfied with such simple amorality. In all his work, he treated ethics and politics as one and the same thing. To him, the "state of war" is a moral scandal because it is the mark, and to a considerable extent, indeed, the cause, of man's failure to fulfill his moral development in civil society. As he described it in the second *Discourse*, men entered civil society in order to live under laws, so as not only to escape from the murders and fights of *de facto* society, but also to be able to follow the dictates of "rational natural law"—which cannot have any force unless men are protected by the civil laws of society. But instead of the reconciliation of ethics and politics, the citizen is faced with a new and worse moral dilemma.

To begin with, man's very effort to assure domestic order, peace, and justice (by setting up the state) has provoked chaos and conflict on the international level; the nations remain vis-à-vis in a "state of nature" similar to the fallen state that had been man's tragic lot just before civil society was founded. "We have prevented particular wars only so as to start general ones which are a thousand times worse"; "all the horrors of war stem from men's efforts to prevent it."[32] Consequently, the citizen is caught in what Rousseau calls a *système mixte*[33]—torn between the laws of the domestic social order and the violence that results from sovereign states in a

---

[31] *Discourse on Inequality*, Vaughan, I, 182. It can be seen from what precedes that Rousseau finds the causes of war not only in the structure of a milieu of clashing sovereignties, but also in the corrupt nature of existing states, and in the "evil propensities" of man, the last due not to his original nature but to the "fall" that society entailed and almost all states have perpetuated.

[32] Vaughan, I, 295, 365.

[33] Vaughan, I, 304–6; *Emile*, Vaughan, II, 158.

world state of nature. Now, to be morally torn is the greatest misery; to be "dragged by nature and by men into opposite directions" obliges man to "end his life without having been able to come to terms with himself."[34] Rousseau implies that the chance for autonomy in the domestic order—where the citizen can hope for the fusion of force and a law that would be his own—does not exist in the international (dis)order because of the fragmentation of sovereignties. Thus, as long as the world competition lasts, even the citizen of the ideal state may find no opportunity for moral action beyond the limits of the state; the human conscience may remain unhappy.

On the other hand, this global competition does more than thwart moral action beyond the state: its very existence gives political leaders a good pretext for putting or keeping man "in chains." Even the establishment of the first civil societies is described as a sort of trick by which the rich ensnare the poor and consolidate inequality under the pretext of mutual protection against outsiders.[35] Later, princes are able to stunt domestic efforts toward self-government and to perpetuate tyranny because of the "necessities" that war entails.[36] Thus, international insecurity and tyranny reinforce each other. Man is not merely caught between domestic order and external chaos, but torn by yet another contradiction: within civil society—whose order, being corrupt, preserves the evils of *de facto* society, *minus* internal wars but *plus* tyranny—the contradiction between nostalgia for the independence he has lost and a yearning for moral and political autonomy.

War, therefore, does more than curtail the scope of such autonomy: it threatens to make its achievement *within* the state impossible. Precisely because of this peril, Kant put the imperative of peace at the center of his philosophy. But Kant noted that the increasing costs of war would oblige rulers "not to hinder the weak and slow independent efforts of their people" to move toward constitutional government.[37] The experience of this century has confirmed Rousseau's gloom rather than Kant's hopes.

Rousseau's study of international relations raised the question whether it would not be better to have no civil society at all than to have many, for the *système mixte* is the worst evil. Not only is

[34] Vaughan, II, 147.
[35] *Discourse on Inequality*, Vaughan, I, 179–81.
[36] *Critique of St. Pierre's Project*, Vaughan, I, 389 ff.
[37] Kant, "Idea for a Universal History," in *The Philosophy of Kant*, C. J. Friedrich, ed. (New York, 1959), p. 128.

the present state far bloodier than the fallen state of nature; it is also one in which—although the causes of war are ever more remote from the citizens' lives—killing has become a duty taught by the state.[38] The moral tragedy is that, "by uniting with some men, we become the enemies of mankind"—which we had never been before.[39]

In a summary of the Abbé de Saint Pierre's peace plan, Rousseau analyzed the special bonds that history, legal institutions, and religion had forged among European nations. Precisely because of these bonds, he remarked, the condition of those nations was worse than if no European society existed at all.[40] It is his same concern for moral *oneness*, his same insight that it is better to be isolated (and thus not experience the agonies of moral choice) than to be dependent on others (and thus be unable, because of competition or inequality, to practice the moral virtues that society both engenders and frustrates).

A fourth crucial difference between Hobbes and Rousseau relates to how they view techniques for mitigating international conflict. Hobbes assumed that different "reasons of state" could converge on common interests. Rousseau demolishes this major part of the liberal (or neo-liberal—I mean, "realist") ideology of international politics, with arguments of enormous importance for the theory of international politics.

1. Rousseau first deals with what might be called restraints through explicit or tacit agreements. Neither international law nor the balance of power can really restrain international competition. Though not instances of actual war, they are tactics in the strategy of the state of war.[41] The balance of power may block major conquests, but it perpetuates instability and preserves or aggravates each participant's dissatisfaction.[42] International law is both weak and dangerous: its fragility is inherent, and due to the very nature of international obligation. It is but the expression of the "law of nature," superseded within states by civil laws but still operative among states. It consists neither of the commands of self-preservation and compassion, which faded after the fall from the original

[38] *Discourse on Inequality*, Vaughan, I, 182.
[39] Vaughan, I, 365. Man was not the "enemy of mankind" either in the original state of nature, when he was a peaceful being, or even in *de facto* society, when his contacts with others may have been bloody but were limited in scope; see Vaughan, I, 453.
[40] Vaughan, I, 374.
[41] Vaughan, I, 300.
[42] Vaughan, I, 371 ff.

state of nature, nor of the dictates of moral reason, which have force only within the ideal state. Instead, it is the law of corrupted nature, the law of *amour-propre* and competition, tempered merely by the attempt to replace compassion with conventions. These are weak substitutes indeed, for the basis of obligation is shaky: nothing guarantees the efficacy of international law but the particular interest of the state to which it applies.[43] Moreover, international law is often worse than fragile. Alliances and treaties (like the laws of imperfect states) merely perpetuate inequality.[44] States often use international law as an instrument against one another in the state of war: not only are peace treaties nothing but stratagems, but recognition and the regulation of foreign trade can also be diplomatic weapons.[45] Peaceful international politics, of which international law is one aspect, is but the continuation of war by other means.

The foundation of Rousseau's reasoning here is his conviction that in a competitive situation as fierce as that among nations, common interests are evanescent and hardly significant. Each player in the game is after his own interest. Consequently, one must distinguish the *real* from the apparent interest of the players. Rousseau calls the apparent interest what the scholar (who superimposes on the competitive situation a fictitious community independent of the players' moves) is normally tempted to call the real—i.e., the common interest in self-restraint. Something close to a miracle would be needed, Rousseau thought, to make the separate calculations of individual advantage converge on a solution favorable to all. Furthermore, advantages are appreciated only "by their differences": if they are common to all, *they will be real to none.*[46]

It is easy to see how so gloomy an analysis applies to contemporary schemes of arms control. These assume that the main powers have a common interest in peace, which could be strengthened by the adoption of measures that would preserve existing advantages (the possession of national armaments) and add new ones (guarantees against surprise attack). Efforts to agree on such schemes have foundered precisely because of the asymmetries in the position of the major powers: each tries to annihilate the enemy's

[43] Vaughan, I, 304–5. Compare Aron, *Peace and War*, chap. 23.
[44] Vaughan, II, 308.
[45] Vaughan, I, 299.
[46] Vaughan, I, pp. 389, 391, 392.

advantages while keeping its own factors of superiority.[47] Each acknowledges a risk of war but remains unwilling to deprive itself of the freedom of action that an unfettered right to use (or threaten to use) its weapons gives it. Each is confident that it can handle the danger of war by unilateral measures of restraint.[48] Rousseau wrote that princes who make war do so not because they are unaware of the perils but because they are confident of their wisdom.[49]

Rousseau's refutation of the "common-interest" argument, and his conviction that commerce only exacerbates greed and the competition among nations and among men, thus led him also to reject a view that Kant and liberals of the eighteenth and nineteenth centuries found too attractive to resist—that commerce breeds peace.[50]

2. If restraints based on common interests are fictitious, what about the possibility of self-restraint, resulting from each state's own effort to define a rational line of conduct, as one can define a rational strategy for a commercial firm? Rousseau's analysis shows why it is futile to try to reduce risk and uncertainty in international affairs by defining *a* rational foreign policy.[51] Economic competition has the simplifying feature of a currency in which all gains and losses can be calculated—money, but Rousseau realized that stakes in international competition cannot all be converted into monetary units or into any true measure[52]: land, men, spoils, prestige, or "degrees of power." (He had no clear idea of an ideological competition, although his remark about the passions of states can easily be extended to it. Such competition is even less "quantifiable.") On the other hand, the "rules of the game" are too fluid, its purely psychological elements too important, to allow for a meaningful definition of rationality: in the absence of a law subordinating the separate interests, or of legal procedures to chan-

[47] E.g., the U-2 affair in 1960, the United States' insistence on piercing the Soviet wall of secrecy; the Soviet Union's inclusion of proposals aiming at the dismantling of America's foreign bases in all its disarmament plans.

[48] See Hoffmann, "Les règles du jeu," *Les Cahiers de la République*, March, 1962.

[49] Vaughan, I, 390–91.

[50] Vaughan, I, 391.

[51] The most brilliant contemporary analysis is in Aron's *Peace and War*, "Introduction" and "Final Note." Rousseau's and Aron's arguments contradict the faith in moderation advocates of the "national interest" as the norm of foreign policy have so often proclaimed in recent years.

[52] Vaughan, I, 391.

nel them, states are condemned by their very independence to the hazards of *fortuna*.

3. Any analyst of international relations who sees world politics as a state of permanent war is tempted to propose radical remedies —to suggest that men and nations spontaneously move into a broad daylight of reconciliation. Rousseau's writings contain more or less explicit criticisms of many schemes that the imagination of men of good will had invented. So far as St. Pierre's peace plan was a forerunner of modern international organization, Rousseau's critique of it goes to the very foundation of that halfway house between state sovereignty and world government which flourishes today and which Kant presented both as a moral imperative and as the object of a hidden plan of nature. Rousseau suggests, in terms close to those Walter Schiffer applied to the League of Nations,[53] that as long as states behave as they have customarily behaved, they are unlikely to be willing to achieve lasting peace through international organizations; and, if their behavior were sufficiently reformed to make their adoption possible, the need for such a league would become much less pressing.[54] On the other hand, anticipating Kant's philosophy of history, Rousseau argues that "what is useful to the public" can be introduced only by force, because of the resistance put up by selfish interests. But he adds that if wars and revolutions are necessary to impose federative leagues on men, they are fearful means indeed and may do more harm than the leagues could ever prevent.[55] This is an admirable, though depressing, comment on the dialectic of history in our own century, which required two world wars to establish two rather weak world organizations. It places a major reservation on Kant's hope that the hidden plan of nature would bring states together through a process of ever more damaging wars.

Rousseau did not deal with disarmament plans, which did not proliferate until the nineteenth century. But his analysis of unevenness and international insecurity, and his refutation of the "common-interest" argument, cuts through hundreds of pages of peace plans.[56]

We are left with a frightening picture of world politics. Nations

[53] *The Legal Community of Mankind* (New York, 1954), esp. p. 199.
[54] Vaughan, I, 388.
[55] Vaughan, I, p. 396.
[56] A recent study has aptly pointed out the three main reasons why all disarmament negotiations have failed: the desire of states to catch up when they are behind in the race, security fears, and difficulties of enforcement. Evan Luard, *Peace and Opinion* (Oxford, 1962), chap. 2.

are apparently condemned to a "state of war." The only restraints are unilateral and temporary; islands of peace are always threatened. Rousseau does not deny that these islands may exist: he assumes not a war of all against all, but a struggle in which the existence of even one "relationship of major tension" may make amity impossible and neutrality difficult.[57] Here, precisely as in his analysis of society in the *Discourse on Inequality,* Rousseau's vision is not historical, but of an ideal-type: it is "the essence of things, not events," that he wants to account for.[58] Consequently, one cannot refute him by pointing out that a few permanent neutrals (like his own Switzerland) have succeeded in staying out of the competition; or that some international systems are more moderate or some restraints more lasting than others—not so much because they are based on common interests as because they operate in times when the range of stakes (the scope of the competition) is narrower than at other moments. Rousseau's answer is obviously that nothing guarantees the preservation of oases of peace or the perpetuation of moments of grace: whenever the system becomes revolutionary again, his analysis is valid.

Yet Rousseau proposed a way out of the *système mixte* of the domestic order—a way of making *être* and *paraître, amour propre* and *amour de soi,* less incompatible. What about the international conditions of physical violence, moral division, and psychological bad faith? For his answers here, we must turn from his empirical theory to his normative theory—or to whatever we can find in its stead.

The loss of Rousseau's manuscript on confederations makes it difficult to know in full detail his solution to the problem of international "anarchy." But it is possible to put together pieces of the puzzle and to assess the relevance of the result to present-day world politics.

More than once Rousseau has been victimized by his interpreters. Recently, it has been fashionable to make him the father of "totalitarian democracy." This is not the place to deal with such a distortion, but two points need to be made. One is to establish Rousseau's intentions without projecting into his work the intentions of disciples or others. The second is to deal with his views on their merits. This may entail showing that his ideal is incapable of execution and of any enforcement that would not thwart his inten-

---

[57] Compare Arnold Wolfers, "The Pole of Power and the Pole of Indifference," *World Politics,* IV (October, 1951), 39–63.

[58] Vaughan, I, 297.

tions.[59] There may be, therefore, serious difficulties in making his work relevant to the world in which we live, but one should absolve him of responsibility for the perversions of his thought that have been produced by attempts to apply his vision.

Let us start with what Rousseau's intentions were not. He did *not* suggest that the way out of the international jungle was the establishment of a world state, nor was he the father of modern nationalism. It is true that his analysis of the international milieu provides what Waltz has called the third image, in which the absence of any common superior over the states is seen as the "permissive" cause of war.[60] But Rousseau does not therefore propose a European or a world federation to put an end to war. The passage Waltz quotes[61] in order to show that Rousseau endorsed such a formula appears in Rousseau's digest of St. Pierre's peace plan, which he thereupon mercilessly destroys in a subsequent critique.

But it is not enough to note the absence of any "world federalist" or "world government" solution in Rousseau's argument; the important question is why Rousseau brushed it aside. For we have an apparently puzzling contrast. He had shown that the "state of war" in *de facto* society convinced men to become citizens, i.e., to establish states so as to put an end to violence at least within civil society. And he had described this movement as having spread because some men (the rich) were able to convince others of their common interest in security under laws[62]—even though he had also said that men in the fallen state of nature were as incapable of making common interests triumph over antagonistic ones as sovereign states were in the international jungle.[63] If, then, men were driven by insecurity to heed the common interest after all, in Hobbesian fashion, why should not nations reach the same conclusion? Their "state of war" Rousseau himself described as worse than the state of violence among men in *de facto* society. If the social contract would set up an ideal state endowed not only with a monopoly of force but also with the capacity to make men morally free and virtuous, why should not a similar compact establishing a world state be the basis of universal peace and the guarantee of "republican government" in each component unit?

[59] This is what I attempted to do in: "Du Contrat Social, ou le mirage de la volonté générale," *Revue Internationale d'Histoire Politique et Constitutionnelle*, October, 1954, pp. 288–315.

[60] Waltz, *op. cit.*, p. 232.

[61] *Ibid.*, pp. 185–86.

[62] *Discourse on Inequality*, Vaughan, I, 180–81.

[63] Vaughan, I, 450–51.

The answers to these questions are only implicit in Rousseau's work. They can be summed up as follows: in the world as it is, such a universal state is impossible; in a world composed of ideal states, it would be neither desirable nor necessary.

Let us first take the world as it is. The prospects of peace and unity are dim precisely because fights among nations are worse than feuds among men before states appeared. Men finally became aware and convinced of their common interest in establishing civil societies, but their purpose was to protect the "ins" against the "outs." It was not an end to competition, merely a *displacement* of it. There is, then, a difference not merely of degree but of essence between the creation of a state and the building of the world state: the former merely *orders* conflict (in the sense of abolishing domestic violence, but allowing and indeed fostering external turmoil); the latter would *eliminate* the competitive use of force.[64] Moreover, this ordering of conflict, to the extent that it makes international war so much more formidable than the state of war in *de facto* society, further weakens the influence "common-interest" arguments can exert upon states. The earlier violence was still anarchic and mild enough to be overcome by such reasoning, but wars among states have become institutionalized; the more intense the fighting, the higher the stakes (in the sense of being greater and being more distant from the citizens' lives, with such elements as national pride and prestige involved), and the more devastating the effects, the less likely are rational arguments of common interest to be heard. Indeed, Rousseau suggests that one component of the original "law of nature," the remnants of which may have played a role in convincing men to abolish war among themselves, has left even fewer traces (and thus kept far less vigor) among states—compassion.[65] So we are faced with units—the states— whose *amour-propre* (hence insecurity) is far more inflated than finite man's could ever be and whose compassion is practically nil. Finally, we must not forget that international conflict is a safeguard for tyrants: world insecurity assures domestic security; for them, would not world peace entail domestic insecurity?

Thus one comes to a triple and dismal conclusion. The only combinations of states likely to emerge in the world are competitive ones, alliances and leagues whose members temporarily agree to suspend the competition among themselves in order better to

---

[64] Or, more accurately, it would reserve to the world-state the monopoly of the legitimate use of force.

[65] *Discourse on Inequality*, Vaughan, I, 182.

resist or to attack other contenders. The "general society of mankind," which existed neither in the original state of nature nor in the corrupt state of *de facto* society, is not likely to result from the international world either. Lastly, should the domination of one state be imposed on all others through conquest, the resulting world empire could not be the carrier of world peace, for the rule of force can never become legitimate: the compact between conqueror and conquered, "far from liquidating the state of war, assumes its continuance."[66]

But what about the ideal world—that of *The Social Contract?* Here again, a world federation or a world state is ruled out. A federation with a legislative body and coercive powers would conflict with the character of sovereignty as defined in *The Social Contract*: sovereignty is indivisible. The essence of the general will—indestructible, inalienable, incapable of being represented—is such that any formula of shared legislative powers, which federation requires, would destroy that identity of freedom and authority which *The Social Contract* purports to achieve, and would restore heteronomy.[67] Moreover, such a federation would rule over far too vast a territory; Rousseau believed that chances for autonomy exist only in small states; like Montesquieu and like the Greek philosophers, he saw large states as major threats to freedom.[68] A world-wide "city of the Social Contract" was inconceivable, since the legislative general will could not assemble in any given place. The bigger the state, the weightier the bureaucracy; the greater the need for a strong (i.e., dangerous) executive, the greater the need for intransigent virtue among the citizens; the smaller the likely "ratio in which the wills of individual citizens stand to the general will or, in other words, customs [*moeurs*] to laws," the greater the need for repressive force.[69]

All those arguments convinced Kant, too, of the impossibility of a world government. If we start with Rousseau's conception of the ideal state—small, ruled by an indivisible general will—then the only links among states that do not conflict with it are confederations, which may have common executive organs appointed or instructed by the legislators, but in which the legislators (i.e., the general wills) would remain separate national entities. Associations of governments are possible, but not of peoples, just as Rousseau's

[66] Vaughan, II, 31 (and in general, Book I, chap. 4 of *The Social Contract*).

[67] See the reasoning in Windenberger, *op. cit.*, chap. 6.

[68] See Vaughan, I, 484 ff.; II, 56 ff., 64 ff., 154, 442–43.

[69] Vaughan, II, 66.

idea of sovereignty rules out genuine local self-government except in the form of regional delegations from the executive.[70]

Thus the road to a "general society of mankind" does not pass through a world government. Rousseau's constant sarcasms about "cosmopolitans" should be kept in mind.[71] The arguments of a number of Frenchmen opposing European supranational institutions have a clearly Rousseauistic ring: there is, at present, no European nation, only a variety of European nations that wish to cooperate; *legitimate* decisions among them can be taken only by the agents of the separate popular wills; otherwise, the decisions would only represent either the will of one of those communities imposed on the others, or the will of "technocrats"—executive agents operating in a political vacuum. And not all Frenchmen who object to European supranationality (or to the spread of majority rule in the U.N.) are conservatives. In this respect (as well as in some of his constitutional ideas), General de Gaulle appeals to a certain Jacobin tradition that justifiably claims Rousseau as one of its prophets.

However, Jacobinism (not to mention General de Gaulle) brings to mind modern nationalism and particularly the militant nation-state that has often turned a war into a crusade. On this score, Rousseau has been accused of being the father of a form of social organization that has been a worse enemy of peace than the princes he so bitterly denounced. Who can deny that he did indeed constantly celebrate patriotism, identify the good citizen with the good patriot,[72] lecture the Corsicans on the need for a national character,[73] and give the Poles a formidable list of recipes for the deliberate creation of a Polish national spirit that could defy the invaders and the ages?[74] In particular, the pages on national education in Rousseau's essay on Poland foreshadow the missionary zeal of the French First and Third Republics in this essential area of public life.

Here again, however, we must be careful. National pride: yes, Rousseau thought it essential, for it would lend its dynamism, indeed its substance, to the general will; but nationalism as we know

[70] See Hoffmann, "A Real Division of Powers in the Writings of French Political Thinkers," in A. Maass, ed., *Area and Power* (Chicago, 1959), pp. 120–24.

[71] Vaughan, I, 182; II, 144–45. See also the passage on Socrates and Cato in *Economie Politique*, Vaughan, I, 251–52.

[72] Iring Fetscher, *op. cit.*, pp. 194 ff.

[73] Vaughan, II, 319.

[74] Vaughan, II, 319, 348 ff., 431 ff.

it now, definitely not; not because Rousseau was unaware of its consequences—having noted that every patriot is harsh to foreigners, he added that this explained why the wars waged by republics are often worse than those waged by kings.[75] But, as we have observed, to Rousseau war was a source of tyranny and the perpetuation of all those evils of society which the "good society"—that of *The Social Contract*—aimed at eliminating. Indeed, he rejected *la religion du citoyen* as doubly evil: it made the citizens "bloodthirsty and intolerant" and it threatened the nation's security by impelling it into wars with all other nations.[76] Because he thought princes had a vested interest in war, he attacked them vigorously in his critique of St. Pierre's project—where republics are never mentioned.[77] Whoever wants to be free must refrain from becoming a conqueror, he told the Poles. Yet in order to be free, to obey only one's own (higher) will, one must keep invaders out—or if (like the Poles) one is too weak to do so, one must at least be able to prevent them from forcing the inner sanctum of the citizens' conscience into submission. This makes Rousseau's enthusiasm for a citizens' army understandable: to him, it is essentially a defensive army, incapable of undertaking aggression (to which a professional army is more suited), but more capable of making an aggressor's life untenable.[78]

Aggressive nationalism would have destroyed Rousseau's ideal. For he wanted a *polis* in which the irreversible consequences of man's entry into civil society—the development of passions and desires, the urge to look at one's reflection in other people's eyes, the mirror game of social vanity—could be channeled to good, i.e., moral, uses. Patriotism is such a good use, for it combines *amour-propre* and virtue.[79] The building of national character is an attempt to dissociate the two elements of *amour-propre*, vanity and pride, so as to smother the former under the latter. Vanity is the result of comparisons with others and of "the fruit of opinion"; pride is born of one's own achievements.[80] The competitions that he advocates for schools and public games, the medals and distinctions he recommends, the national (but not nationalist) celebrations he describes, are all efforts to make the seeds of human vanity

[75] Vaughan, II, 144.
[76] Vaughan, II, 129.
[77] Vaughan, I, 389–92.
[78] Vaughan, II, 486–92.
[79] Vaughan, I, 251. See Fetscher, *op. cit.*, pp. 62 ff.
[80] Vaughan, I, 217; II, 319, 344–45, 441.

sprout into flowers of legitimate collective pride.[81] Rousseau favors a kind of Stakhanovism among citizens, but one that aims at civic virtue, not at national power: the citizens are invited to compete with one another to such a purpose, not to compete with or compare themselves to foreigners.[82] And if he wants them to celebrate work, it is not in order to promote the state's grandeur, but because work is the condition and guarantee of civic virtue; whereas leisure and luxury, credit and speculation are the surest roads to corruption.[83] The Switzerland of his days or the United States of Tocqueville's would be much better examples than any of the new nations of the postwar world—precisely because events have made Rousseau's ideal impossible, as we shall see.

For the community of peaceful but proud nations Rousseau had in mind was a very special sort. Interdependence, the result of our proliferating needs and wants, is evil whenever it engenders dependence. (Rousseau's most eminent quality is one his critics have often denied him—consistency.) Independence, once society appears, is possible for man only in the modern form—not as isolation but as autonomy.

Autonomy can be sought in one of two ways. If man lives in an already corrupted society, he ought to be educated so as to be preserved from corruption and to fulfill himself apart from the polity: autonomy here means following the universal precepts of individual moral behavior, i.e., enjoying the benefits of civil society (a moral sense) without participating in its evils. This is the way of Émile. If man lives in a society that is still pure, autonomy means behaving as a citizen, following the imperatives of the general will —i.e., of man's higher self defined as the self that participates in and wants the common good of his community. This is the way of *The Social Contract*. But this latter kind of autonomy (the only one that really protects man from the disastrous effects of political decisions made without his consent and participation) can be achieved only in small communities. So, if they are to avoid becoming the stakes or the tools of others, these communities must be as self-sufficient as possible. They must aim at an autarky as different, as Iring Fetscher has shown, from the pre-belligerent

[81] Vaughan, II, 434 ff.; Fetscher, *op. cit.*, pp. 194 ff.

[82] See esp. Vaughan, II, 437 ff.

[83] Vaughan, II, 346–47. See also the remarkable passage: "In all that depends on human labor, one must carefully rule out machines and inventions capable of making work shorter, of reducing the amount of manpower needed, and of producing the same results with less effort." Vaughan, I, 320.

autarky of Nazism as patriotism is from aggressive nationalism.[84] In the original state of nature, man, enjoying the "absolute existence" of an "absolute whole,"[85] was both independent and self-sufficient; in the ideal society, his independence is transmuted into autonomy, and independence and autarky become the attributes of the state. Indeed, only if the state is an "absolute whole" can the citizen be autonomous. Otherwise, the tyranny of world competition will rule the state, and the citizen can be neither free nor virtuous. "The nation will not be famous, but it will be happy. Others will not mention it. It will have little prestige outside. But it will have abundance, peace and freedom within."[86]

Rousseau's philosophy remains consistent also in its discontinuities. There is a break between man in the state of nature and man in society. There is a break between man-in-society brought up for himself and man brought up exclusively as a citizen. A third break lies between the ideal society, in which, so to speak, man is reconciled with himself, and the international milieu: so as not to live any longer in any sort of mixed system, the citizen of the good state will do his best not to be an actor on the world stage. Were the whole planet covered with small, essentially self-sufficient republics, endowed with civic pride but no national vanity and equipped with purely defensive militias, then the world would *ipso facto* be at peace. A general society of mankind would emerge, composed not of "cosmopolitans" or "world citizens" but of good citizens—men who would have arrived at the modern, or social, equivalent of natural man's *amour de soi* and compassion, by curbing *amour-propre*, overcoming those passions which "speak louder than [their] conscience,"[87] and practicing patriotism without belligerency. However, this general society would not entail a "real union," with formal links between its member nations, just as there was no real union between men in the original state of nature.

The state of nature was a state of independent men who followed, in their rare encounters, the dictates of the (non-rational)

[84] *Op. cit.*, pp. 241 ff.

[85] Vaughan, II, 145.

[86] Vaughan, II, 353. Abundance here means the welfare that accrues from the citizens' work, not from private wealth: "everybody must live and nobody must get rich. . . . Poverty became noticeable in Switzerland only after money had begun to circulate." Rousseau's distrust of commerce and finance runs through *The Social Contract*, the second *Discourse*, and the *Project for Corsica*: the Corsicans are invited to be a pastoral nation, for in agricultural self-sufficiency lies independence; in commerce lies wealth, but wealth brings dependence. Vaughan, II, 330, 322, 311.

[87] Vaughan, I, 452.

natural law of self-preservation and compassion; the ideal international society would be like pearls juxtaposed but not on a string: independent states that would observe, in their infrequent and relaxed contacts, the commands of "rational natural law," the rules of the original natural law re-established, by reason, on new foundations.[88] Thanks to the self-sufficiency of each nation, our natural reluctance to inflict harm (i.e., our compassion) would no longer be stifled by fear of being harmed.[89] Whereas only through the social contract can man both escape his fallen state of nature and fulfill his moral development, it is now clear why there is no need to envisage a similar compact among states founded on the contract's formula.

Thus, the solution to the problem of war and peace, in Rousseau's mind, is really a "second-image" solution: establish ideal states all over the world, and peace will follow—without the need for a world league *à la* Kant. It is also a "first-image" solution: in the ideal state, man's nature is rescued from the despondency of mixed systems, and he is again at peace with himself. Here, we are very far from contemporary schemes for world peace and very close to the Greek ideal of the primacy of domestic politics: the road to peace passes through the ethical (small) state.

However, there is no guarantee that all states will ever be ideal or ever be capable of practicing the austere virtues of the frugal, self-sufficient nation. Some may continue to depend on others for food or other supplies and thereby risk becoming objects in the international competition; others may be so naturally wealthy as to excite the envy of the "have-nots." All the causes of conflict, that is, may still be with us. Moreover, even if the princes disappear, we have no assurance that in some state the general will could not be corrupted, and superseded by a mere will of all, expressing nothing but human passions, or by a particular will. So, purely domestic reasons may also bring a return to international competition. Finally, when republics occasionally clash, the patriot's tendency to be "harsh toward foreigners" may once again overcome the "reluctance to inflict harm."

For such eventualities, and *not* for a world of peaceful, "general-will" states, Rousseau advocates confederations.[90] Those leagues

---

[88] Vaughan, I, 138.

[89] Vaughan, I, 494.

[90] Here, again, Rousseau learned much from Montesquieu. See *L'Esprit des Lois*, Book IX, chaps. 1–3. On Rousseau's confederations, see Vaughan's discussion, I, 95 ff.

are not the crowning of his theory, as Kant's league of states is for Kant the summit of mankind's grubby ascent. As in Montesquieu, confederations mark not the *end* of conflict but a way for a number of small states to get together, without sacrificing sovereignty, for defensive purposes in the world conflict. They do not signal international sunshine; they provide a shelter against the storm. This is the logic of peace-via-deterrence, rather than of peace-through-law.

Thus, Rousseau's answers to the problem of peace are two. On the one hand, a world *not* composed of ideal states admits of only two ways of mitigating conflict: the observance of those "true principles of the law of war," which he opposes to Grotius' precepts, and which are based on the postulate that war is a contest among states but not men[91]; the other, the confederation. But the former is obviously too fragile to be effective: Rousseau himself tells us that nations obey legal rules only as long as they believe they have an interest in obeying them.[92] And the latter formula does not end folly: it merely provides small states with a way of being wise among fools;[93] it tells them to be hedgehogs in the midst of insecurity. We can only speculate for how long Rousseau thought such associations could be made to last; his analysis of international competition leads to skepticism about the solidity of the leagues he had in mind.

On the other hand, his principal answer—the ideal world of small, self-sufficient, self-centered states governed by the general will—is a "solution" to the problem of war only because it is an evasion of politics. Here, we find the most serious of the difficulties of realization to which I alluded earlier. Rousseau's ideal is utopian, in the first place, because it can hardly be achieved so long as the whole world is not covered with such communities; in the second place, because even if they had spread over the whole planet, they would remain what he wants them to be only under conditions that are hard to imagine. In order not to be dragged into the competition again—in order not to be diverted from the closed-circuit practice of patriotism into the open contest of ambition and vanity—the small community ought to be not just self-sufficient but *insulated*. Should its citizens have more than accidental or occasional contacts with foreigners, then they may be tempted to revert to the evil practice of "comparing oneself in order to know

91 Vaughan, II, 159.
92 See Windenberger, *op. cit.*, pp. 143–44.
93 Vaughan, I, 387; II, 158.

oneself." Presumably, the general will—which is always right—will remain unaffected by those contacts and comparisons. However, the judgment that discloses the general will is not always enlightened.[94] The broader the range of relations among communities, the greater is the peril of a resurgent collective *amour-propre* at the expense of the common good, and the risk of a rising tide of envy, fear, aggressiveness, or greed to corrode the general will. If the outside world is *not* to become the crack in the domestic synthesis of freedom and authority, then the world must remain a distant and very lightly pressing reality. Otherwise, the citizen's autonomy will be threatened.

These conditions are met only exceptionally, and never on a sufficient scale to abolish the state of war. Not every community can be an island, and even Corsica got into trouble. America in the nineteenth century would be a partial example, but, even then, she found herself in contact with others to the north and south.

Lessons may be learned from her experience. When a nation puts into practice Rousseau's teachings about patriotism and national character in a context not of isolation but of intercourse with other nations, the thin line between patriotism and nationalism tends to vanish, despite Rousseau's intent. The general will itself becomes corrupted, and the national institutions, however closely patterned after those Rousseau wanted, may be diverted toward the quest for all those stakes that princes traditionally pursue. Competition among citizens for patriotic distinctions can all too easily turn into competition in xenophobia. Whenever this happens, Rousseau's ideal is perverted in a particularly ugly way. When the state is the expression of the general will, and not just the secular arm of a tyrant or prince, then Rousseau's formula about wars being waged among *states* and not among *peoples*, affecting individuals neither as men nor even as citizens but only as soldiers, loses its point.[95] When the states *are* the peoples, when all the citizens are soldiers, wars come close to that evil from which Hobbes hoped the state would shelter the people—shocks in which whole populations are thrown against each other. Total war instead of complete peace; a general will that is right because it is national, rather than rational: Rousseau would have been aghast at such a perversion. He wanted the ideal of the general will realized in a context of isolation, but events have decreed other-

[94] Vaughan, II, 50.
[95] Vaughan, I, 300 f.

wise. Self-government and self-determination spread in a context of international conflict.

In addition, not only has the historical context thwarted the ideal, but the evolution of the world economy and of communications has made nations even more interdependent and increasingly eager to join the race for wealth. The modern world has repudiated Rousseau's ideal of a community pleased with its frugality, proud of its austerity, hostile to machines and to division of labor, opposed to big cities or feverish social mobility. If nations want to be self-sufficient, it is only in the sense of having an economy balanced enough to withstand external shocks, but this implies a domestic expansion of production and wealth. Today's new nations behave as if there were an international obligation to furnish aid for their development—an obligation that increases mutual dependence and leads to a more frantic pace in the growth of the induced desire that industrial society engenders.

Paradoxically, Rousseau, who recognized that man could never revert to the state of nature, advocated for nations a return to an isolation that the march of history had proved impossible long before he wrote. But the paradox is more apparent than real, for he recognized also that most of the states of his day were too corrupt ever to be capable of applying the principles of *The Social Contract*: only a few small nations could still be saved—obviously not enough to make universal peace possible.[96] It follows that if that peace is obtainable only on Rousseau's conditions, we are condemned to the competition he so searchingly described. The question arising from this depressing conclusion is whether, despite Rousseau, peace cannot be reached in our world instead of in utopia. Here we must turn to Kant.

III

Both Rousseau and Kant identify peace and morality; both consider that the man who listens to the imperative of morality within him must want peace, and that the good community shuns war.[97] However, a sharp difference in their conceptions of man's nature and of society's role explains the different outcomes of their quests for peace. The battle between man's selfish desires and his moral

[96] *Oeuvres*, IX, 287; Vaughan, II, 146.

[97] On Kant's philosophy of peace, see C. J. Friedrich, *Inevitable Peace* (Cambridge, Mass., 1948), and Pierre Hassner's admirable study, "Les Concepts de guerre et de paix chez Kant," *Revue française de science politique*, Vol. 11 (September, 1961). I have followed Hassner's demonstration.

imperative Rousseau describes as a consequence of *society*, which was responsible for the former and in which the latter emerges. But Kant sees this battle as a permanent feature of *man*: the moral imperative is already at work in the state of nature; it is that very imperative which creates a duty to get out of the state of nature; for, like Hobbes and in opposition to Rousseau, Kant argues that precisely because of those selfish desires, the state of nature is a state of war.

Consequently, society, which is the *cause* of a fall for Rousseau's man, since it frustrates and perverts the very moral sense it brings forth in him, Kant sees on the contrary as a *condition* of moral progress, since it is the prerequisite to the establishment of law and to moral action (obstacles to which it is the function of law to remove). But if society causes no fall, reform of society cannot bring redemption, either. In the ideal society of *The Social Contract*, man succeeds in subordinating his particular interests to the general will; thus, authority and freedom are reconciled, and the drama of man's moral division, the battle between the lower and the higher self, comes to an end; political and moral problems are solved together. For Kant, the best society is not the one that *makes* man behave morally, it is the one in which man is most *free* to behave morally if he wants to. If world peace presupposes republican states, it is because they are least likely to be bellicose. Kant's conception of constitutional government is less demanding than Rousseau's: it is almost the opposition between the open and the closed society. On the other hand, the establishment of republics all over the world does not eliminate the problem of war, as a world of "general will" communities would: man's evil propensities may still prevail. Hence there is a need for *additional* legal guarantees to make eternal peace less shaky, in the absence of the world republic that Kant rejects.

So, whereas Rousseau's solution to the problem of war is in the establishment of the good society, Kant, who found the root of war in man's nature, not in society's "denaturation" of man, could not fulfill the imperative of peace with the setting up of ideal states —hence the league for eternal peace. Yet, because man remains free either to heed the categorical imperative or to follow his selfish drives, Kant's peace plan would have set up merely a desirable goal, had it not been accompanied by a philosophy of history that turned this moral end into an historical terminus. Kant's paradoxical conception was of world peace achieved not because of man's moral progress but despite man's moral failings, and brought about not by man's deliberate efforts but by a hidden plan of nature that relies on two highly non-moral factors—catastrophes and the convergence of selfish interests. Both are supposed to lead nations to harmony through interdependence—the very opposite of Rousseau's ideal.

Rousseau's empirical theory contradicts in advance the main assumptions of Kant's system. Concerning the league of republican states, Rousseau pointed out that there were major differences between law within each of those states—law backed by the force of the citizens—and the law among them—law whose strength depends on the plausibility of ending conflict and competition, rather than the other way around. Rousseau's argument is that such an end to conflict is possible only as long as contacts between states are limited—in which case no such international law would be necessary. Should these contacts be intense—and intensity is precisely what Kant's philosophy of history counts upon—then the league itself would become an arena and a stake for conflicting ambitions.

One international development of the past twelve years may serve as a test of these respective doctrines. Is not the West European community that has grown since 1950 an example of a league of states with similar constitutional regimes, having established among them what a modern writer has called a "security community,"[98] because of the lessons of two disastrous world wars and because of the convergence of particular interests, especially in trade and production? Ernst Haas' fine analysis of the uniting of Europe[99] has shown that it is precisely through this convergence of interests, interests that now focus on the common institutions Europeans have erected, that the European communities have expanded. Does Kant's philosophy of politics and history provide a better guide to peace than Rousseau's rejection of a philosophy of progress and his apparent conviction that nations have only a choice between abolishing foreign politics or doing their best to survive in the competition?

I doubt that the West European experiment would have dispelled Rousseau's gloom. He would have thought the nature of the enterprise much closer to his idea of a confederation against "unjust aggressors,"[100] than to the federal ideal advanced by many

[98] See Karl Deutsch *et al.*, *Political Community and the North Atlantic Area* (Princeton, N.J., 1957).
[99] *The Uniting of Europe* (Stanford, Calif., 1958); "The Challenge of Regionalism," *International Organization*, Vol. 12 (Autumn, 1958).
[100] Vaughan, II, 158.

present-day optimists. On most matters that affect the vital interests of the participants, supranationality fades away, and decisions must be made in a very traditional manner. (See, for instance, what happened during the European coal crisis of 1959, in the negotiations on a common agricultural policy, and those on the admission of Great Britain to the European Economic Community.) The legislative powers of the Common Assembly are nil, and the enforcing powers of the European civil servants remain sharply limited. To be sure, such a confederation suspends the use of force among its members. However, the reason why such an oasis of peace can bloom is not that world peace is getting nearer, but that an external danger has brought threatened nations together. There is a shift of alignments within a continuing state of war: no less, but no more. In relations among the confederates (due to the very persistence of the state of war), considerations of prestige and calculations of power count as much as cooperation for peace. The politics of the participants display enough jockeying for leadership, enough disagreements on purposes, functions, and institutions, and enough divergent estimates of the "common interest" to make Rousseau's pessimistic analysis relevant.[101] A defensive *external* common purpose does not eliminate the *internal* rivalries that international competition and the clash of *amours-propres* in close contact perpetuate.

In addition, the forces that have bought about the confederation are not unmixed blessings. Rousseau was dubious about the value of harmony forged out of catastrophes. He might say now that all the gains Europeans have made do not quite erase Europe's political collapse through world wars, or eliminate Europe's dependence on the United States for military security. He was dubious, too, of the contributions that selfish and commercial interests make to peace. He would have noticed that the very prospects of wealth and power—which attract members and applicants to the European community—also turn so successful an enterprise into an added cause of tension and fear in world politics as a whole. Those who are left out resent their exclusion. Those who want to enter produce divisions among those who are there already. Outsiders protest about discrimination. Insiders warn against dilution. After all, military conflict was only one aspect of the state of war as Rousseau defined it. He saw greed as a major source of trouble, quite capable of causing states to want to weaken one another—an intention that is the essence of the state of war.

[101] Compare Aron, *Peace and War*, pp. 729 ff.

IV

Whoever studies contemporary international relations cannot but hear, behind the clash of interests and ideologies, a kind of permanent dialogue between Rousseau and Kant. Kant put forward an ideal of international organization for peace that does indeed correspond to the categorical imperative of autonomy which survives in man's heart; this imperative will be frustrated as long as war prevents man from being his own master. Far from displaying the easy optimism and the underestimation of conflict into which later liberals fell, Kant draws the picture of a world dragged into peace by conflict and by greed; if the hope of progress is a duty that the imperative of autonomy imposes on us, the expectation of linear progress is a major fallacy. Rousseau tells us, however, that the very intercourse of nations breeds conflict; that if it is not possible to end such intercourse, the only remedies are fragile mitigating devices; that it is not enough to try to suppress violence, which is the mere expression of drives that are the essence of international politics—a point that contemporary writers and international organizations tend to forget, in their fascination with the nuclear monster. He reminds us that there can be no assurance that each nation will be able to remain its own master, for the competition itself may always become the overriding tyrant. Just as there is no real middle ground between the general will's austere democracy and *"le Hobbisme le plus parfait,"*[102] so there is no lasting shelter between the state of war and the utopia of isolated communities: there are merely differences of degree in the intensity of the struggle. Citizens are thus condemned to remain in a *système mixte* that permanently threatens the reconciliation of law and force which *The Social Contract* tries to accomplish.

The statesman's difficulty is that he *must* play the game of international competition, from which he can escape only exceptionally, and at the same time he *ought* not to lose sight of Kant's ideal. He ought not to give up the hope of a future world community, but he cannot act as if it already existed. Thus, his task comes at least as close to squaring a circle as the job Rousseau had set for himself in *The Social Contract*: how to fight for the particular interest of the nation so as not to jeopardize the eventual reconciliation of national interests, without which no "international community" could ever emerge. Only when the statesman succeeds in this is the tyranny of world conflict alleviated for the citizen.

[102] Vaughan, II, 161.

Rousseau's contribution is in the nature not of a solution but of a warning. Total success cannot take the form of a world Leviathan, which would be either artificial or arbitrary. Although total success requires, in Rousseau's vision, a world that the evolution of history has ruled out, nothing short of total success can be more than a temporary relief from that plague which, as in Camus' Oran, may at any time wake up its rats and send them to die in a happy city.

FOUR

INTERNATIONAL SYSTEMS AND INTERNATIONAL LAW

MY PURPOSES IN THIS ESSAY ARE two: to undertake, in introductory form, one of the many tasks a historical sociology of international relations could perform—the comparative study of a type of international relations that appears in almost any international system, i.e., international law; secondly, to present the rudimentary outlines of a theory of international law that might be called sociological or functional.[1]

[1] These adjectives are borrowed from Julius Stone, "Problems Confronting Sociological Enquiries Concerning International Law," *Recueil des Cours de l'Académie de Droit International*, 89 (1956), I, and Hans J. Morgenthau, *Dilemmas of Politics* (Chicago, 1958), chap. 11, respectively. The only additional works that try to establish a political sociology of international law are Charles de Visscher, *Theory and Reality in Public International Law*, tr. by Percy E. Corbett (Princeton, N.J., 1957); Percy E. Corbett, *Law in Diplomacy* (Princeton, N.J., 1959); B. Landheer, "Contemporary Sociological Theories and International Law," *Recueil des Cours* . . . , 91 (1957), I; and, to some extent, John Herz, *International Politics in the Atomic Age* (New York, 1959), and Morton A. Kaplan and Nicholas Katzenbach, "The Patterns of International Politics and of International Law," *American Political Science Review*, LIII (September, 1959), 693–712—the last two pieces being concerned more with politics than with law. See also Hoffmann, "Quelques aspects

International law is one of the aspects of international politics that reflect most sharply the essential differences between domestic and world affairs. Many traditional distinctions tend to disappear, owing to an "international civil war" that projects primarily domestic institutions (such as parliaments and pressure groups) into world politics and injects world-wide ideological clashes into domestic affairs. But international law, like its Siamese twin and enemy, war, remains a crystalization of all that keeps world politics *sui generis*. If theory is concerned primarily with the distinctive features of systems rather than with the search for general laws that are valid for all systems, international law becomes a most useful approach to international politics.

I propose here to examine the relations between international law and international systems, first in general terms and subsequently in more concrete form with evidence derived from history. Finally, in the light of such a historical presentation, I will examine briefly two of the main politico-legal problems raised by international law.

I

Most theories of domestic politics start with an ideal-type of (1) a community—an unconditional consensus on cooperation, a belief in a common good (however vague) and in the precedence of this common good over particular interests; and (2) an organization, the State, which has created this community or was established by it, and which is endowed with the monopoly of the legitimate use of force. The theory of international politics must start from the ideal-type of milieu in which (1) the behavior of the members ranges from, at best, that of partners in a society—who cooperate on a limited number of issues, rarely unconditionally, and give primary allegiance to themselves, not the society—to that of accomplices in chaos (the social group made up of the states is always on the verge of becoming a fiction); and (2) there is no monopoly of power, over and above that possessed by the members. Thus, whereas procedures for cooperation, for the creation and expression of consent, exist in both domestic and world politics, the permanent possibility of free and legitimate recourse to violence remains the mark of international relations.

du rôle du Droit International dans la politique étrangère des Etats," in Association Française de Science Politique, *La Politique étrangère et ses fondements* (Paris, 1954), pp. 239–77.

This simple point of departure is of decisive importance both for the understanding of international law and for the delimitation of international systems.

Law is a body of rules for human conduct established for the ordering of a social group and enforceable by external power. Domestic law orders the national group by acting directly on the individual citizens and by regulating all the problems that are deemed to be of social importance; it is enforced by the power of the state, exerted directly on individuals. By contrast, international law suffers from three forms of precariousness. The first is its low degree of institutionalization. The second is its unique substance: in the domestic order, which regulates a great mass of individuals, law is an instrument of homogeneity; the international order regulates a small number of subjects and consequently, its law is a law of differentiation, caught between the Charybdis of universality at the cost of vagueness and the Scylla of precision at the cost of heterogeneity. The scope of the subject matter is limited by the reluctance of the subjects to submit themselves to extensive regulations and by the inefficiency of premature regulations: hence, numerous gaps in the body of rules. The third is the limited amount of solidity or authority in international law. I do not refer here to efficiency in Kelsen's meaning of the term, for it is true that most forms of international law are obeyed, but to the obscurities or ambiguities that mar existing rules, since they are established by the subjects themselves; to the fact, analyzed by de Visscher, that the greatest solidarities exist in matters that least affect the power and policies of the subjects, and vice versa; and to the fact that, in Julius Stone's words, international law is the one legal order that provides for its own destruction by the mere force of its own subjects.[2]

An international system is a pattern of relations among the basic units of world politics, characterized by the scope of the objectives pursued by those units and of the tasks performed among them, as well as by the means used to achieve those goals and perform those tasks. This pattern is largely determined by the structure of the world, the nature of the forces that operate across or within the major units, and the capabilities, patterns of power, and political cultures of those units. Such a definition corresponds to accepted definitions of domestic political systems, which are also characterized by the scope of political objectives (the limited state versus

2 *Legal Controls of International Conflict* (New York, 1954), p. 1.

the totalitarian state, the welfare state versus the free-enterprise state) and the methods of organizing power (constitutional relations among the branches of government, types of party systems).

The international system is both an analytic scheme and a postulate. It is a way in which the scholar tries to give structure and meaning to a complex and confusing mass of data. It is also the expression of an assumption that is indispensable to the scholar— that history can be ordered, that there are distinguishable patterns of relations and key variables that can be discerned without artificiality or arbitrariness. A historical sociology of international politics must try to study the international systems that have emerged in history just as political scientists study real (by contrast with imagined) domestic political systems.

Yet here the difficulty begins. The domestic political system is easy to delimit. Its existence is certain: it manifests itself through the combination of positive legal norms and laws of political behavior that result from the social structure, economic regime, traditions, formal institutions of the country, etc. Its limits in time are indicated by easily recognizable changes in the key variables: a revolution that substitutes a new constitutional order for the old one, a radical transformation of the electoral system or of the party system, etc. The international system is much less easy to delimit.

To begin with, its existence is more hypothetical. The analytic scheme corresponds to a historical reality only if three conditions are met. Relations among the units must be regular; they must reach a certain amount of intensity. Secondly, for the system to be more than a hypothesis, of which reality is merely a vague approximation, the units must have a modicum of awareness of their interdependence. In a domestic political system, given the underlying consensus and the overriding central power, the actors (parties, interest groups, etc.) are aware of the existence and structure of the whole. They are system-conscious even if they are competitive or antagonistic. But the international system is more open and more problematic. Such system-consciousness (much in evidence after 1648, much less so in the sixteenth century) is even less synonymous with solidarity than in a domestic system: the lack of consensus and of central power makes it clear why awareness of the interdependence and hostility are perfectly compatible, since the former entails only that the moves and calculations resulting from the latter take into account the existence and possible reactions of the other parts of the system, not that the maintenance of the system be the unit's goal. The third component is specificity. In a domestic system, differentiation between the social system as a whole and the political system is always difficult, but there is always a visible (if partly dependent) subsystem of political institutions. In international affairs, the difference between what is "within" and "without," between domestic affairs and trans-unit relations is not always clear. I am not referring to periods when domestic affairs become stakes in the international competition (when the boundaries between domestic and foreign affairs, although transgressed, are still recognizable), but to periods when the boundaries that separate "within" from "without" fade away. It is hard to discuss an empire's international relations as if it were itself an international system; it is equally difficult to apply the concept to feudal periods during which territoriality is scrambled.

Secondly, the limits of an international system in space are also often problematic. At times, different systems coexist on the map but ignore each other. It is also possible for a single system (say, the European one in the seventeenth and eighteenth centuries) to be composed of different subsystems, within each one of which relations were far more intense than in the over-all system.

The problem of the limits in time is the most serious of all. As Raymond Aron has observed, periodization is both necessary and dangerous: the historian is free in his choice of criteria, but he should refrain from attributing to the periods he establishes consequences that only empirical evidence can prove.[3] The choice of criteria is obviously dictated by one's concerns as a scholar: one will say that there has been a change of system (rather than change merely *in* the system) when the key variables one has selected have undergone a decisive change; the choice of the key variables and of the amount of change deemed decisive depends on the purpose of the study. Given my own conception of international politics and the resulting emphasis on conflict, the criteria I would propose are what I would call the *stakes of conflict*. A new system emerges—

1. When there is a new answer to the question: what *are* the units in potential conflict? —i.e., when the basic structure of the world has changed (as in the passage from the city-state system to the Roman Empire; from the Empire to the medieval system; from the medieval hierarchy to the modern "horizontal" system of multiple sovereignties).

2. When there is a new answer to the question: what *can* the

[3] "Evidence and Inference in History," *Daedalus*, 87 (Fall, 1958), 11–39.

units do to one another in a conflict? —i.e., when there is a basic change in the technology of conflict. (Such a change may also transform the basic structure of the world: as John Herz has reminded us, the gunpowder revolution ushered in the era of the "impermeable" territorial state.[4]) Even within the same type of basic structure, a fundamental innovation in the technology of conflict changes the nature of the international system: the atomic revolution rendered obsolete previous multiple-sovereignty systems because it meant the passage from a relative to an absolute power of destruction and consequently the end of great-power "impermeability." An effective diffusion of nuclear power could mean still another system.

3. When there is a new answer to the question: what do the units *want* to do to one another? Here, we try to distinguish systems according to the scope of the units' purposes and to the techniques they use to meet their objectives or to prevent rivals from achieving theirs.

If we combine the criteria, we come to the fundamental distinction between stable systems and revolutionary ones. A stable system is one in which the stakes of conflict are limited; relations among the actors are marked by moderation in scope and means. Whatever the system's basic structure and the state of the technology of conflict, the units act so as to limit the amount of harm they could inflict upon one another. In a revolutionary system, this moderation disappears. When one major actor's decision to discard it coincides with or brings about a revolution in the technology of conflict or a change in the basic structure of the world (or both), the system is particularly unstable.[5] In other words, in a stable system, the life or essential values of the basic units are not constantly in question, and the main actors agree on the rules according to which competition among them will take place; in a revolutionary system, the incompatibility of purposes rules out such agreement.

[4] *International Politics in the Atomic Age* (New York, 1959).
[5] The *number* of violent conflicts is not involved in these definitions. A stable period may be marked by frequent wars as long as they remain limited in objectives and methods. A revolutionary period may not necessarily be marked by all-out general war, if the technology of conflict introduces a mutual interest in avoiding the total destruction such a war would entail. But as long as this restraint does not bring back moderation in the purposes and means of conflicts other than all-out war, the system remains largely revolutionary, although it disposes of an element of stability—a fragile element, given all the other circumstances.

For each kind of basic structure in the world and each kind of technology of conflict, we may arrive at the ideal-type of stable system by asking: what are the conditions from which moderation in scope and means is most likely to follow? At times, actual historical systems meet these conditions, but often they do not; and they are, of course, marked by constant change in all their elements. The changes (1) do not affect the system at all, when they do not hurt or remove the essential conditions of stability; (2) merely weaken the system, when they cripple some of those conditions but do not wholly destroy the moderation in scope and means; (3) ruin the system altogether if such deterioration, instead of leading to temporary disturbances, brings about a breakdown in moderation, a revolution in the technology of conflict or in the basic structure of the world.

Whether a change affecting the essential conditions of stability damages the system decisively depends on the circumstances. A breakdown requires the collapse of a large number of such conditions. This can happen either when one of the main actors decides to overthrow the system and succeeds in removing so many of the conditions of stability that the system does indeed collapse—i.e., when the actor's move leads not simply to *any* kind of conflict, but to a revolutionary one; or when previous deterioration leads to a conflict that may not begin as revolutionary but becomes so because it develops into a decisive additional factor of disruption. In both cases, the end of the stable system is marked by general war.[6]

In the world of multiple sovereignties before the appearance of absolute weapons, it was the balance-of-power system that brought stability to international politics, a pattern of relations among states which, through shifting alliances and the use of various diplomatic techniques, tends to limit the ambitions of the main units, to preserve a relative equilibrium among them, and to reduce the amount of violence among them. The ideal conditions for such a system are the following:

1. In the structure of the world: a greater number of major

[6] Besides making the fundamental distinction between stable and revolutionary systems, we have to distinguish among stable and among revolutionary ones. Here, our criteria should be, in addition to the basic structure of the world and the state of the technology of conflict: in the case of stable systems, the *kind* of means used by the actors in their competition and cooperation (see below, pp. 100 ff., for the distinction between the stable system which preceded the French Revolution and the stable system which followed the Congress of Vienna; both were "balance of power" systems, but the latter was more institutionalized than the former); in the case of revolutionary systems, the type of *objectives* for which the conflict takes places (religious allegiance, form of government).

states than two; relative equilibrium of power among them; the existence of a frontier zone where the major states can expand without fatally colliding, which is a prerequisite of the kind of flexibility that a balancing system needs.

2. Related to transnational forces: technological stability; a common outlook among the leaders of the major states, provided by either similar regimes or a common attitude to religion or similar beliefs about the purpose of the state. A common outlook allows for horizontal ties as strong as or stronger than the political ties that attach those leaders to their domestic communities; a common conception of legitimacy can thus develop.

3. Related to domestic affairs within the major units: the existence of political systems in which the state exercises only limited control over its citizens' international loyalties and activities.

The outcome of these conditions is a system in which the major units' objectives are limited to only moderate increases in power or prestige, and in which many of the tasks that could be performed through the processes of world politics remain beyond their pale. The means used by the major units in their mutual relations are coalitions, designed to prevent any single unit from disrupting stability, either by rewarding him for his cooperation or by punishing him for misbehavior (but not, however, making it impossible for him to cooperate again).

The ideal conditions for international stability can be defined as *evenness* in the situation of the major units—just as a large degree of identity among the members of a state is necessary for the emergence of the general will. Conversely, the process of deterioration that leads to disturbances within the system and might provoke its breakdown can be summed up as the re-introduction of unevenness or heterogeneity.[7] This process includes the appearance of the following conditions:

1. In the structure of the world: irrepressible ambitions of individual rulers;[8] ambitions kindled by disparity in power between one major actor and its neighbors or other major units; the end of the frontier zones, which increases the likelihood of and stakes in direct clashes between the major units.

2. In the forces that cut across these units: a technological revolution, which leads to instability when it produces competition;

[7] Panayis Papaligouras, *Théorie de la société internationale* (Geneva, 1941).

[8] They do not, by themselves, destroy the balancing system, but they make its operation uncertain and increase the likelihood of "in-system" wars, which may in turn destroy the system if other essential conditions for an ideal balance have also disappeared, or if the logic of war destroys previous limitations on the instruments of conflict.

the destruction of transnational ties either under the impact of national integration, which inevitably submits diplomacy to greater internal pressures, or because of an ideological explosion set off by a disparity of regimes or beliefs.

3. In the domestic affairs of the major units: strong integrative trends leading to nationalism; the expansion of state control over the foreign activities of the citizens for either economic or ideological purposes.

Let us turn now to the relation of international law to various international systems. International law can be studied as a product of international systems and as a repertory of normative theory about each one of them. On the one hand, it is shaped by all the elements that compose an international system:

1. It reflects the structure of the world. The nature of the actors determine whether the law of the system is the "law of coordination" made by territorial states or the external public law of an empire, or whether it will disappear altogether, as it did during much of the medieval period. The size of the diplomatic field determines the degree of universality of the legal order. The degree of unity of international law and the efficiency of a good deal of its provisions depends on the existence, duration, and seriousness of a relationship of major tension.

2. It reflects transnational forces. Technology is of considerable importance: the intensity or density of legal relations among the actors depends largely on the state of the arts. The unity and authority of the legal order depend on the presence and number of transnational ideologies and conceptions of legitimacy.

3. The domestic situation of the major units is also relevant to international law, which has always reflected the patterns of power and the political cultures of the main actors.[9] The development of law by treaties and the reception of rules of international law within the national units depend on provisions of constitutions and decisions of domestic courts.

4. Finally, international law reflects relations among the units. It is shaped by their scope: the breadth and nature of the subject matter regulated by law vary according to the range and character of the goals the units try to reach and of the tasks they try to perform. In particular, rules of law often express the policies of the major units. Moreover, customs and treaties reflect the methods by which units try to meet their objectives, and they regulate at least some of the techniques used.

[9] See Corbett, *op. cit.*, especially chaps. 1–3.

On the other hand, if we turn from empirical systems to norma-tive theories of international law, we find a critical assessment of international systems from the viewpoint of world order. In any political system, order is achieved if the following three require-ments are met: security—i.e., dealing with the problem of conflict by assuring the survival and safety of the members of the system; satisfaction—i.e., dealing with the problem of assent, and obtaining it through constraint or consent; flexibility—i.e., dealing with the problem of change (which is crucial, since assent is never definitive or total), by establishing procedures capable of absorbing shocks and channeling grievances. In a world divided into many nations, order is always threatened. Legal theorists ask whether order is pos-sible at all; if so, whether the system is capable of ensuring it; and if not, what kind of measures are necessary to obtain it. On the whole, in each period of history, there have been those who deny either the possibility or the desirability of a stable legal order; the utopians, who also question the effectiveness of the existing system but propose to substitute a radically different one; and the adjust-ers, who try to show how and to what extent order can be estab-lished or preserved within the existing system. We learn a great deal about the nature and operation of a given international system if we study the range of disagreements among these three groups; the more stable the system, the narrower this range.

Since international law constitutes the formal part of the reign-ing order and expresses the more lasting interests of the actors—their long- or middle-range strategy, rather than their daily tactics —the link between the solidity or authority of international law and the stability of the international system is strong. The basic function of international law is to organize the coexistence of vari-ous nations: this presupposes that their existence is assured. In stable international systems, it is possible to distinguish three kinds of international law:[10]

1. The law of the political framework—the network of agree-ments that define the conditions and some of the rules of the politi-cal game among states. By "conditions," I mean such provisions as the settlement of borders after wars, the main alignments as expressed in treaties of alliance, periodic conferences among major powers; by "rules," I mean provisions that determine the mutual commitments of states or procedures for the settlement of major disputes.

[10] See Georg Schwarzenberger, *Power Politics* (New York, 1951), chap. 13, and Morgenthau, *op. cit.*, pp. 228–29.

2. The law of reciprocity, which defines the conditions and rules of inter-state relations in areas that less vitally affect the power and politics of the states. This is a large zone in which states can be assumed to have a mutual and lasting interest in common rules —a zone of predictability, on which the competition in politically more sensitive areas rests and depends. We can distinguish two kinds of laws of reciprocity: the law of delimitation, which defines the rights and privileges of states—in peacetime over such matters as diplomatic relations, territory, and people, in wartime over weapons, military objectives, noncombatants, etc.; and the law of cooperation, which regulates joint interests, particularly in commerce.

3. The law of community, which deals with problems that can best be handled, not on the basis of a reciprocity of interests among states understood as separate and competing units, but on the basis of a community of action independent of politics—problems of a technical or scientific nature to which national borders are irrelevant.

These distinctions are sound and legitimate in a stable period, for when the survival of the nations involved is insured, a hierarchy of interests becomes possible. The law of the political framework deals the cards with which the players try to reach such objectives as greater power, or prestige, or the triumph of ideals; the law of reciprocity provides the underpinning of national security and defines those functions and attributes of the state that are not at stake in political contests. But in a revolutionary system, the distinction between these two kinds of law becomes extremely fuzzy; when survival is not assured, the limits that the law of reciprocity sets to states' privileges or jurisdictions become obstacles in the quest for greater security and power, while cooperation over joint interests is replaced by conflict or competition which challenges previous rules. In such a system, the power and policies of states are directly involved in almost every aspect of international activity.[11] Thus, in a revolutionary system, the great bulk of interna-

---

[11] Scholars may argue that important mutual interests still exist and that states have little to gain by turning the zone of predictability into a battlefield. But what seems irrational to the scholar from the viewpoint of international society seems rational to the statesman from the viewpoint of his own national calculation, given the peculiar logic of such calculations in fiercely competitive situations. An "objectively" common interest might not be perceived by the antagonists, and, even if it were, there remains an abyss between such perception and a formal legal agreement that might still sanction it. On these points, see Kenneth Waltz, *Man, the State, and War*, pp. 192 ff.

tional law partakes of the somewhat shaky authority of the law of the political framework.

The difference in the solidity of law in revolutionary and stable systems is reflected in the contrasting impacts of political change on law. Changes that do not destroy a stable system do not lethally affect the legal order, precisely because customs and agreements express strategic rather than tactical interests. To be sure, the body of rules reflects such changes if they are of sufficient magnitude: in particular, the disappearance of some of the essential conditions for an ideal stable system has repercussions on the law of the political framework, which is the most sensitive to such tremors; it may also leave its mark on the law of reciprocity, because certain kinds of agreements become increasingly rare, or codification becomes more troublesome, or difficulties appear in the discharge of treaties. However, the law of reciprocity may continue to develop even when the ideal conditions for stability are no longer present (as was shown in the flowering of such law just before World War I) precisely because it reflects mutual interests that the fluctuations of politics do not impair so long as the stable system lasts. Also, while the essential moderation in the scope and means of international relations continues, the gaps and uncertainties of law are not disruptive factors: in the areas which are not regulated or in which the rules are ambiguous, a purely political decision or interpretation by the states concerned will be needed, but, given the system, no destructive effects are likely to follow.

In a revolutionary system, however, gaps and ambiguities become wedges for destruction or subversion of the international order in the interest of any of the actors. The absence of agreement on the rules of the game, the increase in the stakes of conflict, and the reign of insecurity mean that political changes will have the following effects on international law: (1) just as theories and concepts outlive the system that justified them, regulations that have become obsolete nevertheless continue to be considered valid (although they are less and less respected) because of the increasing difficulty in agreeing on new rules, or because they serve the interests of some of the contending units; (2) new problems thrown up by political or technological change remain unregulated, for the same reasons; (3) new regulations appear which attempt to deal with some of the changes but turn out to be incompatible with the new system; and (4) since international systems change essentially through general wars, the collapse of previous laws of war is usually the first effect of the change on the legal order.

This conglomeration of ruin, gaps, and "dysfunctional" old or new rules denotes the major areas of friction and tensions in world politics during the lifetime of revolutionary systems and particularly in periods of passage from one system to another.

Thus, it is in balance-of-power systems that the authority of international law has been greatest: as Oppenheim stated, the existence of the balance is a condition of the flourishing of authoritative international law.[12] However, this condition is at the same time a limitation:

1. Even when the balance functions under optimum conditions, the political framework may remain largely unregulated. We must distinguish between systems in which the balance is more or less automatic or mechanical and systems in which it is institutionalized to a greater degree—a distinction among stable systems based in particular on the law of the political framework.

2. Even under optimum conditions, the balance sometimes operates at the expense of law. In a system of "sovereign" states, the principles of equality and consent are essential to the legal order. But daily practices may conflict with these norms: a preponderance of power often forces small, or isolated large, states to assent to measures that go against their objectives or detract from the formal equality of all the units.

3. Among the many power configurations that characterize the relations of units in a balance-of-power system, there is one that threatens the solidity of international law (especially the law of the political framework) more permanently: when optimum conditions are met, the most likely result is the "mechanism of imbalance"—a coalition of a majority of the main actors against an isolated would-be disrupter; but when those conditions are not all present, there may develop an opposition of blocs of comparable strength, so that alignments stiffen instead of remaining flexible. The authority and unity of international law may then be imperiled.

II

Three concrete examples of relations between international systems and international law will support the preceding generalizations.

The first example is that of international law during the balance-

[12] See the first editions of his *International Law: A Treatise*, Vol. I (London, 1905 and 1912).

of-power system that lasted from the Peace of Westphalia until the French Revolution.

The balance operated effectively because the treaties of Westphalia had redistributed territory so as to create a number of major states capable of neutralizing each other and had also removed the poisonous element of religious conflict. Within the main units, mercantilism and absolutism gradually weakened. New transnational ties developed; the "corporate identity" of monarchs, diplomats, and officers across national boundaries led to a consensus on the legitimacy of the balance, just as the community of European intellectuals produced a consensus on the values of the Enlightenment. The political result was a mechanical balance, frequently disturbed however, either because a state could never be sure in advance whether or when others would try to curb it, or because of individual ambitions. Hence, numerous limited wars occurred: stylized wars of position that only rarely affected the civilian population.

Although there was little international law of the political framework, the law of reciprocity developed in a way that reflected both the moderation and the volatility of a balancing system. In the area of trade, statesmen came to realize that law was the best technique for obtaining an increase in national wealth and power (as in past mercantilist practice), but safely; the idea of harmony of interests replaced the earlier expectation of conflict—hence, numerous measures to protect commerce at sea, especially in wartime. Neutrality for the first time became possible, a good bargain, and a subject of legal regulation. Yet, the balance of power imposed limits to the development of law. To preserve the system, it was required at the end of wars to restore equilibrium among the major powers at the expense of small states; these compensations proved that the norm of territorial integrity was effective only as long as it was backed by force and that it was subordinated to the preservation of the balance. Also, there were gaps wherever rules would have restricted state power too sharply: maritime warfare remained anarchical; there was no adequate procedure for the settlement of disputes developed except in rare instances of delicate arbitration.

The response of theory to these developments was most interesting. In the previous revolutionary system, a large gap had separated destroyers of the medieval dream of unity—like Machiavelli, creators of new dreams—like Crucé or Sully, and the numerous would-be rescuers of the medieval theory—who reasserted the supremacy of natural law and the doctrine of just war, but who secularized the former, hedged in the latter with qualifications, and came to recognize the existence of an international law created by the will of states. Now, in a system of increasing moderation, the gap narrowed. Even those who denied the efficiency of "covenants without the sword" showed that self-restraint might prevent all-out war. At the other pole, the Kantian utopia also reflected the new optimism: to establish order among the states was going to require an essential change in the regimes but not the end of the division of the world into separate units, and it would be effected by the invisible hand of history. The theorists on the middle ground, still trying to save the idea of a legal community of mankind, gradually abandoned the idea of natural law as the bonding cement of this community—a retreat that would have been taken as an invitation to and confession of chaos in the preceding period, but that could now be accepted without anguish; a positivistic emphasis on the fundamental rights of states as the foundation of order no longer seemed necessarily self-defeating. The expectation of a harmony of interests had been fed by the system.

The collapse of that system was a sudden, swift chain reaction. The decisive factor was the change in France's regime—which shows that the study of international systems must extend to the analysis of the political ones they include. The French Revolution, in turn, destroyed transnational links: the heterogeneity of regimes introduced an explosive element into Europe; after a brief period of idealistic pacifism—a revulsion against maintaining the balance of power, that sport of kings—the revolutionaries, turning to messianism, lit the fuse. This attempt to destroy old regimes everywhere removed another essential condition of the balance: nationalism in France led to the imposition of full government control on its citizens' acts and thoughts. Next, equilibrium among the major powers was destroyed by the French victories—an incentive to exploit unevenness even further. Then, Napoleon's ambitions produced the first modern instance of total power politics, based on an ideological inspiration and waged by total domestic and international means. A further series of changes in the conditions of stability resulted: constant shifts in the map of Europe; a transformation of the domestic order of many of the units involved, who moved away from feudal absolutism to defeat France's nationalism with its own weapons; the creation of two opposed ideological camps. Consequently, international law was thoroughly disrupted: the law of neutrality collapsed; wars of total mobilization, movement, and extermination of civilians replaced the ballet of limited wars. We have here the example of a system breaking down because of the deliberate attempt by one of its major component units to destroy it and because of this unit's capacity temporarily to succeed by exploiting the dynamism of revolution.

Let us now examine the international system of the nineteenth century. The defeat of the force that had destroyed the previous system—France—and the apparent collapse of French-inspired ideals seemed to make a return to stability possible. The victors of 1815 decided to restore a balancing system, which they saw as the pattern that could best ensure stability, by giving security to the main powers, providing the greatest amount of flexibility, and obtaining the assent of all participating units, including France (on which only a far tighter organization than the victors were capable of maintaining could have imposed a punitive peace with any chance of success).

Some of the victors wanted a new kind of balancing system, however; what is interesting here is the discrepancy between their intention and performance. Although England was willing to return to a mechanical balance of power, Austria and Russia wanted to extend the scope and means of world politics. Whereas the eighteenth-century balance had excluded intervention in domestic affairs, Metternich and Alexander now wanted an organized balancing system that would include a formula for domestic order in its concept of legitimacy and dispose of means of enforcement against the rise of liberal and nationalist forces. The international law of the political framework would have become an explicit and powerful instrument of the great powers' common policy of preserving the Vienna order in both its international and its internal aspects. But this was not to happen, for it soon appeared that a voluntary system of cooperation was too weak to control developments within nations that a previous balancing system had already been powerless to prevent. In other words, so extensive a community could not be created by superstructural means alone. The failure of the Holy Alliance proved that an effective new balancing system could be obtained only through a return to moderation, not through an ambitious extension, in scope and means.

In the beginning, almost all the conditions for a successful balance were present. The structure of the world was marked by a double hierarchy: the distinction between a civilized core and a frontier, and, within the core, between small and large states. No permanent relation of major tension emerged until after 1870. In the core area, technology expanded but never to a degree that gave one major actor power of life and death over another. Despite the clash of political ideologies, supranational ties persisted: the dominant ideologies were themselves either supranational or favorable to the maintenance of bonds between national elites; the *Internationale* of diplomats allowed for a consensus on the rules of the game. Although regimes were far from identical, the limited state developed everywhere. The conduct of foreign affairs could be divorced from domestic passions. Constitutionalism, marked by the legalization of public affairs and the growth of the judicial apparatus, made notable advances. Liberalism led to a separation between state and society.

Consequently, relations among states were once again characterized by moderation in scope and means. First, the number of tasks performed by the processes of world politics was limited to conflict and political accommodation. The failure of Metternich's hope meant that, within the core area, domestic developments were not a legitimate object of international politics: the "neutrality of alignment"[13] necessary to the effectiveness of the balance required neutrality toward regimes as well, which was possible so long as internal revolutions made no attempt to disrupt the international system. The separation of state and society removed another vast zone from world politics—the field of private transnational activities, especially economic ones. Secondly, the objectives of the major units also remained moderate in scope: they sought limited increments of power and influence within the core area and, on the whole, avoided the destruction of value systems or national existences in this area. As for moderation in means, it was shown by the return to limited wars, the practice of nonintervention within the core area, and the multiplication of international conferences of all kinds.

In this system, international law—the law of the European core area—appeared in all three of the aspects described above, within the limits defined. The law of the political framework was the law of the Concert: as the instrument of the society of the major powers whereby they could supervise small states and control the individual ambitions of each member, it consecrated the power relations that developed for this purpose—hence the prevalence of legal techniques of neutralization and internationalization. These techniques implied agreement on common abstention from or common action in a given area or problem; they resulted from the

[13] See Kaplan and Katzenbach, *op. cit.*

consensus on moderation and cooperation.[14] But since this law was a balancing technique, not a way of overcoming the balance, its development was hampered by the usual limitations. Many rules merely expressed the independence of states: for instance, the principle of unanimity in Concert meetings. Law was violated whenever the maintenance of the system required it—e.g., at both ends of Concert activities: the composition of the meetings violated the principle of equality, and the process of enforcement often twisted the independence, integrity, or free consent of small powers. Lastly, there were major gaps in the law of the framework, as exemplified by the purely voluntary character of Concert meetings and by the total freedom to resort to war. These limitations and violations became increasingly dangerous for world order during the 1860's, when the balance was too fluid—i.e., when the mechanism of imbalance did not function, owing to the divisions or passivity of a majority of the big powers—and during the last years before World War I, when the hardening of the blocs produced arteriosclerosis in the Concert.[15]

The law of reciprocity was a projection of the constitutional state into world affairs, a reflection of mutual interests, and a product of the balancing system, which curtailed states' objectives. The law of delimitation became firmly established. The law of cooperation progressed considerably in commerce, where the retreat from mercantilism opened a "depoliticized" zone for free trade and for the free establishment of aliens, and in the settlement of disputes, as states became willing to resort to judicial procedures in a variety of cases involving either private citizens in the "depoliticized" area or state interests directly, but which the actors found convenient to arbitrate since the balance of power had made resort to force less profitable, or because the development of domestic legal institutions had given greater prestige to legal than to diplomatic mechanisms. But, in all its branches, the law of reciprocity suffered from the same weakness as the law of the political framework. Different standards for the treatment of foreigners applied by the major states to "civilized" nations and to backward areas showed the limit of the norm of equality. The treatment of debtors by creditor nations proved that the law often identified right with might. "Depolitization" came to an end either when

---

[14] For a more detailed analysis, see Hoffmann, *Organisations internationales et pouvoirs politiques des Etats* (Paris, 1954), Part 1.

[15] It was in 1871 that Russia denounced the Black Sea provisions of the Paris Treaty, in 1908 that Austria annexed Bosnia-Herzegovina.

citizens ran into trouble abroad and appealed to their country of origin, or when a dispute fell within one of the numerous areas excluded by reservations in arbitration treaties. Spectacular failures at the Hague Conferences left many gaps in the laws of war and for the settlement of disputes. Again, these weaknesses became more severe when the Concert did not function well; at the end of the period, a return to protectionism, tariff wars, and the failure of the London Conference on maritime warfare were signs of deterioration.

The law that best reflected all the elements of the system was the law of war and neutrality. Since war was a legitimate method of settling disputes, and since law attempted not to curtail the ends sovereignty served but to regulate the means it used, war was entitled to a *status*: it received a legal framework, which distinguished sharply between peace and war (hence the need for a formal declaration at one end, a treaty at the other) and between international and civil strife. Within this framework, the means of war and the various categories of war victims were regulated.

Secondly, since total war practices were banned by the balance of power, and war had once again become a method of settlement of disputes but not a way of eliminating one's antagonist, war was considered to be merely a *moment*; it was a dispute between states, not between individuals—hence the customs and court decisions on the effects of war on treaties and, more importantly, the crucial distinction between combatants and noncombatants in war, between the duties of the neutral state and those of neutral citizens. Furthermore, it was a political dispute, not an interruption of economic processes—hence the protection of the neutral trader, who was maintaining the continuity of these processes, and the inviolability of as much of the belligerents' private property as was possible, both at sea and in occupied territory.

The law of community also expanded, through countless conferences, conventions, and even institutions; it regulated an increasing number of administrative and technical functions.

Consequently, the law of the nineteenth-century balance-of-power system, in matters that directly affected the power and the policies of the major states, was the transcription of the balancing process in normative terms, the expression of a system in which each state submitted to law insofar as the rules were supported by the pressure of stronger force. In other matters, law grew out of the restrictions to which power consented, in a liberal century, for the development of nonpolitical forces of reciprocity and for the devaluation of borders.

One result of this double role of law was a fairly effective system of world order. Security was achieved in the core area, especially for the major national units; lesser ones bought survival at the cost of supervision and, often, partial sacrifices of sovereignty. The Concert tried to preserve flexibility by acting to legalize and harness revolutionary changes. Assent was never complete, but as long as the major powers preferred, or had no choice but to prefer, the maintenance of the system to the gains they might hope to reap by destroying it, this was enough.

Another result was a new *rapprochement* among the three groups of theorists, who now agreed on a number of crucial points: the possibility of avoiding chaos; the basic character of the state as the foundation of world order (and the definition of the state in terms of will); and, paradoxically, the weaknesses of international law in the world as it was (an admission that, as in the previous stable period, could be made because of the general moderation of world politics). Even "deniers" such as Hegel believed in a European family, or a "higher praetor," which would prevent the warring states from turning inevitable war into inexpiable hate. Even the visionaries no longer dreamed of supranational utopias: they thought the world was moving toward a community of harmonious nation-states, thanks to free trade and public opinion. The positivists dealing with the previously avoided problem of the basis of legal obligation, could come up with auto-limitation, *Vereinbarung,* or an indivisible community of interests, without feeling that these were circular answers. At an earlier period, stressing the differences between international and municipal law, and the individual rights of the state, they had sounded almost like the cynics. Now, on the contrary, the positivists and the visionaries were close.[16] Both saw a new world almost without power, but they failed to realize that the retreat of power from certain spheres had been the result of a highly political balancing process—which was in its death throes just when the theorists believed the millennium was coming.

The deterioration of the system had, once again, started with a change in the domestic order, but this time it was a change that occurred in most of the major units, and it was gradual, not deliberate. The emergence of the modern nation-state weakened some of the essential conditions for an ideal balance of power; for in a

[16] See Walter Schiffer, *The Legal Community of Mankind* (New York, 1954).

nation-state, the population is mobilized around national symbols, and the development of the machinery of the state reinforces international integration at the expense of transnational ties. After 1870, the army's weight in domestic affairs increased everywhere, pushing the nations toward imperialism. Consequently, a change occurred in the structure of the world that almost obliterated the difference between disturbances within and destruction of the system: the end of the frontier. In addition, horizontal links between major powers were progressively weakened by the rise of mass nationalism, the success of philosophies of conflict and of national or racial superiority, and nationalities' movements that sought allies among the major powers. The legitimacy of states that were not based on the national principle was challenged; thus, international legitimacy was concerned again with domestic affairs; heterogeneity returned to the system. As a result, relations among states took on new and threatening aspects. The very frequency of disturbances, due to the uncertainty of the balance, created a climate of dissatisfaction in which small powers tried to escape the control of bigger ones. The big states, also looking for a way out, could agree only on temporary adjustments, which would not tie their hands for the future but which infuriated the small powers. In such a climate, the freezing of the balance of power after Bismarck's departure meant the end of "neutrality of alignment"; the replacement of the hierarchical system of the Concert with a vertical one, in which blocs composed of large *and* small states faced each other; hence a change in means (the decline of the Concert, the return to arms races) and an increase in scope (economic affairs became vital again in international politics). Another change in means— the resort to general war—dealt the death blow to the system; the "technical surprise" of World War I, to use Aron's expression, made the objectives of states once again incompatible and increasingly more universal.

Lastly, I would like to discuss the relation of international law to world politics in the present revolutionary system.

The structure of the world today is characterized by one consolidation and two deep transformations. On the one hand, the diplomatic field, which the previous system had gradually extended and unified, embraces the whole world for the first time. On the other hand, bipolarity has replaced the multiplicity of major actors (and put an end to the mechanism of imbalance); and the splintering of the frontier into a large number of new units has obliterated the distinction between a core area and the rest.

Secondly, a gigantic technological revolution has led to a competition to be foremost in industrial power, and it has not been accompanied by the restoration of universal transnational links. The diversity of regimes, "isolationist" reactions in many nations (especially new ones) to the intrusion of foreign affairs into all spheres of life, the tendency of the dominant forms of political regime to project and promote themselves throughout the world —these conditions have resulted in the absence of any clear and extensive conception of international legitimacy, and in huge ideological rivalries. New transnational links have emerged as a consequence of the latter, but they are divisive, competitive, and often negative solidarities.

The spiritual and temporal control of the state over its citizens has increased everywhere. Just as the old territorial essence of sovereignty was becoming obsolete, the spreading ethics of nationalism and the universal practices of public welfare have given to sovereignty an incandescent "personal" core.

The outcome is a series of revolutionary changes in the scope and means of world politics. There is no longer a "depoliticized" zone of major importance. The collapse of empires has made economic development, once dealt with by private investment or behind the walls of empires, one of the largest issues of world politics. Nor has the separation of domestic and international affairs been sustained: the logic of intervention, either to enforce a degree of conformity within one's own camp or to subvert the adversary's, has made the diffusion of political "ways of life" one of the tasks performed by world politics.[17] Consequently, the objectives of states have expanded so that the full realization of the goals of one unit or bloc would often involve the physical or moral death of another unit or camp, and such goals include blueprints for domestic as well as for international order. As for means, they have never been so varied: "total diplomacy" ranges from highly institutionalized military alliances to economic warfare, from propaganda to a host of international organizations; quasi-Doomsday machines and traditional limited wars coexist with revolutionary guerrilla wars. There is one moderating force that makes this revolutionary system an original one: the possibility for one power alone to inflict unacceptable damage on its enemies, however numerous. This makes a return to the principle of imbalance unlikely in case of a

[17] Many of the difficulties of the U.N. operation in the Congo stemmed from the attempt to distinguish between domestic and international aspects of the crisis—an exercise in fiction.

new multipolar system, but it also makes the actors hesitate far more to resort to violence than the dynamism of a revolutionary system would otherwise allow—hence the appearance of an extremely delicate and uncertain restraint.

In comparison with the pre-1914 system, the present one is marked by extraordinary and continuing changes and by great complexity.[18] Such changes and complexity have had an enormous impact on international law; the European legal order of the past could not be stretched to the dimensions of the new system without major changes.

Let us look first at the impact of these changes. In the first place, huge chunks of the traditional body of rules have been destroyed.

Basic distinctions which established in the legal order the restraints of the balance-of-power system have lost their meaning or justification. The distinction between matters of domestic jurisdiction and matters regulated by international law has practically vanished, in a period when the choice of a regime largely determines the international conduct of a state. The distinction between civilized nations and the others is challenged by the new states' objections to many traditional rules (e.g., in regard to territorial waters or even diplomatic representation). The distinction between private acts for which the state is not responsible and public acts has been destroyed through the intervention or subversion of "private" groups manipulated by their governments, and through the growing importance of transactions between large foreign or international "private" companies and the state. The distinction between war and peace has been replaced by what Philip Jessup has called situations of intermediacy: a period of irreconcilable oppositions, ideological clashes, *and* fear of total war could not but engender wars without declaration, armistices without peace, non-belligerency without war, and aid to insurgents without recognition of belligerency.

Consequently, many traditional rules have been destroyed by massive violations. Many provisions of war and neutrality could

18 We speak of a "loose bipolar system" in which "bloc actors" tend to become more important than unit actors—but, at the same time, the rate of obsolescence of strategies and the diffusion of nuclear power challenge such a view. Inversely, we refer to the fragmentation of the old frontier into multiple new sovereignties, but, at the same time, the necessities of the struggle against colonialism and for development might lead to the gradual emergence of "bloc actors" there. We discuss the atomic age, but, as Herz observes, many interstate relations are still in a pre-atomic phase. We have both a revolutionary system and a tacit agreement on one rule of the game—to avoid total war.

not outlive the technological and political conditions of the nineteenth century, nor could the law forbidding states to help foreign insurgents or subversives. Similarly, many rules that governed territorial jurisdiction have vanished: instead of a fairly clear distinction among a number of separate zones and the sharp definition of the conditions in which state power could be exercised in each of them, there are now blurred, overlapping, and multiplying zones. The size of those on which states claim rights has grown; the claims themselves have steadily expanded, even over the open seas and often through unilateral moves. Traditional rules on the treatment of foreign property have been generally disregarded. These changes have reflected all the transformations in the international system: the increase in the number of nations often leading the least viable or secure ones to demand the fullest amount of control over the greatest amount of space; the technological revolution provoking a rush into air space; the decline of the old transnational consensus affecting the freedom of the seas; the modern welfare state and the totalitarian regimes attempting to grab resources wherever possible and to remove previously accepted restrictions on territorial sovereignty; the cold war leading to U-2 flights and to weapons tests in the ocean, and adding military overtones to the struggle over the extent of the territorial seas; the anticolonial revolution becoming a basic force in this struggle and in the spread of expropriation; the Arab-Israeli conflict having repercussions on canals and straits.

Many of the gaps in the body of rules have created opportunities for chaos. The silence of international law on the upper limits of air space may lead to dangerous and conflicting claims. International law has little to say about most modern methods of propaganda, subversion, and intervention short of the actual use of force. Nor did it foresee that traditional privileges of domestic jurisdiction—such as the right to grant nationality, regulate the conduct of aliens, treat citizens as the state sees fit, and recognize new states or governments—would be used as weapons in the struggle among states. Here we find what is probably the best example of the different meanings for world order of gaps in stable and revolutionary systems. In the nineteenth century, recognition was deemed a political privilege, not a legal duty, but no arbitrary consequences followed because, on the whole, very simple tests were applied: a check on whether the state existed, whether the government was in control, and whether the state accepted the existing framework of international law and politics. Since international law was flexible and contained no requirements about regimes or alignments, there was little trouble. Today, the same privilege has become a nightmare because the collapse of the old consensus on international legitimacy (states now use criteria for recognition that are nothing more than tests of conformity to their own concept of legitimacy) and also because of a new aspect to legitimacy: the nature of the regime or the way it came to power. This is as true in the case of anticolonial conflict as it is in the cold war. Finally, international law has nothing to say about most of the weapons that have appeared since 1914.

Other traditional rules have become simply more uncertain in their operation because of changes in the international system. Those dealing with state immunities were established at a time when the state did not engage its "majesty" in trading or manufacturing activities; court reactions to the development of these activities have been conflicting and shifting. The validity of interventions in the domestic life of another state at the request of its government becomes dubious when there is a domestic contest about the legitimacy or legality of that government. Treaties also reflect the forces of disintegration that have appeared: the increase in the number of nations has led to the "individualization of rules" through reservations, or to the use of vague expressions (as, say, "genuine link," used in the recent Geneva provision dealing with flags of convenience) or to conflicts between obligations accepted by one nation in agreements on similar matters but binding different groups of states. Domestic hostility to the increasing scope of international treaties has brought about difficulties in their ratification and has led to moves such as the Bricker offensive. The intensity of inter-state conflicts has made resort to the *rebus sic stantibus* argument more frequent than ever.

Thus, much of present international law is obsolete, precisely because it reflects a dead system. But the new international system has had a second kind of effect on international law: some rules that are supposed to be valid today, which express attempts to impose a new scheme of world order that has drawn the lesson of the balance of power's ultimate failure, are premature; the scheme from which they derive has proved to be unfit for the present revolutionary world.

On the one hand, there was an attempt to give to the law of the political framework a greater scope than it had in the past, by curbing state sovereignty in matters as vital as the settlement of political disputes and the resort to war, by subordinating the conduct of states to rules administered by international organization. The success of this effort presupposed a stable world that was not to be deeply divided by ideological conflict, in which existed a basic homogeneity of regimes and beliefs, and in which the transnational forces of public opinion and "world parliamentarism" would keep disputes at a reasonably low level.

The fundamental flaw of the formula is in the ambiguous nature of international organization: it is an "as if" international community, which leaves the basic character of the world system unchanged and in which decisions are still made by states. Consequently, its success depends entirely on whether there is a system of basically satisfied, democratic units tied together by a common concept of legitimacy; if there is not, the organization itself has no power to bring such a world about. If this indispensable happy world does not exist at the start, the major powers must bring it to life—and their ability to do so is totally absent. As a result, a new and dangerous discrepancy has come to plague world order—between the United Nation's Charter provisions and practices on disputes (the power of the U.N. organs is limited to frequently ineffective recommendations), and the Charter's sweeping ban on the use of force—which encourages states to refine their techniques of offensive action short of force, and which drives victims of such tactics to disregard the ban.[19] The attempt to revert to a "just-war" concept has proved to be impossible or absurd in a world of conflicting legitimacies.

The other effort was a direct projection into the international sphere of the legal relationships that exist between groups or individuals in a constitutional state. International jurisdiction for the settlement of many disputes, international protection of human rights, the establishment of a criminal code thanks to which the punishment of warmongers would be the judicial side of a coin whose political side was the outlawing of war—all these measures reflected a utopian legal community of mankind. They have suffered a fate even worse than the fictitious political community. International adjudication can be effective only when international relations are not fundamentally at variance with the conditions of a liberal state—when a large zone of private activities is not con-

[19] See, for instance, the arguments of D. W. Bowett, *Self-defense in International Law* (New York, 1958), pp. 145 ff., and Julius Stone, *Aggression and World Order* (Berkeley, Calif., 1958), chap. 5. *Contra*, Joseph Kunz, "Sanctions in International Law," *American Journal of International Law*, LIV (April, 1960), 324–47.

trolled by governments, when state objectives are not so incompatible as to rule out a joint resort to the judge. The predominance of the desire to change the law over mere disagreements on interpretation of it, and the opposition in the values of the major ideological camps, have led to a decline in the importance of the World Court and a full-scale revolt against international adjudication. Human rights are unlikely to receive adequate international protection at a time when the core of sovereignty lies in the bonds between the state and its subjects.

Out of the dialectic of the obsolete and the premature, contemporary international law has managed to show a third effect of the changes in the international system. There is some evidence of a "third way" that is neither a return to the old system nor a realization of the Wilsonian utopia, but the elaboration of rules that do correspond to the few elements of stability in the present system. Although U.N. Charter provisions are used by all nations to enhance their own interests, procedures and institutions that correspond to the general desire to avoid total war have been developed by the U.N. If the competition of East and West for the allegiance of the "Third World" tends to become constantly more intense, it nevertheless remains peaceful on the whole; consequently, an international law and numerous international organs devoted to technical assistance and economic development have appeared, which correspond to the convergent interests of all three groups in channeling some measures through the procedures of a "universal actor." On the ruins of the nineteenth-century law of reciprocity, a few new conventions of delimitation and cooperation have been signed, dealing with the "humanitarian" side of war, or the continental shelf, or the joint exploitation of sea resources or the Antarctic.

This is not much. Some of those developments (e.g., concerning the continental shelf) reflect a very traditional kind of agreement to increase, not curtail, states' powers. The U.N. apparatus designed to prevent extension of conflict is an improvised one; the contemporary internationalization of trouble spots remains an *ad hoc* practice despite efforts to turn it into a general rule, and mutual East-West interests in preventing nuclear war have expressed themselves in parallel unilateral measures more often than in firm agreements. Only in the area of community—scientific research, health, communications—have there been few obstacles. Nevertheless, such developments suffice to give contemporary international law a Janus-like aspect: it has one face that announces chaos, and one that promises order.[20]

Contemporary law also reflects the heterogeneity of the present system—indeed, of every element in the system; hence, there is a permanent contradiction between such heterogeneity and the formal homogeneity of a legal system whose members are supposedly equal.

Contemporary law reflects the heterogeneity of a structure in which, although the nation-state is the basic unit and also a common aspiration, more than ever before there is a major disparity between states that meet the traditional criteria of statehood—a population, a territory, a government—and those that are governments still in search of their nation, governments that operate within explosively artificial borders.[21]

Present-day law also reflects the asymmetry of domestic regimes: the difficulties met by various attempts at codification, or at regulating international trade, air communications, and commerce in raw materials, or at establishing common standards of inspection for arms control, have shown how much the attitudes of a welfare state and a free-enterprise state, and, even more, of an industrialized state and an underdeveloped state, differ in international economic matters, or how radically the conceptions of secrecy in a democracy and a totalitarian state diverge.

Contemporary law also reflects the heterogeneity of the system with respect to transnational forces. Technological unevenness has left its mark: pressure has come mainly from the underprivileged states for legal regulation of space; the opposition of the nuclear "haves" and "have-nots" has limited the effectiveness of international cooperation for the peaceful uses of nuclear energy. As for ideological asymmetry, even though Soviet international law appears to differ little in its *rules* from Western law, there are significant variations in the interpretation of and general attitude toward law, which correspond to the differences in the nature of the regimes;[22] in particular, there is a considerable difference in the attitude toward the use of force within each camp's sphere. Efforts

[20] Similarly, during the period of the Thirty Years' War, legal developments were ambiguous, for the war destroyed the previous unity of the Civitas Christiana and the secular authority of the Church but, at the same time, brought into shape the modern territorial state through a succession of wars.

[21] See Rupert Emerson, *From Empire to Nation* (Cambridge, Mass., 1960), chap. 6.

[22] For a recent discussion of those points, see the *Proceedings of the American Society of International Law*, 1959, pp. 21–45.

to negotiate various agreements on human rights have shown the incompatibility of competing concepts of world order on crucial issues.

Present-day law also reflects many contradictions in the relations between national units. In the first place, it shows traces of a basic contradiction that affects the policy of every state: between determination to increase national power, security, welfare, and prestige as much as possible by one's own means, and dependence on others for those very purposes. If we look at the principal source of law—treaties—we see that at the same time as such agreements suffer from the weaknesses I have mentioned above, they extend to objects never before regulated by world law (labor, human rights) and never before subjects of law (international organizations). If we look at the military function of the state—the state as fortress— we see that every state tries to ensure its security by expanding its sovereignty as far as it can (especially in the air) or developing its own weapons systems or armies, and also by participating in military alliances, which often involve a radical transformation of its traditional territorial sovereignty. If we look at the economic function of the states—the state as provider of welfare—we see that each tries to develop its own resources and acquire additional ones wherever it can (for instance, under the sea), but also that each has to join with others in order to promote the welfare of its own citizens or to receive indispensable aid.

In the second place, international law reflects the complexity of international legal situations in the face of the main issues of contemporary world politics. On the one hand, some of the provisions of the Geneva Conventions on the law of the sea, most expropriation practices, and votes in the U.N. on the question of self-determination all reflect an alignment over one main political issue, a coalition of nations interested in overthrowing the norms of the nineteenth-century system against the *status quo* Western states that are the heirs of this system. On the other hand, on cold-war issues, there are layers of states belonging to different ages of politics. On the top, the two super-powers enjoy a large amount of independence (except from one another) and extensive advantages within their respective alliances (military bases, status-of-forces agreements). Under them, there are allies who are developing their own deterrents; they continue to depend on one or the other super-power for their ultimate protection, but they are capable of bargaining hard before conceding privileges to it. Next, we find other allies who are more or less reluctant, more or less gilt-edged satellites (depending on the ideological camp to which they belong): hence, outbreaks of neutralism and of fear of war. Fourth and last, we find the states that have joined no military camp and live in a kind of fictitious nineteenth-century world of territorial sovereignty.

Lastly, law reflects the bizarre coexistence of revolutionary international relations and elements of stability introduced by the "mutual dependence" of the balance of terror, just at the time when the role of the military establishment in national decision-making has become greater than ever and weapons have begun to live a life of their own almost apart from events in the political universe.

The reactions of theorists to these developments reflect both the heterogeneity of the international legal order, and the impact of changes in the international system on this order. On the one hand, there is little in common between totalitarian theories of law and non-totalitarian theories: we have here both conflict and asymmetry. The former are non-scholarly analyses of the international system from the viewpoint of a desired world order: they are instruments at the service of a state strategy. They are not normative examinations of the ideal order and of the discrepancy between the actual and the ideal: they are policy sciences showing how the actual should be used or abused in order to reach the ideal determined by official doctrine. On the other hand, within the non-totalitarian theories, changes in the international system have shattered the fragile *rapprochement* that had once united the main tendencies. Both nineteenth-century extremes have disappeared. It has become impossible to believe in a dialectic of clashing units with a happy ending and in a vision of a world that moves inevitably toward law, order, and harmony. Even the middle group—positivism—has suffered severely from the marks that the free wills of states have left on world order. Gone is the common faith in the avoidance of chaos, or agreement on the indispensability of the state as the basis of the international system: theories today range from ones that nevertheless maintain this claim to those that make anguished pleas for world government. Vanished, also, is the agreement on differences between international and domestic law: some still stress these differences and some offer subtle, if unconvincing, demonstrations of the similarities.

It is characteristic of revolutionary systems that doctrines not only multiply but often pose as what they are not. Thus, today, "deniers" or cynics are either sorrowful (rather than gloating), or else are disguised as "policy-oriented" theorists who dissolve rules and principles into a maze of processes, messages, and alternatives. Today's utopians are either straightforward adepts of world government, outright natural-law revivalists, natural-law thinkers in pseudo-sociological disguise, or "pure theorists of law" who derive normative order from empirical chaos by what I would call a parthenogenesis of law. In the middle, there are persistent, but troubled, positivists and sociologists of law who seem more adept at examining the weaknesses of law than at finding formulas which would disguise them, as positivism used to do, more adept at maintaining that it is absurd to separate the legal order from its political roots than at attempting to close the gap between the aspiration for order and the practice of chaos.

III

The basis of obligation is the same in every legal order: a consciousness among the subjects that this order is needed if one is to reach a common end. Law is not obtained by deduction from a preexisting natural law or objective law *à la* Duguit; it is a creation toward an end. Thus, the purpose and the legal order cannot be separated, Kelsen's theory notwithstanding. The solidity or authority of a legal order depends on the nature and substance of the common end—which, finally, depends on the group: if the group shows a high degree of community of purpose and is organized by central power, the binding force of the legal order will be great, not otherwise.

The feeble consciousness of a common end among multiple units that allow no central power to impose its vision or to promote theirs, permanently weakens the binding force of international law by comparison with domestic law. But there are variations in the degree to which such a common end exists in international politics and, consequently, in the binding force of international law. There are variations in *level*: as we have seen, there are, in stable periods, three superimposed groups with different common ends and therefore with an international law of varying force. The law of community is strongest because it rests on a common positive purpose. The law of reciprocity is only relatively strong, because it is the law of a limited partnership whose members' common end is a set of mutual interests. The law of the political framework is weakest, for it is the law of a collection of units engaged in a struggle whose common end is limited to a narrow sphere—the rules of the game— and subordinated to the fluctuations of the balance of power.

Secondly, there are variations in *time*: it is not the same in stable and in revolutionary systems. The legal order of the nineteenth-century system was modest, because of the moderation in the scope and means of international relations and because national freedom of action was curtailed by the balance of power rather than by law, and it was efficient, because it was able within these limits to serve as a restraint on the states and also to consolidate their interdependence. Legal theories reflected both this modesty and efficiency. Contemporary law, on the contrary, must serve a system in which the extension of international relations seems to require a far wider range of common purposes but in which heterogeneity has drastically reduced this range. There is consequently a divorce between the difficulties of practice and the delirium of theory; the practices of international law are both highly ambitious and relatively inefficient. The increase in the scope of law's subject matter demonstrates the ambition, but, on vital issues, "society" is limited to a few identical or convergent interests that are sometimes even too narrow or too flimsy to provide a firm basis for developing any law. There is today no strong enough consciousness of or representation of a common legal order of mankind.[23]

Finally, there are variations in *space*. Given the narrow range of common ends and the absence of central global power, regional solidarities, institutions, and legal orders have appeared. They differ in their political foundations: the Soviet bloc used to be a "Roman" system in which the common ends were largely imposed by central power; the Atlantic "community" is really a modern limited partnership, whose sharing of ends is far from total and where cooperation is far from unconditional. The organizations of the European "Six" try to go far beyond inter-state cooperation and to build a trans-national community. They also differ in degree of institutionalization, and in the subject matter they cover. The binding force of law depends on all the factors.

Another problem to be treated in the light of a theory of the

---

[23] Statesmen have mutually exclusive images of world order, in which the highest power remains the state; individual citizens have no way of breaking the statesmen's monopoly: the citizens' efforts at promoting their transnational common ends through law rarely succeed in transcending the borders of the state, which continues to fulfill most of their needs and to be seen as the best protection against outside tempests. Indeed, the development of contemporary law has occurred especially in those areas where individuals raised demands which the state could not satisfy alone: hence the law of international functions and economic integration, whose binding force seems quite strong.

relations between international systems and international law is
that of sovereignty.[24]

Let us start with the classical definition given by the World
Court in the Wimbledon case. Sovereignty means that the state "is
subject to no other state and has full and exclusive powers within
its jurisdiction without prejudice to the limits set by applicable
law."[25] Thus, sovereignty is the situation of the state that has no
political superior but is nevertheless bound by international law.
First, the exercise of its sovereignty—for instance, signing agreements that may restrict its legal freedom of action—does not ex-
haust, indeed is a demonstration of, its sovereignty. Secondly, the
relations between sovereignty and international law are characterized by the principle of domestic jurisdiction: matters not regulated
by the former fall within the latter. Thirdly, relations among states
are marked by the principle of equality (whatever their size, all
states are in the same situation: their only superior is international
law), by the duty of nonintervention, and by the right of self-
preservation.

The trouble with this set of definitions is that their neatness is
illusory. If we look at relations among states, we see a broad gamut
of situations—from the mythic state-in-isolation, which exercises all
the privileges of sovereignty without any other limit than that of
general international law, to the member state of a federation.
There is, in fact, a hierarchy of legal status determined according
to the amount of sovereignty whose exercise has been given away
to, or restricted in favor of, other states or international agencies.
The nature and range of this hierarchy vary with each international
system. Sovereignty, rather than being a reservoir that is either full
or empty, is a divisible nexus of powers of which some may be kept,
some limited, some lost. The point at which sovereignty can be
assumed to have vanished is a matter of definition. Given such a
hierarchy of situations, the equality of states is mythical.

If we look next at the relations between states and international
law, we find that the definitions are illusory because the term "international law" is fuzzy: the "limit" or "restraint" it imposes is
ambiguous and shifting—ambiguous because of the conditions of
elaboration and enforcement of international law, which are the

---

[24] For a sharp analysis, see W. J. Rees, "The Theory of Sovereignty Re-
stated," in Peter Laslett, ed., *Philosophy, Politics and Society* (New York,
1956).
[25] Permanent Court of International Justice, Series A, No. 1 (1923).

product of the states, shifting because the norms of international law vary from system to system.[26]

Thus, the actual substance of sovereignty depends on the international system and, in each system, on the position of a state on the ladder I have mentioned. In a stable system, such as the nineteenth century's, sovereignty is a fairly clear nexus of sharply defined powers: the world appears as a juxtaposition of well-defined units whose respective rights are neatly delimited, which allow few exceptions to the principle of full territorial jurisdiction, and which have few institutional links among them; cooperation is organized by diplomacy and the market; limits on sovereignty are set by general international law (customs and general treaties). In today's revolutionary system, on the other hand, sovereignty is infinitely more complex. The diversity of legal status is great, owing to multiple patterns of military, economic, and political cooperation, which introduce various forms of inequality—hence the predominance of treaties over customs and the prevalence of less-than-universal treaties. Secondly, the sum of powers of which sovereignty is composed, and the limitations imposed by law, are in constant flux and are increasing, because of the intensity of international relations. (The same paradox had marked the revolutionary system in the early seventeenth century.) Thus, the edges of sovereignty have become blurred. Although the basic legal unit remains the state, powers of action in the world are widely scattered among states, blocs, and international organizations, yet concentrated among the major industrial centers or (in matters of life and death for the planet) full nuclear powers.[27]

After the dust has settled, a new stable system will probably be one in which many state powers will be permanently redistributed among global and regional actors. Despite the general aspiration (especially among new nations) to return to a world of non-inter-

---

[26] The best combination of ambiguity and change is provided with the concept of domestic jurisdiction. On the one hand, the area regulated by international law has been drastically expanded; on the other hand, this increasing "legalization" of inter-state relations could become an effective restraint only if there were institutions able to prevent states from extending the plea of domestic jurisdiction to issues where it does not apply—and from rejecting the plea when it is still justified. Instead, we find that states successfully invoke the argument even in areas clearly regulated by law (cf. the Interhandel dispute) and refuse to listen to it whenever a problem is of international concern, although it may not be regulated by law (cf. the attitude of the General Assembly of the U.N.).

[27] On the impact of such concentration, see François Perroux, *La coexistence pacifique* (3 vols.; Paris, 1958).

vening sovereign states, the traditional substance of sovereignty is barely compatible with the political and technological conditions of the present world. However, we are bound to remain with the present system for quite a while; a decline of military blocs in the missile age would not make the competition of East and West any less fierce; the emergence of new nations does not make their resentment of their former masters, their demands on the well-endowed states, and their own political uncertainties any less dangerous; the spread of nuclear power does not make the international system any less explosive. We are in the midst of a succession of revolutionary systems—not on the verge of a stable one, and the solidity of international law will continue to remain in doubt.

FIVE

THE STUDY OF INTERNATIONAL LAW AND THE THEORY OF INTERNATIONAL RELATIONS

T HE STUDY of international law by social scientists is in decline. There are many reasons for this loss of interest, among the main ones being:

1. A sense of the irrelevance of international law as a factor in world politics, which stems from the spectacle of nations revolting against the rules of law, disregarding them altogether, or choosing to apply only those laws which conform to their interests. When there is a discrepancy between the way groups actually behave and the norms that prescribe how they ought to behave, social scientists, whose primary concern is the former, tend to discard the latter.

2. A sense of the futility of traditional methods of teaching international law. Social scientists are impatient with a discipline that seems to focus exclusively either on a closed universe of norms—their logical consequences, their hierarchy, their interconnections—divorced from the political and social universe in which they appear and which they try to regulate, or on doctrinal interpreta-

tions and desiderata that, while they take political and social purposes into account, represent only the idiosyncratic views of irrelevant if respectable writers.

3. The tendency of some international lawyers to agree with earlier criticisms so much that they throw out the legal baby with the stale bath. They analyze law in policy terms that miss the distinctiveness of law as a method of social control and that iron out the normative essence of law under the pretext of straightening out the discipline.

4. The growing number of social scientists who tend toward a kind of scientism concerned with arriving at general laws of behavior and developing deductive models from which valid and meaningful predictions can be derived. To the extent to which they shy away from the study of institutions, these social scientists pay less attention to law than did (or do) their more traditional colleagues. When they express interest in law, their habit of operating at a very high level of abstraction and concentrating on concepts and variables common to "systems" of all sorts interferes with their understanding of the originality of international law—and of the unique features of international politics.

It is my conviction that the neglect of international law by specialists in international relations is a mistake. What I would like to discuss here is the contribution historical sociology can make to the study of international law, and *vice versa*. The general conception I wish to apply is *not* primarily concerned with "social-science methods." Methodology has become the bane of the social sciences; in each field, the proper methods are those which are effective, and the effective methods are those which are consonant with the nature of the field. Our first task must therefore consist of asking what the nature of international relations is.

I

The social scientist is interested in studying certain forms of behavior, or social action; the specialist in international relations deals with a particular social action with unique features, which Aron calls "diplomatic-strategic behavior," or foreign-policy conduct.[1]

It differs from domestic political action and from the types of social action studied by sociologists and economists in that it is concerned with the competition of units linked neither by strong consensus (fragmentation of mankind into groups that feel "differ-

[1] See Aron, *Paix et Guerre Entre les Nations*.

ent") nor by a central, common power. Consequently, it is a form of action that takes place permanently under the shadow of violence.

Although the competitive essence of diplomatic-strategic conduct obliges the actors to calculate their forces and their moves, this type of behavior is undetermined in two ways:

The theory of international relations is concerned first with analyzing the logic of foreign-policy behavior; since the latter is political behavior, it consists in both instrumental action (like economic behavior) and action oriented toward values and goals. Economics is a science of means, politics a science of means and ends, international relations the science of a competitive action with multiple, unmeasurable, often contradictory ends and uncertain rules; for power is neither measurable nor the measure of foreign policy. The calculation of available means introduces no criterion of rationality or predictability, both because the means are to a large extent shaped by the ends and because of the competitive and consequently uncertain nature of the "game."

Secondly, the theory of international relations deals with material and social causes of foreign-policy conduct. However, the nature of causal relations in the social sciences is such that it is impossible to reach valid generalizations about the effects of a single factor, except at a level of generality that approaches platitude.

Concerned, thus, with a form of behavior that is uncertain both because of the diversity of causes and because of the adventurous essence of foreign policy, the study of international relations cannot hope to elaborate *a* single theory or a global network of general laws allowing for prediction. Causal theory can, at best, develop probabilities and study systematically the partial relations among sectors of social reality; theory dealing with the logic of the game can, at best, provide us with sharper concepts, with empirical tests of models and hypotheses, and with typical schemes—such as the analysis of systems formed by competing units. Both kinds of theory can also study the scope, causes, and variations of the fundamental uncertainties of international relations. It is obvious that this approach entails the use of traditional social-science methods—in particular, the resort to history as the raw material, object of investigation, and touchstone; but nothing prevents one from resorting to so-called modern techniques, be they derived from communications theory or from game theory, to study those (rather limited) sectors of social reality to which they are relevant and in which they are fruitful.

The approach suggested here requires that due attention be paid both to the complexity and to the originality of international relations. Some contemporary efforts at theory are over-simplifications or over-generalizations that are particularly harmful to the study of international law.

It is essential, first, to remember that foreign-policy action is not totally determined and dominated by the international competition or system. Indeed, the international system itself is the outcome of a number of developments many of which originate in the component units.[2] Any "systemic" study of international law that tries to explain the legal order of a given system exclusively in terms of the number of main units or of the kinds of characteristic alignments neglects such important considerations as the impact of domestic practices and beliefs or the state of technology on the system, on the competition, and on law.[3]

It is also necessary to remember, inversely, that the essence of international relations is a political competition among separate units. Consequently, analyses of international law that put too much weight on the "common law of mankind," or studies of international affairs that stress too much the similarities between domestic social systems and international systems and suggest the transposition to the latter of methods of conflict resolution effective in the former, are wide of the mark. In the development and crises of international law, cultural similarities and differences are often less important than, and manipulated by, political calculations.

II

The contribution that a historical sociology of international relations could make to the study of international law strikes me as far from negligible. At the start, there is, it seems to me, a double *theoretical* contribution. First, it might help to put in better perspective the old debate among theorists as to the "legal" nature of international law. This conception of international relations throws light at the same time on the originality of a "system" deprived of any broad consensus or central power and on the "systemic" aspects that are nevertheless due to the interdependence of the units and their calculations. This should help one realize

[2] See Richard N. Rosecrance, *Action and Reaction in World Politics* (Boston, 1963).
[3] This point is well made by Robert W. Tucker in his review of Kaplan and Katzenbach, *Political Foundations of International Law* (New York, 1961), in *Journal of Conflict Resolution*, VII, No. 1 (March, 1963), 69 ff.

both that international law, the law of a milieu that has many features of a society, meets the minimum requirements of a legal system (inherent ones, which distinguish law from morality or religion, and external ones—i.e., a sufficient amount of obedience) *and* the imperfections of a body of law that regulates a "group" which is racked by violence, and whose peaceful interrelations are *also* partly relations of competition and antagonism.

Secondly, such an approach may be of help in enlightening us on the other perennial problem—the foundation of obligation. The international milieu is neither complete chaos nor genuine community; there is both a transnational society and—above it—a set of juxtaposed, competing sovereignties. Hence, international law must present aspects of both the *jus gentium* and the state of nature described by Hobbes or Rousseau.[4] Inevitably, the solidity of international law will be greatest in the law of community, which expresses the transnational order, and weakest in the law of the political framework, which reflects temporarily identical or convergent interests of the competing states. As for the law of reciprocity, it reflects lasting mutual interests of the states as competing units, and norms of the transnational society over which the states exercise vigilant control; the solidity of such law necessarily depends on the intensity of the contest.

A historical sociology of international relations also helps to put the study of international law in *situation*, i.e., it takes it out of the vacuum that has sometimes been created by the pure theory of law or by the liberal brand of legalism so prevalent among international lawyers.[5]

A first task would consist of stressing the underlying political realities. Such a task is much less necessary in the study of domestic legal systems: there, the political context is usually well known and taken for granted; domestic law, being much more institutionalized, lives a life of its own. But the unique features of the modes of elaboration, enforcement, and change in international law mean that there is between it and the international system not just an umbilical cord but a tight harness. Thus it is necessary to ask: how did the rules of international law come about? Whose will or interests do they express? What geographical scope do they actually cover? Do they constitute a restraint on the use of state power, or

---

[4] See Aron, *op. cit.*, chap. 23.

[5] For a splendid analysis of the latter, see Judith N. Shklar, *Legalism* (Cambridge, Mass., 1964).

do they consecrate or even increase the state's liberty of action?[6] The international lawyer who does not ask himself those questions condemns himself, in times of trouble, to unwarranted despair or unjustified utopia.

The approach I suggest—to stress the links between international law and historical international systems, the latter analyzed as complex sets of variables dominated by competition—may help the teacher or writer put some order into the huge mass of norms. It should provide him with criteria: just as the constitution of the United States ought to be of greater interest to the scholar than the constitution of a tiny, politically irrelevant state, those parts of international law that are most connected with the competition of states should be more important than the rules most distant from the contest.[7] Secondly, it should make it possible systematically to trace the elaboration of the norms (and attitudes of states in carrying them out) back to the different elements of the system (domestic political and economic regimes, ideologies, technology, etc.). Thirdly, it should allow one to distinguish between the various roles played by international law in world affairs: from the viewpoint of foreign policy, a tool or an ideology; from the viewpoint of the system as a whole, a framework and a stake.

The forms of an historical sociology of international relations depend not just on the competitive essence of international relations but on the changing schemes and patterns of the international contest. In this respect, our conception may bring important insights to the study of the "progressive development" of international law.

To the extent that it emphasizes the role of violence in world affairs, this concept leads to a classification of systems based on the scope and types of conflicts and, in particular, to a distinction between moderate and revolutionary systems. It thus draws the scholar's attention to the conditions and limits of reciprocity within each system and to the changes that either strengthen or undermine it. Any suggestion for the development of a legal order whose basis is reciprocity must be tested with reference to those underlying conditions and limits. Furthermore, our concept of foreign-policy behavior as competitive action should warn the scholar against inventing or proclaiming "common interests" suitable for law-making in

---

[6] A brief but fine example of an analysis of this sort by an international lawyer is Oliver J. Lissitzyn, "International Law in a Divided World," *International Conciliation*, No. 542 (March, 1963).

[7] Since the competition requires restraints and cooperation, along with antagonisms and violence, this remark does *not* suggest that the most important rules are the shakiest (although it is often the case).

areas where states behave as if only antagonistic interests existed.[8] Advocacy of law in such areas must be preceded by the formidably difficult exercise of enlightening statesmen on how they "ought" to view their interests.

The same emphasis on the central role of violence should help to put in proper perspective suggestions presented about conflict resolution. Our approach shows that there are several levels of "causes of wars." There is the fundamental level of what Kenneth Waltz calls the permissive cause—i.e., the fragmented nature of the international milieu (which can in turn be divided into two sets of causes, the absence of consensus and the absence of central power). Then, there is the level of the "effective" causes, which turn potentially violent conflicts into actual wars and which consist of myriads of factors that can be traced to each element of the system. Conflicts exist because we are neither materially nor psychologically in a world of plenty; dissatisfaction leads to war when the contest becomes too intense and because in a fragmented world resort to war is both available and tempting. Consequently, prescriptions for peace that concentrate exclusively on action at one level are inadequate—as, indeed, are many proposals for peace-through-law (the level of consensus), peace-through-collective-force (monopoly of power), or peace-through-action (against one specific set of concrete tensions only). Our approach, which stresses the dependence of legal norms on political realities, should also put us on guard against proposals or attempts aimed at banning the resort to force before adequate machinery for law enforcement has been established: as long as this remains a fragmented world, self-help (which may often, of course, lead to chaos) may be at times the only available method of law enforcement; to condemn it altogether because of its potential dangers might well preserve peace at the cost of justice and law, and thus ultimately undermine peace.[9]

Our approach may also help us to find the most likely general directions for change and development in international law. For it emphasizes not only the way states behave, but also the meaning they give to their conduct and the ideological garb in which they clothe their acts; in other words, it illuminates the principles that are not quite norms of law yet but that are guidelines of political action which tend to become law sooner or later, often after hav-

---

[8] Such as human rights today. The same remark applies also to proposals to expand international adjudication.

[9] This has been Julius Stone's argument in many of his recent works.

ing served as explosives against existing norms. Among the relevant principles at the present time, we find self-determination, equality, sovereignty, coexistence: the very stress modern states put on such slogans should deter us from announcing too soon the coming of a revolutionary new international law based on recognition of the obsolescence of the nation-state.

All these ideas are familiar. None of those tasks requires of the "science" of international relations more than it can provide now or is likely to produce in the future. Much has already been accomplished in this direction by lawyers with a keen eye for political realities or by political scientists with an interest in law. But much more remains to be done, and the job is never finished. One does not at all weaken respect for law or appreciation of the distinctive features of law if one tries to clarify and understand the social and political underpinnings of the legal order.

International lawyers would have many reasons for complaining, however, if social scientists came to believe that a sociology of law or a policy science of law took care of everything. After one has explained the origins, political implications, and effects of a rule, one has not yet disposed of the rule itself. If the social scientist can broaden the horizons of the lawyer, the lawyer's domain remains indispensable to the social scientist.

III

All legal norms are rules prescribed *for* social conduct; when they are obeyed or enforced, they become part *of* social conduct. The task of social science at least consists in studying how people actually behave; it ought also to consist in studying how people think they should behave and what they try to institute and legislate to carry out their views. A social science that, under the name of behaviorism or whatever, neglected law as a form of social control would be poor indeed.

This is not to say that the social scientist must be concerned with all aspects of law. The political scientist realizes that much of the legal system is of no political significance, either because of its subject matter or because, although the subject matter (say, a constitution) is highly relevant, political realities do not at all conform to the legal prescriptions. Conversely, much political life has nothing to do with law, being concerned with "strategies" and "policies" that do not take the form of rules. However, a great deal of political activity has either law-making (or law-amending, or law-destroying) purposes or legal consequences; a great deal of legal activity has political significance. There is, then, a continuum: legal decision-making is *a* form of policy.

This is as true of international law as it is of domestic law. The specialist of international relations who is trying to make sense out of the chaos of data, variables, hypotheses, etc., with which diplomatic history, international economics, cultural anthropology, etc., provide him, and who uses the concept of system in order to do so, will realize that international law gives a cast and shape to his inquiry. A study of the substance of the norms that are valid and efficient at a given time will tell him a great deal about the restraints on, and scope of, the contest among states, about the nature and solidity of the zone of predictability or comity that lies outside the contest—in other words, about the degree to which the system resembles or differs from the Hobbesian model of the war of all against all. Since every state wants to turn its interests, ideas, and gains into law, a study of the "legal strategies" of the various units—i.e., of what kinds of norms they try to promote, and through what techniques—may be as fruitful for the political scientist as a study of more purely diplomatic, military, or economic strategies.

It is essential, however, to understand that law in the hands of statesmen is not merely a policy among others, but that it has very special characteristics and roles: the social scientist who forgets this and advises the Prince accordingly will debase the instrument and mislead the Prince.

Law is distinguished from other political instruments by certain formal features: there is a certain solemnity to its establishment; it has to be elaborated in a certain way. More significantly, the legal order, even in international affairs, has a life and logic of its own: there are courts and legal experts who apply standards of interpretation that are often divorced from underlying political and social factors. For instance, the courts use, for the interpretation of treaties, such principles as textual analysis, the original intentions of the parties, or the purposes or functions of the legal instrument—principles often at variance with the parties' actual desires or interests and unconnected with how the rule came to be established or its political effects. Law may be an instrument of policy, but it is one that has an "artificial reason." Not every legal norm can be traced back to political or social realities: this fact should, in turn, give to political sociologists of law a sense of perspective and modesty.

Most important is the fact that law has a distinct solemnity of effects: it is a normative instrument that creates rights and duties. Consequently, its function is both symbolic and conservative; it enshrines, elevates, consecrates the interests or ideas it embodies. We understand, thus, why law is an important stake in the contests of nations. What makes international law so special a tool for states is this solemnity of effects, rather than the fact that its norms express common interests, which is far too simple, since some legal instruments (peace treaties) reflect merely the temporary, forced convergence of deeply antagonistic policies. A situation of dependence or superiority that is a mere fact of life can be reversed through political action, but once it is solemnly cast in legal form, the risks in taking action to change the situation are much higher: law is a form of policy that changes the stakes and often "escalates" the intensity of political contests; its constraint is comparable to force in effect. To the extent that the study of international relations is one of a "strategy of conflict," it must therefore include the strategy of law-making and law-changing and recognize its distinctive features. A better understanding of law's nature as a symbolic "trip-wire" and of its constraining quality would make political scientists realize that, in a revolutionary world, advocacy of *informal* restraints on the use of force may be wiser than advocacy of explicit agreements. For unstable conditions and intense political competition would make such covenants unsteady, but their very solemnity could lead to formidable crises in case of violations or evasions: the breakdown of an informal restraint carries fewer risks than that of a solemn treaty.

I want here to restate briefly what I have written elsewhere: the social scientist in search of models for the interpretation of world politics, whether he tries to use "new" tools such as those provided by abstract systems analysis, or old concepts such as those of community and society, could do far worse than study the theories presented by writers on international law—philosophers or theologians, lawyers or judges. To any theorist of international relations, the central concern is peace; this is and has been the problem all the theorists of international law put at the heart of their investigations. There may be more to learn about the present stakes, conditions, and directions of world politics even from so debatable and shabbily argued a statement as the World Court's opinion on the financing of United Nations peacekeeping operations (perhaps even because it is so shaky an opinion) than there is from many "developmental charts" and "quantitative approaches" recently concocted by social scientists.

IV

It is my hope and belief that social science may be as Jaurès said patriotism was—that narrow patriotism pushed one away from mankind, but that deep and broad patriotism brought one back to humanity. A little bit of social science may widen the chasm separating it from international law, by heightening their mutual hostility; more (and more adequate) social science should do the opposite. A sound social scientist will realize that the so-called failure or fiasco of international law is not the fault of law but the product of the very kind of system he tries to study; he will understand that if international law has unique weaknesses due to unique features of international relations, it is found at the same time on a continuum of legal orders reaching from, say, domestic civil law at one end to international law at the other. It is as legitimate to distinguish between all types of "public" law (such as public international law, constitutional law, much of labor law) and all types of "private" law, as it is to distinguish between the ideal-type of "domestic law" and the ideal-type of international law.[10] Simultaneously, the international lawyer will realize that social science, putting law in perspective without denying its distinctiveness, guides him away from the alternatives of gloom or illusion.

It is my conviction that these results can be achieved only if social scientists show the necessary amount of modesty about their disciplines and methods. In the case of international relations, there can be no general laws to account for the undetermined and no meaningful predictions to chart the unpredictable; flat predictions about the development of international law tend to be either vague or rash. The task of the social scientist in international affairs is the inventory and delimitation of uncertainty. When he envisages the future, he can show the likely limits on action, the impossibility of controlling all the effects of one's action, and the general (but usually ambiguous) directions of the play. All the rest—i.e., action itself—is left to the actors and to chance.[11]

[10] In the subject matter covered by all types of "public" law, the balance between "arbitrary" domains (unregulated by law) and law-regulated sectors tends to be weighted against the latter, and law itself is only partially the expression of generally accepted standards of justice: the more open and organized conflict we find, the greater the range of arbitrariness and the smaller the consensual quality of the law.

[11] For another approach, see Richard A Falk, "The Adequacy of Contemporary Theories of International Law: Gaps in Legal Thinking," *Virginia Law Review*, L, No. 2 (1964), 231–65.

SIX

ROULETTE IN THE CELLAR: NOTES ON RISK IN INTERNATIONAL RELATIONS

Let us imagine a large gambling place. Around a large roulette table stand players of all sizes and all ages. Behind them are their families. Depending on the stakes, and on the fancies of the roulette ball, the families' fortunes increase or collapse. Sometimes one player dominates, sometimes the struggle focuses on two main rivals, sometimes a great number of players share the bulk of the gains. Occasionally, the accidents of the game do not simply ruin a family but kill it. But the game never stops.

Such are international relations. They are features, *par excellence*, of the realm of uncertainty. Within normally constituted states, the solidarity among groups and the presence of a constraining framework of Power reduce the scope and intensity of uncertainty for leaders, parties, classes, etc. But the universe of international relations is still in the state of nature described by Hobbes, in the state of competition denounced by Rousseau. Without even mentioning the uncertainties provoked by forces the players do not entirely control, such as technology, one must list three basic factors of uncertainty that result from the players' actions. The goals they seek are multiple, irreducible to unity or to a unit of measure. Even when the goals seem identical, the means they may reasonably propose to use in order to reach them are diverse. The gambles on which the choices of goals and means are based are contradictory, and the calculation of forces and the quest for power are as hazardous as they are indispensable. For force means little without the ability to use it well—and that ability does not easily lend itself to quantification; power, like a liquid, takes the shape of the receptacle statesmen try to provide for it; reactions to a calculation of force and a quest for power can always foil the latter and render the former useless.

The sphere of international relations is, therefore, a perfect breeding ground for risks. Competition is total, rising all the way up to the actual use of force, and it is the threat of such war that gives international relations its political uniqueness and even its structure. There are risks for the citizen, whose private life, whose welfare, or whose allegiance is threatened whenever the states' moves and the dynamics of the international system put his nation at stake. (This is why Rousseau and Kant believed that reason and freedom would rule in public affairs only when peace could be insured among states.) There are risks for states, either because their own ambitions or their own mistakes created those risks or because they are the victims of an international system that works against them. (Thus, eighteenth-century Poland suffered not only from its own weakness but also from a so-called balancing system which led the major powers to practice compensations at Poland's expense. The risks that France faces at present are isolation on account of de Gaulle's policy but also decline as a result of a bipolar international system that may turn lesser powers into passive objects rather than active players on the world scene.) Finally, there are risks for the international system, whose stability is only relative at best. Even the stablest of systems, such as that which characterized Europe in the nineteenth century, is nothing better than a mechanism that moderates conflict; it does not eliminate wars. The system is always at the mercy of national moves that either tend to destroy it—deliberately, in Hitler's case; accidentally, in 1914—or submit it to dangerous shocks—Bismarck in 1870, the Soviet Union in Cuba in 1962. Other forces also threaten the system: revolutions in major states, such as France in 1789 or China in 1949, innovations in weapons technology, a population increase greater than the increase of available resources. What is true of the global system is true of the partial ones, alliances or organizations of states, as well.

The uncertainty that is of the essence of international relations —relations indeterminate in their logic and in their causes—is responsible for this accumulation of risks. In turn, the risks entail a number of consequences, which will remain important as long as the nature of the game is unchanged. First, the citizen, the state, and the system have no way of avoiding risks. Risks exist for all those whose misfortune it is to be located not only in the circle of the contestants, but even in the farther reaches where the contestants are able to perform their feats: the tribes of Africa, the slumbering peoples of Asia discovered this in the days of colonialism just as did the Poles, the Danes, or the Belgians. A French proverb says that he who risks nothing gains nothing, but in international competition, where everyone risks something, he who risks the most always risks gaining the least or the worst (cf. Hitler); he who has nothing incurs risks anyhow, for the well-endowed participants may compete for even the poorest land. According to Rousseau, the only way for the citizen and the state to escape these risks was for the states to be democratic enough to reduce ambition, and self-sufficient enough to reduce temptation. But this amounts to abolishing international relations, which is both utopian and hopeless. According to Hobbes, as soon as international competition actively threatens the nations' safety—which he did not think was the case of international relations in his time—the remedy is to create a Leviathan, a power superior to the players and in possession of the monopoly of force. Again, this amounts to abolishing the contest and abolishing international relations. As long as international relations last, so do the risks, which Hobbes deemed tolerable but which may not be so today.

The very complexity of international relations prevents us from speaking of risks indiscriminately. The real question is, who risks what? The threat of violence creates a risk of war, but the *real* risk of war is intermittent and migratory; the *latent* risk is permanent and universal. The latent risk, since it flows from the very essence of international relations, is as foreseeable as the passing of the seasons. The *real* risk, since it flows from the uncertainties of the game, is much less easy to foresee. In the spring of 1914, few people predicted the coming of four years of war; in the United States, few Americans believed their country would eventually enter the war. Moreover, war, one of the crucial facts of the game, is only one means at the players' disposal, only one of the possible outcomes. This is why the range of stakes is so broad. A state may put its very survival at stake—its survival as a state or its survival as a collection of human beings—if its geographical position and its active or passive role in the game require it. Or else the risks may put the state's security at stake, if its position or role in international life threatens its tranquility. Or else its power may be at stake, if a domestic or foreign conflict threatens its resources or its capacity to use them, or simply if forces it does not control decrease its might and increase the means with which others can play. Great Britain's decline comes from the convergence of these two kinds of threat, due as it is both to losses inflicted by war and fall of empire, and to the advantage that states of continental dimension and huge demographic and military capabilities enjoy today. Another risk is that of losing one's independence, if a competitor's moves or the system's evolution turns one into a protectorate or satellite or leads to one's merger in a larger unit. There is still another risk, and not a minor one in a game where intangibles count for so much, where symbols are often at stake, and where the creation of the illusion of force or serenity is often tantamount to the creation of power: the risk of losing prestige, a paper currency with no gold to back it but without which banks would go broke. Finally, there are risks that threaten the values a nation promotes or represents, as often as international competition or historical evolution seems to relegate those values to the museum or graveyard. Many people believed throughout the 1930's that liberal values were doomed. Many people today see in the cold war a duel of values as much as a duel of power.

Risk is fatal; and risks are multiple. The players must choose among risks. No one state can avoid them all; that which takes none incurs many. The nation that devotes its resources and attention to domestic welfare risks losing its prestige or even its independence if it leaves other major decisions to other states. Whoever acts to minimize the risks he deems most dangerous will thereby create new risks, either because the means he chooses worsen the condition he wanted to cure or because the price he must pay for the cure provokes other diseases. When the French decided that the most dangerous risk was that of allowing their security to be threatened, the Maginot Line—symbol of a defensive mood and defensive strategy—proved costly for French prestige and power (since to maintain it France in fact had to sacrifice its allies), ultimately for French independence as well; all the while, it increased the risks for French security too because it bred illusions.

If the Soviet Union decides that the risks of a world holocaust make it imperative to move cautiously, the price it may have to pay for survival may be a loss of prestige and power and a diminution of the values that Communists had seen as their duty to propagate.

At all times, the line separating smaller from larger powers has corresponded to two different attitudes toward risks. Small powers are forced, by their resources, their location, and the system, to be satisfied with establishing a hierarchy of risks and with attempting to minimize the risks they consider to be most serious. Those attempts, as we have just seen, are fraught with dangers and always require some renunciations. A country like Switzerland that choses permanent neutrality must still run the risk of having that neutrality violated, and it also condemns itself to a reduced freedom of action. This is the price it must pay for insuring its independence, which deliberately is kept without glamor, and its security, which is preserved necessarily without assurance. Larger powers are those which, while trying to minimize the unbearable risks the system or other states create, nevertheless do not hesitate deliberately to engender new risks—in addition to incurring the other new risks that come from the effort to minimize the intolerable ones. For only in this way can they attain their statesmen's goals, which lie beyond the minimum objective shared by all states: to survive and be secure. Bismarck, while binding together the alliances designed to insure Germany's security, did not refrain from resorting to the threat of war in order to increase his nation's power, and Hitler played with such threats with virtuosity between 1936 and 1939. The main object of a large power is to maximize gains (defined in a variety of ways) rather than to minimize risks.[1]

Consequently, for a great power, the great statesman is not the one who risks least. Those who consider that a statesman risks too much, yet who do not share the illusion that risks can be avoided, are actually blaming him for having goals that exceed the country's possibilities, for using the wrong means toward admittedly valid ends, or for not having the right hierarchy of stakes and values. The decisive question is: what is it wise to risk, and

[1] There is another difference between large and small states. The great power does not really have to ask whether it ought to mortgage its independence; the alliances it negotiates may well restrict its freedom of action but do not force it into dependence. A small power, when it establishes a hierarchy of the risks it must minimize, must choose between security and independence whenever it cannot simultaneously curtail the risks that threaten both.

what for? —a question to which the reply is never completely provided by always ambiguous and somewhat adjustable data. The great statesman's daring is rewarded; this presupposes that he has made an intelligent *guess* on future relations among states, an accurate *calculation* of the limit of his action and its chances for success and a *choice* that is in harmony with the wishes of his countrymen. The most spectacular mistake for the statesman of a large power to make is to create senseless risks (Hitler, fighting on too many fronts); the most obvious mistake for the statesman of a small power to make is to choose the wrong way of insuring his nation's survival and security (Poland, 1934–39). Less obvious but equally serious mistakes are made by states in an intermediate situation: by a major power that refuses to risk anything or that sacrifices its ambitions in order to reduce the risks that threaten its security or survival; and by a small power that ignores its weakness and pretends it can act like a great power.

Thus, France, during the 1930's, was incited by so many of its citizens to behave as a second Switzerland that it ceased to be a major power; the methods that kept lightning from striking Switzerland could only attract it to France. Conversely, Mussolini created all the risks of independence, power, and prestige on the basis of insufficient resources, in a world that was too constricting, and for a nation that was too apathetic. Since 1940, France is precisely in the intermediate position. Vichy's mistake was not merely to behave as a small nation and to sacrifice to physical survival all the objectives that go beyond it—independence, power, honor—but to do this so that not even survival was insured, and above all to make the wrong bets and calculations—since German victory was not sure, possibilities for French action still remained, and the French people kept their nostalgia for "rank." General de Gaulle's wager then and now is that France can still act as a great power. His critics accuse him of making a miscalculation that is the opposite of Vichy's—of creating risks as senseless as Mussolini's.

As we can see, the game's uncertainty prevents us from knowing for sure whether a risk the statesman deliberately creates is excessive, whether the road he follows to minimize an incurred risk is a dead end, whether the bloated power is mistaken in believing that it can act like a great nation, or whether the power that lies low is mistaken in believing that it must act like a small one. Here we find the second consequence of the fatality and multiplicity of risk. International politics is a battle of wills, and yet it is also the preserve of destiny—if one means by destiny all that lies beyond man's calculation. Whenever they try to minimize a risk or to take one in order to attain their goals, statesmen may end up erring in two ways: first of all, the main lines of evolution are rarely straight and convergent, and it is only later that the historian discovers the direction of the road, that the sociologist discovers the rules of the system, that the political scientist discovers the limits around the statesmen's freedom of action; secondly, even when all the facts are clear, each statesman tends to interpret them in the light of his nation's experiences and desires. Baldwin and Chamberlain saw Hitler as a gentleman and thus projected on the most unusual of history's monsters the memories of the European Concert and the values of liberalism—hence, a long succession of mistaken efforts to reduce the risk of Nazi aggression and war, the long refusal to take risks while there was still time, that would have obliged the foe to retreat. Roosevelt facing Stalin made similar blunders. Conversely, Austria, when it sent an ultimatum to Serbia in 1914, created a risk it thought it could turn to its advantage, for this had been the case in previous Balkan incidents. The Soviet Union in Cuba was hoping to present a *fait accompli*, as it had so often succeeded in doing elsewhere. Even the most experienced players are not masters.

II

Today's roulette game is played with a thermonuclear ball. How much has the game changed? Is the problem of risks different—for the players, as well as in the game itself?

First of all, a change has occurred in the nature of the weapons, hence in the stakes. The players are now able to destroy the game itself simply if they continue to play with the same carelessness as they did in the past. Only two or three among them have this power of death at their disposal, but in ten or twenty years, many more may bear that awesome privilege. True, the cost of delivery systems rises all the time, but the cost of producing the bombs themselves seems to decrease. The possibility that small states can have a stock of bombs to use at close range against their immediate neighbors entails a risk of escalation tantamount to generalizing the peril of annihilation—even if the number of states endowed with long-range means of delivering bombs stays small.

A second essential change is the conspicuous increase in the number of players—about 120 nations today. The existence of an international organization in which majority rule obtains provides even the weakest among them with a place in the sun. To the extent that many are born and live, or rather survive, in stormy and miserable circumstances, the game may suffer from the change.

Thirdly, the tightening of global communications and the increase in population turn the world into a kind of echo-chamber. Each player knows more about the others' games and finds it easier to follow their example or drag them into his own game.

To sum up, there are more people around the roulette wheel; the stakes are higher and more diverse; and the risk of death hovers over every player's shoulder. The risks for the citizen, the state, and the system have been joined by a new risk—for the game itself, for the world. And yet the game continues, for the simple reason that the structure of the international milieu has not been fundamentally transformed. There is still no power above that of the states, the states are still the spokesmen of distinct communities, the communities are still separated by antagonistic claims, ambitions, and memories.

Let us take the risk of war, the identifying mark of international relations. The new international system is so deeply revolutionary that this risk is multiplied rather than limited. Nations, regimes, levels of development are varied; the world lives under the threat of violent conflict between blocs, between states (in the Middle East or Africa), between factions within a state (in which case the echo-chamber is employed and each faction mobilizes its friends elsewhere: in the Congo, or the Yemen, or Vietnam). Yet, the risk of annihilation is such that none of the powers with the means for it can deliberately use nuclear war as an instrument of policy; at least, this has been so ever since the United States and the Soviet Union reached a balance of terror—which is not equality in thermonuclear arsenals but an approximate equality in the capacity to inflict intolerable retaliation, not weapons parity but peril parity.

From this fundamental contradiction, important consequences follow for the players and for the game. One consequence affects primarily the super-powers, possessors of absolute weapons. In a world where the *risk* of total war is unacceptable, but where the very structure of the game preserves the possibility of total war, these powers oscillate between a policy of moderation motivated by the common desire for survival and for the perpetuation of the game (the very stability of the system thrives on the constant threat to the game) and, on the other hand, a strategy that preserves the latent risk of war and periodically revives the real risk, a strategy motivated by the intensity of their rivalry and the need of each to prove that it will not sacrifice its security or its values merely to survival. This latter strategy consists, for example, in exploiting minor conflicts. The further a conflict is removed from the thermonuclear threshold, the more tempting and useful it may be as an instrument of foreign policy for large or small states. This is why expansionist major powers have done their best to exploit such conflicts; each time a major power has been embroiled in a minor conflict, its adversaries have played the game of trying to make it back down by threatening it with escalation. The United States used such a warning to get the Chinese and North Koreans to sign an armistice agreement in Korea; the Soviet Union did the same in order to push the British and the French against the wall at Suez.

The strategy of the super-powers in their direct confrontations has also included the threat of total war, which is known to be intolerable to both sides. In Berlin, each one has tried to trap the other in a vise between holocaust and humiliation, hoping the adversary will give in to avoid it. In Cuba, the United States succeeded in applying this tactic to the Soviet Union.

Finally, the real risk of war reappears without any deliberate move but simply because of the uncertainty that prevents one from knowing at what moment the latent risk becomes real—hence a miscalculation such as Khrushchev's in the Cuban missile crisis, when he based his decision to send missiles to Castro on the idea that the American political system would react slowly enough to allow the Soviet Union to build its bases in the meantime with impunity. The super-powers still play the game of chicken—as in 1914 and after March, 1939—but they are careful not to remove their foot from the brake-pedal.

Other powers, too, are in a paradoxical situation. In terms of capabilities (weapons, population, GNP), there is a real abyss between them and the super-powers. The cold war, both a bipolar contest and an ideological conflict, seemed to condemn the lesser powers to a choice between security obtained at the cost of a protection that was close to dependence, and a most radical insecurity. The reality is different, however. Each time the world is split into opposing camps, the international hierarchy reverses in some way; the super-powers who need allies must take into account the grievances and desires of the small powers who join their coalitions, and they must court those that choose to stay outside. Three different factors have pushed this reversal much further now than in the past: first, each super-power finds itself unable to use its huge scarecrows to frighten reticent allies and annoying neutrals into docility, for, should it try, the chances of its own camp disintegrating and its rival acquiring superb opportunities for gain would be at least as great as its chance of consolidating its own position: the Peloponnesian war remains a precedent and a warning. Two, the United Nations bolsters the small powers, which endow it and themselves with Secretaries General devoted primarily to the protection of smaller powers (partly because there is nothing they can do about the great ones): a countervailing power on behalf of the weak nations' independence. Third, and chiefly, the balance of terror reduces the risk of total war (without eliminating it); it contributes to depriving the super-powers of the use of the very weapons that insure their superiority (if not of the threat to use them); it also seems to lessen the risk that the super-powers constitute for the small powers' security, and thus removes any reasons the latter might have to subordinate their independence to their security and survival, which do not appear greatly threatened.[2] A remarkable divorce between power and influence thus occurs[3]: the greater the power, the narrower the nation's freedom of operation —a position the United States discovers everywhere. The less power weighs (the fewer problems it creates), the broader freedom of action appears to be. Each in his own way—Mao as against the Soviet Union, de Gaulle as against the United States, Nasser or Sukarno versus both sides—tries to maximize the influence of his own country at the expense, and sometimes under the protection, of other nations' power.

There follows from all this a curious change in attitudes toward risk. The super-powers still try to reach objectives beyond survival and security, to be sure. However, not only are they obliged to

[2] West Germany, a country directly exposed to a latent threat to its security and survival, is also the country that has most deliberately chosen to put independence after safety and that has exploited least the revival of influence that these three previously mentioned factors granted to other states.

[3] This should be read as a shorthand expression: power here refers to material *capabilities* (GNP, military potential) and to those *uses* of power that require an application of these capabilities, i.e., essentially the coercive uses of power and the power to reward. Influence I would define as a use of power not based on material capabilities, i.e., a use of power designed (of course) to move others, but without constraints or rewards. What such a use requires from the actor is, on the one hand, the existence of spiritual or non-measurable capabilities, and, on the other hand, considerable diplomatic skill; it will lead to achievements if (as is the case now) the logic of the system makes room for such a subdued use of power.

be cautious when they create risks with which they hope to force their adversary to give in to their ambitions, but often they must also give top priority to minimization of the risks they incur for their own survival; indeed, the imperative to reduce such risks tends to dominate their policies and strategies. In the Congo, in Berlin, in Cuba, in Cyprus, Khrushchev, for all his petulance, seemed to be inspired above all by the fervent wish to preserve the Russian Revolution from destruction. And, at the root of the strategic dispute between the Americans and the Europeans, one finds the Americans' wanting to avoid atomic catastrophe above all, even if this means preparing for wars that would remain limited (for them) in case deterrence fails and even though such catastrophe is unlikely. Precisely because the risk does indeed appear improbable to them, the Europeans would prefer a less "flexible" strategy—which horrifies the Americans, since they view such a change as an almost infallible recipe for turning an accident into an apocalypse.

Conversely, the small powers, now reassured (perhaps too soon) about their survival and safety, and even though they disagree on how to consolidate both (with a small striking force based on the theory of graduated deterrence, or by having one's finger on some-one else's trigger, or by taking refuge in a non-nuclear zone?), try to reach objectives beyond survival and safety and no longer hesitate to create for others and for themselves the enormous risks that must be taken to reach these goals. This is what Nasser does in the Yemen, Sukarno against Malaysia, the Romanians of 1964 toward Russia—not to mention, of course, Mao and de Gaulle.

Insofar as the game rather than the players is concerned, the uncertainties provoked by the risks the players incur or create are partly traditional and partly new. The uncertainties of deterrence are familiar. The idea that one can insure peace by creating so great a risk of damage for a potential troublemaker that he will prefer to find his interest in moderation or abstention, although it appears new, is not original at all. The balance-of-power system also tried to contain the restless nations by giving them the choice between the somewhat bitter but not always unrewarding advantages of moderation (under the guise of compensations, for instance) and the risk of losing prestige, power, and security at the hands of a coalition as mighty or mightier than they. The collective-security system tried to go even further and turn the risk for the trouble-makers of a coalition of equal or greater might into the certainty of a police operation launched by all against one or a few. The strategy of deterrence merely adapts older techniques to new weapons; it also, therefore, inherits traditional uncertainties. The troublemaker can always hope to benefit from the hesitations or divisions of his opponents; he may even try to induce such falterings by resorting to provocations that would appear too mild to be sanctioned by lightning, just as he was able to benefit from the excessive abstraction, rigidity, and absolutism which kept collective security in the realm of theory, and just as the balance-of-power system before 1914 had been honored in the breach at least as much as in its triumphs.

Nor can one call it new that the decisive uncertainties are those that derive from the risks run by the super-powers. The influence of lesser states seeps through the dikes built by the large states' power. In areas or issues where the risk of general war is most central—Berlin, Vietnam, Cuba, disarmament negotiations—the game is most obviously dominated by the players with the highest stakes. The small states may advise, intrigue, and complicate matters, but they do not decide. France may advocate the neutralization of Vietnam, but Vietnam will be neutralized only if the United States approves, and neutralization will be different from a barely diluted expansion of Communism only if American might bolsters it. Cuba may ask for and try to keep Soviet missiles on her soil, but both the taking and the abandoning of this risk are decided in Moscow.[4]

But two new uncertainties have made the game even more dangerous. The first is a new uncertainty of deterrence. Yesterday, deterrence was unsure because the troublemaker was never certain that he would be faced by the coalition of his rivals; in other words, the threat was not always there. When it was there, it was real (credible) insofar as its execution was in the interest of those who had proffered it: their resort to force in order to stop an antagonist was a reasonable policy. Today, deterrence is unsure because the troublemaker creates situations in which the threat of retaliation is blurred, and because even when the stakes are huge, carrying out the threat would be foolish for both threatener and threatened; in other words, the threat's credibility is dubious; today's troublemaker knows that his opponent's threatened attack may boomerang. Insofar as even a barely plausible threat of absolute war suffices to preserve peace, deterrence works (also, the theorists of small striking forces are encouraged), but insofar as it

---

[4] This explains why, despite the current advantages of influence and the relative impotence of force, the smaller states that think power is within their grasp use their influence to reach it.

becomes increasingly less credible, deterrence is increasingly fragile. Not only the basic elements of the system (political and economic regimes, ideologies, conflicting ambitions) but also the very logic of the new weapons works to multiply conflicts that are not total war: the less possible total war becomes, the more the other forms of violence take its place. True, the danger of escalation is a countervailing factor, but, on the one hand, even as this danger injects caution into the strategies of those who plan or abet local conflicts, it also worsens the risk that each conflict creates for the game; on the other hand, the more each antagonist believes in the others' "rationality," the less seriously will he take the risk of escalation. The pendulum that swings from hope to panic often comes to rest on anxiety.

The uncertainty of what one might call "deterrence as a bluff," which is due to the technological revolution in weaponry, is not the only one. Order and system are not synonymous: the system is a situation, order is a normative state; a system may be execrable, but order requires a minimum of peace, justice, and flexibility. The multipolar balance-of-power systems had a certain kind of order, not strong enough to keep the system going forever, but enough to make it last. This order was due in part to the limited number of players, in part to the fragmented and limited stakes. (The subsystems had a measure of autonomy; equilibrium was primarily political and military.) It was also due to the fact that the big powers' resort to force served both to restrain each other's ambitions and to limit the damage that the excesses of small powers could create. Order enforced by the sword of the mighty could do no more than insure a very elementary kind of justice; it was therefore precarious. But at least, in a world that obeyed neither the rule nor the ethics of law, force was a way of limiting the rule and ethics of war and of insuring observance of the law —even if such law expressed essentially the interests of the strong. Today, however, the uncertainties of precarious, relatively unjust, too inflexible order are replaced with the uncertainties of chaos, lessened only somewhat by the general determination to avoid Doomsday.

The world lives between the fear of disaster, brought on each time force is used in any considerable quantity, and the fear of lawlessness, provoked when states (especially small states) make moves more or less arbitrarily and do so with impunity so long as the moves do not involve military force (Nasser during the Suez crisis in 1956), or even when their excesses can be justified as a legitimate use of force against colonialism or neocolonialism or on behalf of the peoples' right to self-determination (Sukarno in Irian, or Nehru in Goa). As we have seen, the great powers' reluctance to use force either as an instrument at the service of a challenged international law or as an instrument of national policy makes it possible for the lesser powers to increase their influence. This influence often has as its purpose the development of their own power, as one can see in the French and Chinese cases. The present system, although so far it has insured the survival of all, does not serve equally the other concerns of all: thus, now as before, revisionists are ranged against a system that deprives them of power; they are determined to use the freedom of action it gives them to subvert it for their own benefit. Hence there is a clear and present danger: the relative stability of the nuclear bipolar system makes the emancipation of lesser powers possible, but this very emancipation threatens in the long run to destroy the system and replace it with one for which history has no precedent and which might well put terror at the disposal of all.

There are other causes of chaos: the high number of players, many of whom are below the threshold of economic, political, or bureaucratic viability; the existence of a single international system that turns all elements of heterogeneity or all factors of regional disorder into universal headaches. The only sure thing is the proliferation of trouble, and there is no tried and tested method for getting rid of it. Never has a principle of order, even one as debatable as the European Concert, been so necessary, and yet, we remain submitted to the hazards of empiricism and the shocks of improvisations.

III

The new conditions of the game of roulette have moved the gamblers from the casino to a sort of dark cellar. The ball keeps rolling, the gamblers and their families continue in a state of mixed social ease and suspicion, but the stakes have become so terrifying, and the overcrowding is so suffocating, that one can hear more and more laments and curses against the game itself: if only one could get out of the cellar and open a way to survival and security! Any reasonable man, be he statesman or scholar, understands that nothing short of a radical transformation of the game itself can be satisfactory; only if one gives up the game will one be able to get out of the cellar. The famous lessons of history are of little use: they tell us that yesterday's relative order was insured by an equally relative cooperation of the great powers. But we cannot be content with that kind of a solution, even though we are still far from having reached it. For in yesterday's world, now so distant, the number and nature of the problems to be solved in common did not exceed the big powers' resources, whereas today, the political, economic, military, sociological, and psychological tensions are so great and so deeply rooted that the super-powers alone simply cannot handle them, especially since they can no longer use force freely to do so. Moreover, in yesterday's world, breakdowns of the concert did not entail the end of the world; today, any crisis between the nuclear powers creates the danger of death.

This is why the problem of international order appears so difficult and so urgent. On the one hand, it is obvious that, in the present complex international milieu, there must be a less elementary organization than before—i.e., there must be a hierarchy, institutions, rules of behavior both flexible and realistic, unprecedented possibilities of participation for all, and sharp limits on the use of force. On the other hand, it is equally obvious that the game's development complicates the problem of international order, even as those complications convince the gamblers of the danger's seriousness; the risk of nuclear diffusion threatens the relative stability of the bipolar balance of terror, and the influence of the small states, backed by the United Nations, subverts the hierarchy. Caught in the vise of contradictory data, many people see no solution other than a sudden mutation, with the gamblers giving up the game all at once, in a *nuit du 4 août* of international relations.

Two kinds of mutations have been suggested. If the stakes have become unbearable because of the weapons, let us change everything by removing those weapons. This is the first prescription, which strikes me as, alas, utopian: it cannot be realized, and even its realization would not be enough. Only on one condition would a world disarmed, in which nations still had the know-how and the means to start an arms race again, be more than a return to the classical game of roulette at a lower level of *real* risk (the *latent* risk of rearmament might be unbearable): the players would have to establish an efficient and impartial police. In other words, there ought to be a world government whose control and purpose would not be the stake of a permanent competition, as in the

United Nations.[5] The problem is thus infinitely greater than that of weapons alone. Weapons serve ambitions: only if ambitions die down will weapons die out. It is hard to imagine that the gamblers will quietly decide to give themselves a master who would make it impossible for them to fulfill their wishes or who would serve the desires of some at the expense of others. It is largely because it is based on a narrow view of the role of weapons that the theory of disarmament is so unlikely to triumph. I do not see how one could draft a disarmament treaty that would not favor some and harm others, that would be equally acceptable to the *status quo* powers and to those who feel victimized by the *status quo*, that would take into account all the political and geographical factors of asymmetry among states, and that would establish an international system (neither too fragile nor too overbearing) of enforcement, inspection, sanctions, and settlement of disputes. As between the risk of death created by weapons states possess, which, in their conceit, they think they will use only when this risk is low, and the risk of a leap into the unknown, which disarmament would bring about, states prefer the former. They are used to the game and naturally lean toward the familiar peril, even if the change of degree is tantamount to a change in kind. Great powers prefer to minimize the risk for survival and security entailed by the new weapons by means of precautions, instead of eliminating it through a mutation, which, as they see it, might not succeed or which would do so at a cost they are unwilling to pay—their giving up all goals beyond survival and security. As long as the game goes on, each player suspects that the others want to keep some hidden stock in their pockets. Nobody is deemed impartial enough to verify on behalf of all that someone has hidden something.

Short of total disarmament, two theoretical possibilities remain. One is a big-power agreement against nuclear proliferation, which would be an agreement by the dominant gamblers to preserve the game, even perhaps by force. Such an agreement presupposes, however, a degree of acknowledged complicity and solidarity among the super-powers that may well prevail only when it will have become meaningless for world order; there is a kind of iron law that enemies draw closer only when new rivals threaten; as long as these potential rivals are weak, the big powers' antagonism, and their resulting need for support, prevent them from acting together at the expense of their respective or prospective allies;

[5] See Hoffmann, "Erewhon or Lilliput," in Lincoln Bloomfield *et al.*, *International Military Forces* (Boston, 1964).

when the rivals become dangerous, yesterday's super-powers may no longer have the means to impose their duopoly. Or rather, they will have a chance to do so only if their rule does not appear as merely the rule of the strong; for justice to be enhanced, the sword of the super-powers would have to be at the service of an organization capable of meeting the aspirations of other states. Once again, the problem of weapons leads to the broader problem of world order.

There remains the possibility of the super-powers taking more modest measures—ones that require fewer inspections, procedures, and innovations—to slow down the race or to relinquish whatever has become superfluous. Such measures make the cellar a little less deadly, but that is all. Since they do not at all affect the competitors' capacity for destruction nor prevent them from resorting to the threat of or use of force to reach their goals, such demonstrations of good will are nothing but a mixture of common sense at low cost and easy-going cynicism.

In no way can they be compared to moves for unilateral disarmament, which have been suggested rather naïvely here and there, especially by social psychologists; these men seem not to know (1) that it is of the essence of the game that any such initiative taken by a super-power might be exploited, rather than imitated, by others; (2) that any such initiative taken by a lesser power would only put it at a disadvantage in the game, without in the least pushing the other players into some trance of abnegation; and (3) that the players gamble not because the "image" they have of each other is twisted, sick, or hysterical, but because they have conflicting ambitions: the image is perverted because the ambitions clash and not the other way around. Whoever gets up first from the gambling table so as to move toward daylight will lose his seat: since everyone is crushed together in the overcrowded cellar, the problem is to get everyone to the exit together, not one of individual escape. However, as long as the players remain what they are, each super-power will suspect the other of wanting to disarm it under the guise of mutual disarmament, and the small powers will suspect the great ones of the same thing. How can an agreement be established on such a basis?

Here we find the other blueprint for a mutation. Since the problem of weapons leads to that of world government, and since the mushrooming of murderous yet precarious stakes makes the game too risky, one should end the game not by emptying the pockets of gamblers who might still find a way of playing, with matchsticks instead of weapons, but by changing the players. The best method for eliminating the roulette game would be to get rid of those to whom it has become as necessary as opium to drug addicts. Either one thus envisages a world government that would bring competition to an end by following Hobbes' formula, or one suggests ways to replace the sovereign state with larger communities in which the functions presently performed by the state would be dissociated. In both cases, one would abolish the state as the sovereign player, as the decision-maker without any legal superior or *de facto* superior other than the will of more powerful decision-makers. Instead of indicting the weapons, we indict their owners; instead of the stakes, we put the players themselves in question.

This is a familiar theme—the condemnation of nationalism. Unfortunately, it entails once again ambiguity and confusion. Is the nation-state condemned because it is dangerous for peace or because it is too small to meet the citizens' needs? The champions of the cause of a United Europe, for instance, have not always distinguished between the two motives. Some of the defenders of Jean Monnet's method support it as a procedure of universal validity that would help to solve concrete problems through agencies independent of and superior to the state. As they see it, this procedure creates no risk for the states' survival or safety, but its purpose is to extract progressively the venom from sovereignty.[6] Others, on the contrary, hail supranationality as the most economic way of building a United Europe which would in every respect behave as a regular player, albeit of impressive proportions, at the gambling table. Those who blame de Gaulle for his nationalism should at least divulge which of these two objectives they themselves aim for. If it is the game they resent, they are quite right to oppose his policies, for nobody plays the game with more zest than the General. If it is only the measurements of the gamblers that are at stake, then those critics ought to think twice. If the game is to go on, it is not at all sure that de Gaulle's strategy is the worst one from the viewpoint of Europe. The risk he takes is that of a nationalist epidemic keeping Europe divided: the risk he refuses to take is of building an apparently united Europe either on foundations so shaky that it would have no genuine common policy (in which case there would be a serious loss of national freedom of action without any offsetting gains either for the nations

[6] See Max Kohnstamm, "The Rising Tide," in *Daedalus, A New Europe?* (Winter, 1964); and Hoffmann, "Europe's Identity Crisis," *Daedalus* (Fall, 1964).

or for Europe) or else on the basis of excessive docility toward the American protector. The difference between de Gaulle and the critics who argue against the viability of the wholly independent nation-state is not over whether the game should go on, but over the disputed value and effects of the supranational procedure for national opportunities; it is also a disagreement on France's limits and opportunities of action. A difference in the respective hierarchies of risks follows: for de Gaulle's critics, the threat to safety and survival as well as to all the objectives beyond—power, prestige and values—require a sacrifice of independence; to him, any sacrifice of independence is a sacrifice of the latter objectives without any guarantee for security or survival.

Who is wrong? De Gaulle's strength is precisely his understanding of the strength of nationalism. If the future belongs to the nation-state, then it is certainly the player's duty—even if it would be in his interest to unify nations each one of which is too weak to have a big chance in the game—to move with considerable caution: he must not sacrifice his own stake so long as the new collective stake has not been determined; and, in the clash of wills, he must see to it that his own concept of the new common strategy prevails over the others. Let us go back to Rousseau, whose thought is so often close to de Gaulle's: from dependence on "things," there follows no necessary dependence on *someone else*. We must recognize that the nation-state is not yet in decline. The fundamental choice for any state is not between independence and a larger community that would outgrow and transcend the game; it is between the risks of independence, which are indeed gigantic, and the risks of dependence, which does not in the least reduce the risks that peace and world order incur because of the independence of other states. Insofar as independence is a snare and a burden, the state minimizes its risks by participating in organizations that provide it with what it needs, such as the functional agencies of the United Nations. Unfortunately, those organizations either do not prevent the game from going on or else are themselves the reflections of or the stakes in a clash of wills—such as the United Nations and NATO. In the world as it is, the number of states eager to live and to grow has constantly increased, and the superpowers have not provided an example of scuttling sovereignty or sacrificing power politics. The Soviet Union has fiendishly protected the former and avidly waged the latter; the United States has talked of partnership only when its interests were endangered by the growing power of its associates, and it has resorted to the

United Nations—at Suez and in the Congo (someday perhaps it will do so in Indochina)—only insofar as the U.N. serves its interests. But when it comes to building a brave new world, *noblesse oblige*: unless the lions give the good example, the lesser breeds will flee.

At the present time, the experience of transfers and devaluations of sovereignties is hardly encouraging. Sometimes, they have affected only areas of small importance for the governments, which have thus remained free to promote their policies. Sometimes, as in the case of the European Community, those shifts have succeeded in the area of welfare and economics owing both to the nature of the common objective—to maximize wealth—and to the organic solidarity the division of labor creates. But there has been little or no impact on the area in which each partner's risk of losses cannot be compensated by the lure of material rewards— the sector of diplomacy and strategy, where separate objectives proliferate and where competition develops in a climate of antagonism rather than solidarity. Sometimes, transfers and devaluations have taken place only at the expense of some and for the benefit of others, according to the most traditional rules of the game. We have not escaped from the traditional dilemma: new entities will emerge only when governments agree; and governments are not ready to give up the game.

We have thus had to rule out what one might call mutation through common sense. What are the chances of nevertheless transforming the game so that the risks become bearable once more? There are two conceptually different methods. Nothing prevents both being used, but they correspond to different hypotheses.

If men are not sensible enough to abandon the game that keeps them in the cellar, events may force them to. In the past, disasters never succeeded in convincing states that risks created for them by a steady mechanism for international security and settlement of disputes were less than risks created by their monopoly of force and independent action. In the future, disasters may well convince only the dead. Would the prospect of impending disaster—economic or nuclear—be enough, or would the world need some partial evidence, in the form of a "limited doomsday" or a limited economic collapse? It seems obvious that it would take an almost universal earthquake to convince the weak and the strong, the rich and the poor, the totalitarian and the pluralist of the necessity of ending the game without waiting further for assassins, neighbors,

or rivals to take the first step. In a world where the unity of the
system and the universal scope of the problems are not tantamount
to harmonious reaction or homogeneous attention, one would need
a sizable shock to provoke such attention or reaction. This new
version of "catastrophic optimism" is not very encouraging. But
the troubles are so huge and the available cures so ineffectual that
even so repulsive a prospect cannot be dismissed offhand. "Mutation at the brink" strikes me, anyhow, as less unlikely than deliberate mutation.

Let us assume, however, that everyone's prescriptions will keep
mankind away from the brink. The game will go on. The problem
will then be to widen the walls and break through the ceiling of
the cellar so as to put the players at greater ease. If they are then
faced less often with a risk of death, if they are forced less often
to follow the ethics of cunning and force to survive or to satisfy
their ambitions, they may gradually agree to switch from the game
of nuclear roulette to a game of cards or even to parlor games.
Under what conditions could this take place? —only through coherent and continuous action on all fronts. To concentrate on the
elimination of a single kind of risk would be useless; one would
create or strengthen other risks while doing so. Even an enforced
agreement on giving up national resort to force would soon be
undermined, unless it were accompanied by measures for the solution of the numerous concrete conflicts from which the risks of
war spring, or if it left in the nations' hands all the other, more
insidious but not always less efficient weapons for harming each
other.

This action on all fronts designed to make the cellar liveable and
the game reasonable requires two rules of conduct: first, as long as
the competition goes on, the players cannot be asked to behave
as if it were over; it is absurd to want states to give up their separate interests merely because they have a common interest—diver-
gently perceived—in survival and a modicum of order. But it is not
absurd for states to refrain from pursuing separate interests with
means that are capable of throwing not only their immediate rivals
but all bystanders and themselves into the abyss. In the choice of
means, uncertainties will remain; all one can ask for is that, as between two ways of obtaining satisfaction, between two techniques
of expansion, between two procedures for increasing wealth, between two levers of prestige, the states select the one that appears
to them less dangerous—if not for the international system (which
some nations have good reasons to want to change to their benefit)

—at least for needed world order. This is, of course, a vague standard, since it can be used, for instance, both to condemn the spread of nuclear weapons and to justify the creation of smaller nuclear forces at least by states with no ambition for revenge or aggression. To be sure, concern for order may lead to contradictory results or be used as a pretext for varied ambitions, but its mere introduction into the calculations would be a step forward, even if not a guarantee.

Secondly, the action necessary to establish any kind of order makes resort to international or regional organizations doubly indispensable. The players do not have so much choice: if they want to do everything themselves, they will be condemned to permanent panic; the notion of universal empire—one player winning once and for all, and imposing his will on all the others—has become synonymous with universal disaster, for such a conflagration alone could bring about a situation in which one state was master, hence liquidator, of the game. Only the road of cooperation is left open, then. This means, first, that nations must get used to settling together the problems they can no longer settle separately. (Nothing prevents each one of them from trying to make its views and its will prevail.) It also means that nations must accept resort to third parties, not only so that the players who are doing badly (such as France and England at Suez) can save face, but also in order to find or enforce solutions whose terms could not be set or whose execution could not be imposed if the antagonists remained alone with their resentments and their afterthoughts. (Nothing prevents each one of them from maneuvering so that the solutions will favor it.)

These two rules of behavior correspond to a new reality; their observation requires a third rule, which is both a prerequisite and a sanction; together, the three rules could bring about appreciable results. The new reality is that, for the first time, each player has a *particular* interest in preserving not necessarily the system but the game. Rousseau was right to say that the common interest, precisely because it is common, matters less to the players than the peculiar advantage at which he aims. But when the game itself is at stake, the interest in preserving it (whose disastrous end would be death for the players) becomes a basic concern: the very possibility of obtaining separate advantages depends on it. When the game is played by states both capable of destroying each other and often so weak that their survival as economic and administrative units depends on other nations, even the players most obsessed by the lure of individual gain or the envy of better endowed rivals is obliged to behave with a minimum of caution. Even risks can lead to order—should states make a good use of risks.

Given the capacity of men and states to prevent wisdom from obliging them to behave wisely, this minimum of caution must be reinforced, so to speak, by "secular arms": the state that is tempted to resort to force must be prevented from doing so; the state that is tempted to harm its neighbors must be discouraged; in other words, crime must not pay. International organizations naturally have a part to play here. When the United Nations sends firemen to wipe out fires that national appetites and passions have lit, this is important; especially when any minor conflict may provoke general disorder, there are no minor services. But if persistent vigilance is a duty for all, its effectiveness nevertheless depends above all on the big powers. Precisely because transfers of sovereignty have been meager, and the quarrels and stakes huge, states have strong reasons to resist the impact of or refuse to finance international organizations—whenever the risk of giving up a vital objective or accepting a formula that favors a rival appears higher than the risk of no solution at all. International organizations have neither the means nor the ambition to raise the latter risk deliberately, so as to force reluctant states to opt for the former. Even if one of their first objectives is to limit the area in which the super-powers clash directly (for instance, in appeasing conflicts with forces provided by the small states), they depend ultimately on the super-powers—which are both "secular arms" and deeply involved parties. This is obvious as far as the financing of the United Nations and its aid program is concerned. As for regulating the use of force, the United Nations can play its pacifying role only if the antagonists have not aligned forces and wills that exceed its own. (What would the United Nations have done in Algeria?) And the United Nations can move forward only between the trenches the super-powers have dug: when the lines drawn by the super-powers meet, the United Nations has no resort but to take refuge in the margin; we have seen it in Berlin and in Cuba. In order that crime not pay, one thus needs either the concerted action of states within, or if necessary without, international organizations, at the call or with the support of the super-powers; or else, when a big power is the culprit, one needs the deliberate and traditional action of its rivals and their associates to call him back to order, without, however, provoking thereby the very disorder their coalition aims to prevent.

A return to world order thus requires a return to the practices of deterrence and constraint with which past balancing systems curtailed the ambitions and curbed the policies of large or small states that did not voluntarily adopt balance-of-power *policies*. But, whereas past practices included the use of force against troublemakers, new conditions make such recourse unadvisable. World order must be rescued from the alternatives of chaos-through-collective-impotence and chaos-through-collective-overshooting. That states must now stick to moves of cautious moderation even when they are firm—in contrast to their behavior in balance-of-power systems, where calls to order could afford to be rude—should incite them to invent a subtle range of means of pressure.

We see, then, that the ways of wisdom remain uncertain and narrow, flanked by abysses; but, if they remain open, a kind of cumulative movement toward order could take place. The choice for moderation will be an incentive toward cooperation, and cooperation will strengthen moderation. The more states see (or are forced to see) that they have an interest in pursuing in the least brutal fashion even their most distinctive ambitions, the more they will become accustomed to exploiting the procedures of cooperation in doing so. The more cooperation develops, the more it will provide states with alternatives to isolated action in emergencies and lead them to adopt rules of competition-through-cooperation rather than competition-in-separate-action. As we can see in the European communities, bargaining could replace blackmail, *finesse* replace force, and hypocrisy replace vice. Even though the hunters carried guns, the guns would be loaded with blanks—which is progress, after all. The very existence of techniques of cooperation—from which each nation can hope to benefit or from which each can fear that in his absence others might derive benefits—incites those who find themselves insufficiently rewarded at least not to withdraw and at best to negotiate concessions from the others. Politics would remain the art of manipulation, and the context of manipulation is always important. The advantages of regional or international organizations for cooperation lie in the multiplicity of purposes they can serve, simultaneously or *seriatim*. The super-powers demonstrate this themselves. They see to it, sometimes with savage determination, that these agencies do not too greatly disturb their own moves, and yet they do not really challenge them either.

To turn material interdependence into psychological and political interdependence, to keep the inevitable politics of the powers from being power politics pure and simple, to tame the irrepressible realities of force through agencies for international cooperation, and to resort to appropriate constraint if cunning is not enough: this must be the objective. Short of "mutation at the brink," the risk of death and chaos will be mastered only in the game that breeds it. Relaxing the rules of the game requires that reflexes and habits be domesticated, which can only happen by trial and error. The point where sovereignty must be devaluated because of supranational or transnational links will be reached only if sovereign states consent to it through traditional international agreements. The snowballing movement described above will take place only if statesmen keep pushing all the time. Even more than in the past, international order is a permanent creation. The role played by destiny itself makes the permanent tension and deliberate convergence of wills indispensable; history teaches us that the only chains of events that can occur without men's decisions are chains of catastrophes. Woe to whoever trusts automatic processes, "irreversible" progress, or certain harmony. The game is never up, nothing can be deemed accomplished once and for all.

Men of impatient or utopian good will must choose between catastrophic optimism, with its enormous perils, and caution without illusions, without even the advantage of concealing the risks of the game. Yet such caution has the advantage of being rooted in reality, and it does not mean resignation. For there are two sides to uncertainty: nothing is lost and much can be gained if only one wants it and acts accordingly. The game can be changed only by playing it, but it is necessary that the players' aim be to transform the game. By choosing the least dangerous means—organized forms of cooperation, and pressures on everyone to stick to them—states should prepare for the coming of a world in which legitimate resort to force will be both controlled and centralized—where the great powers will put their weapons at the disposal of others, or where international organization will have means of action that will not be improvised and impoverished. In such a world, the state will probably be part of a network of regional and functional associations constructed so that the functions of defense, welfare, domestic order, cultural promotion, and allegiance—now all knotted together—will no longer be tied around the nation-state. The uncertainties of the game prevent us from knowing what delays it will take to bring the players away from their cellar, nor do we know in what state they will be when at last they turn to play a game other than roulette. But the uncertainties cannot deter us from wanting to reach this stage as the alternative to annihilation or suffocation. "Fallibility is not the same as futility; limited achievement is not the same as unlimited failure; danger is not the same as doom."[7]

We must go on living with risks, and living with the risk of chaos and death, but we must learn to create risks for citizens, states, and the international system *only* with the purposes of avoiding the total risk for the game and creating the opportunity for order.

[7] Inis L. Claude, *Swords into Plowshares* (New York, 1964), p. 403.

SEVEN

RESTRAINTS AND CHOICES IN AMERICAN FOREIGN POLICY

Nor LONG AGO, Henry A. Kissinger commented: "The stagnation of our policy is often ascribed to the fact that our best people are not in government service. But the more serious and pertinent question is how qualified our eminent men are for the task of policy-making in a revolutionary period."[1] Since those words were printed, two new national administrations have done their best to harness "our best people" to American foreign policy, and Mr. Kissinger's question is more pertinent than ever.

It would take a volume to analyze why policy-making is so frustrating a task in America today. My purpose here is to discuss the most important constraints on policy-makers' liberty of action, and to see how narrow or how broad a margin remains for choice. Such an attempt is worth while from at least two viewpoints. For one, recent theories of international politics seem to divide into opposite extremes—some focusing on the international system, tending to describe it as a compelling, even tyrannical, sociological divinity, others scrutinizing national decision-making, patiently listing all

[1] Henry A. Kissinger, *The Necessity for Choice* (New York, 1960), p. 340.

the organs that take part in it and all the "inputs" that go into decisions. Theories of the former type have not yet examined carefully enough the weight with which the system presses on various kinds of states at different times; theories of the latter type tend to be casual about the international environment. A study of the restraints and margins of choice may be useful to both and even begin to build a necessary bridge between them.

For another thing, such a study may be of interest to the observer, often baffled and generally critical of American foreign policy. What baffles him is the massive continuity of American policy —despite the innumerable verbal clashes, the promises of drastic reform, the temporary oscillations around the main trends, and the headlines announcing crises and bankruptcy. The wrapping changes: the substance remains much the same; images multiply, but the reality they mirror is monotonous. Consequently, there is constant clamor for change. The best way to find out why there seems to be this curse of continuity, and to what extent it is legitimate to suggest alternatives to it, consists in analyzing whatever it is that constricts American policy.

Now, various distinctions can be made. Certain restraints operate as prohibitions, others as imperatives: the former tells us what cannot be done; the latter tells us what has to be done. Certain restraints (of both kinds) delimit what United States foreign-policy proposals can try to accomplish; others delineate what kinds of proposal United States policy-makers can put forward. To take the case of prohibitions, let us say that what cannot be accomplished should not be requested (except for propaganda reasons), but that what cannot even be formulated should be expected even less. The most basic distinction is of a different kind. Its criterion is in the origin of the restraints. Some are provided by the international system itself, of which the United States is but one element. The system rules out certain policies and dictates others, but it does not annihilate all freedom of choice. Others stem from the nature of the American political community; either they rule out actions that the international system does not exclude, or they impel the nation to decisions which on the surface may appear as shining examples of free choice but which are actually, in a deeper sense, domestic compulsions. Many critics blame the nation or its leaders for what is the fault of the international system; others indict the system for evils that must be traced to the nation. The vultures that attack Prometheus may be the gods', but the ties that bind him to the rock may be his own.

I

Sensitive souls often object to describing international politics as a game—whether chess, poker, or a complicated play of game theory—but the metaphor has its usefulness. As Raymond Aron keeps telling us, the nations play a game in which payment is in blood, not only cash.[2] Of the restraints the players must observe, some are inherent in the distribution of the cards, others result from the rules of the game. Whether he seeks a better distribution or new rules, the player must exercise self-restraint lest he lose. What those limitations are and to what extent they can be overcome depend on the concrete circumstances of the system and the player.

Let us start with the cards—that is, with the basic elements of the present system as they appear to the United States. The first element is bipolarity.[3] America's power has not been America's choice. As long as the international order could be left in the hands of Great Britain and France, the United States chose isolation; but the United States emerged from World War II as the only nation that could counterbalance the might of the Soviet Union. It literally had no choice, unless one calls abdication from politics and escape from history a genuine alternative. There is a difference between a mistake and a mirage; those who in the 1920's encouraged Americans to cultivate their gardens may have been wrong, but those who suggest today that the United States practice "self-commitment and self-containment" before trying to deal with others are living in an anachronism.[4] The old choice between isolation and involvement is dead; there remains only the purely academic choice between historical sleep and the dangerous life of a great power. The fact that the latter often seems like a nightmare does not make escape into untroubled dreams a genuine alternative.

It is significant that, at the close of World War II, the United States behaved as if the old choice still existed. It opted for a kind of disengagement that did not amount to isolation but behind

---

[2] Aron, *Paix et Guerre Entre les Nations*, "Introduction."

[3] On the significance, origins, stability, and propects of bipolarity, see below, Chapter 8. Bipolarity does *not* mean that only two powers have real freedom of choice: indeed, the combination of bipolarity and nuclear weapons produces the "divorce between power and influence" already mentioned above, in Chapter 6, and discussed again below. One of the most paradoxical constraints produced by bipolarity is on the super-powers' use of power.

[4] For such a suggestion, see William Appleman Williams, *The Tragedy of American Diplomacy* (Cleveland, 1959).

which there was the expectation of a world without a bipolar struggle, or in which other people's conflicts could be arbitrated by the United States. But bipolarity by definition rules out arbitration and entails conflict. On the world scene, de Jouvenel's distinction between *dux* and *rex* is never really valid. In the nineteenth century, the British *rex* had to behave as *dux* more often than theoreticians of the balance of power like to admit; in a bipolar world, there is a clash of *duces*, and no *rex*.[5] Consequently, when the nature of Soviet power and policy and the crumbling of British strength became obvious, the United States simply had to fill the vacuum. President Truman's freedom of choice was strictly limited: it concerned the moment and the manner in which America's taking up the challenge would be demonstrated. Even in this respect, the margin of choice was narrowed by the development of the crisis in Greece in 1947. Thus it is fair to view the great decisions of 1947 as supremely creative acts of statesmanship, but it is also fair to describe America as the nation, in Malraux's terms, "that has won the greatest power in the world but not sought it." Rarely has freedom been more clearly the recognition of necessity, and statesmanship the imaginative exploitation of necessity. America rushed to those gates at which Soviet power was knocking. Part of the trouble, as we shall see, has been that, ever since, so many unexpected challenges to America's power have appeared on the Western side of the gates.

Among the various consequences of bipolarity, two deserve mention: one is the risk of general war; the other is the scramble for allies. Critics occasionally argue as if a specific wickedness of American policy-makers were responsible for the climate of tension and for "pactomania." But the dialectic of reciprocal fear, which accounts for both, appears whenever the game has only two major players. It is legitimate to ask whether each one does all he can to make the atmosphere less electric and to select only those allies worth being defended—in those respects, there may indeed remain some freedom of choice, but it is a very limited freedom, both because bipolarity sets the stage for a pugnacious competition and because of other restraints, to which we now turn.

A second fundamental constraint in the postwar international system is furnished by its ideological character. To make things worse, there are two ideological battles in progress. As is well known, the bipolar struggle is a contest for the minds of men at

[5] Bertrand de Jouvenel, *Sovereignty: An Inquiry into the Political Good* (Chicago, 1957).

least as much as a fight for men, markets, resources, or space. What is at stake is how both domestic politics and the international order are to be organized. In any nonideological struggle (even if it is bipolar), pauses and compromises are much more likely, because their implications are less damaging to the players. In an ideological contest, the psychological repercussions of minor defeats, the use of temporary advantages as springboards, the symbolic nature of every test of will, and the unlimited character of the final objectives (however limited the subject matter of a particular crisis) almost condemn the world political scene to being a desert without oases. Concessions do not disarm hostility, and they may indeed infect the adversary with the exhilaration of success. Thus it becomes almost impossible (and not for domestic reasons alone) for the United States to recognize Red China. A small concession in Berlin may undo the whole tapestry; an East German agent in an international control commission adds nothing to Soviet material power—his only value is symbolic, but this is precisely what the battle is about. In such a context, even mild conditions each camp puts to sign agreements with the other tend to be interpreted as death warrants. To ask that West Berlin not be a teeming nest of subversive activities aimed at East Germany is tantamount to asking to undermine the freedom of thought and speech that are the pride of the West. To ask that the Soviet Union stop bringing aid and comfort to Communist parties or guerrillas outside the Soviet area is to ask it to give up the proselytizing that was the cement, and remains the least dubious tie, binding pro-Soviet Communist nations, and the best Soviet defense against Chinese competition and charges.

In such a climate, the traditional tricks of diplomacy (neutralization or internationalization of certain areas, political armistices that delineate spheres of influence) lose their justification. Domestic affairs cannot be insulated from the competition any more than specific areas. As the old techniques become useless, new methods of intervention become unavoidable, and thus restraints and compulsions converge to decrease freedom of choice.

The other ideological contest, between the anticolonial forces and their former masters, operates as a restraint on the United States primarily because of the link between the cold war and the nationalist revolution: the United States is not free to give full endorsement to this revolution, whereas the Soviet Union can do so, for, in the scramble for allies, the United States lined up with all the colonial powers. Moreover, despite North American reluctance to consider United States–Latin American relations in any way colonial, the danger of anticolonial nationalism reaching Latin America and attacking United States positions is not fictitious. Yet the United States cannot ignore or resist the winds of change, for nothing could be more successfully turned into hurricanes spreading Communism. This is particularly true in Latin America, where, if the United States opposed all manifestations of nationalism aimed at American interests and influence, the nationalists would have no place to turn to but Moscow and Peking, whereas African and Asian nationalists in revolt against Europe have a broader choice.

These two ideological conflicts have one important characteristic in common: asymmetry. One side is on the offensive, one on the defensive—and, in both cases, the West is on the defensive.

The vigor and character of the offensive varies: obviously, neither Soviet strategy nor Chinese moves nor anticolonial forces are as bellicose in their offensive as Nazi Germany was, or Napoleon; Soviet actions since the Cuban confrontation in October, 1962, have been prudent indeed. But all the word "offensive" implies is *direction*: a nation pursues an offensive policy when the moves it makes aim to effect drastic changes in the distribution of power in the world and in the internal order of nations. This policy may or may not rely primarily on military power and military action.

It takes only one nation to start a war; it takes only one camp to launch an ideological contest. The adversary has no choice but to pick up the challenge, unless he is resigned to defeat at the outset. The United States is an ideological contender by necessity rather than choice: in the bipolar struggle, the United States "ideology" (to be examined later) consists of a set of views-on-things rather than a doctrine about the direction of history or instructions for impelling the world along its due course. In the anticolonial revolution, the United States finds itself on the defensive not because of its "public philosophy" but largely because this "philosophy," which is a set of anticolonial reflexes, is neutralized by America's alliances, which prevented the United States supporting with deeds (or sometimes even words) the liberation movements in Africa and Asia, and by those national-liberation movements' frequently intense radicalism, which obstinately insists on seeing America as the richest satisfied power instead of "the first new nation."

Such asymmetry immeasurably complicates the American problem of action. The United States first must try to gain some sort of initiative in the midst of a generally defensive strategy; all too often, the site and the moment of the battle are selected by the other camp, and the United States' freedom of choice is more tactical than strategic. Second, whereas the offense can choose to provoke a limited localized crisis, the United States cannot apply the traditional Cartesian method of subdividing the issue into its component parts so as to resolve them one by one, for this would lead to precisely the kind of piecemeal retreats the adversary wants to impose. Third, because of the absence of a genuine national ideology, and because of the conflict between anticolonial feelings (or the anti-Western feelings of former colonies) and colonial alliances, the way the United States can wage the battle for the minds of men is strictly limited. (Characteristically, the proponents of a "forward strategy" do not do much more than ask for greater vigor in American propaganda activities—and there are other restraints that operate here.)

The third basic aspect of the international system is the most widely discussed one: nuclear power. It is also one of the sharpest restraints with which great powers have had to cope. Does not the possession of the most formidable weapons in history increase the freedom of movement of its possessors? Reality, for better or worse, is more complicated. Such possession is a prerequisite of great-power status, but today, because of nuclear weapons, the discretion of a great power is much more sharply limited than before. A great power armed with nuclear weapons is like Baudelaire's albatross: *ses ailes de géant l'empêchent de marcher.* It may be argued retrospectively that, in the days of its nuclear monopoly, the United States had a freedom of action that it wasted out of timidity; but in the age of nuclear stalemate and nuclear plenty, surely the restraints on the actual use of nuclear weapons are decisive.

What of the threat to use such weapons? If their invention virtually abolished certain kinds of *war* as rational instruments of foreign policy, do not nuclear weapons increase a state's saber-rattling capabilities in *peace?* Here, two different restraints weigh on the United States. First, the more the "balance of terror" tends to stability, the less an American nuclear threat is credible. Indeed, we have reached the stage where both Europeans and Americans wonder whether the threat of a United States first strike against the Soviet Union, in the case of a Soviet conventional attack in Europe and in the absence of a conventional NATO army large enough to be a deterrent force by itself, has not ceased to be plausible. But there may still be psychological advantages resulting from a militarily implausible threat, given the ideological dimension of the contest;

and the Soviet Union has shown (in 1956 at the time of Suez or in 1961 for the "protection" of Cuba) that it was not ready to throw away the benefits of bluff. Here is where the second handicap appears, which applies only to the United States. A nation whose position in a contest is essentially defensive can use the threat of force defensively, for the protection of vital interests and stakes. Indeed, it often must resort to such a threat, when only the prospect of having to fight a battle may still deter the enemy.[6] But a defensive power finds it much more difficult to use saber-rattling imaginatively so as to put the enemy on the defensive. Not only does the American nuclear threat have little military credibility, but the defensive power in an ideological contest tries to win the minds of men by, among other things, stressing the innocence of being on the defensive. The offensive power, by definition, uses all possible techniques in order to push ahead: ideological appeals, subversion, and fear. The defensive power gains by appearing as the mighty champion of the frightened. To frighten back has more drawbacks than advantages.

If these are the disadvantages of the defensive, is the United States not free to switch to the offensive? We must look for the last time at how the cards were distributed at the end of World War II. There is no doubt that the challenge was cast by the Soviet Union and that Western positions were besieged (indeed, often conquered) either by the Communists or by the nationalists in the underdeveloped countries. Nor is there any doubt that the West has in no place tried to roll back the Iron Curtain. In order to preserve its position, the West will have to do infinitely more than sit and wait behind radar screens and barbed wire; but until and unless the world is no longer bipolar and the Soviet Union's ideological drive loses its force (either because of domestic "thawing" or because of failure abroad), the basic conditions of the game will keep the United States in a defensive position vis-à-vis the Soviet Union.

Other restraints and necessities result from the rules of the game. First, there are sharp limits to United States freedom of action in East-West relations. Not only does the ideological asymmetry discussed above narrow the range of common interests, but it also makes the translation of such interests into explicit agreements

[6] Pacifists who usually miss this important point fall into a Soviet trap and interpret U.S. military bases abroad or a U.S. threat of a first strike to deter Soviet conventional attack in Europe as aggressive moves.

very difficult. The fundamental difference between the two political regimes is the major component of this ideological asymmetry and the main reason why such agreements are so unlikely. The most obvious example is the spectacular failure of attempts to get a Soviet-American consensus against nuclear war and nuclear diffusion expressed in any treaty, other than a limited nuclear-test ban that amounts to little more than a joint awareness that nuclear saturation has been reached. Soviet disarmament proposals are tactical constructs. They give propaganda advantages to the Soviet Union if they are rejected, and they would benefit the Soviet Union by destroying the barrage of Western force that keeps Russia from Western Europe, and China from Formosa and Southeast Asia, if they were adopted. United States schemes for disarmament and arms control tend to keep the Western barrage intact. They inevitably raise the formidable question of inspection, and they give a kind of priority to the problem of surprise attack, which is not really the Soviet Union's major fear, since the likelihood of a U.S. switch to the military offensive is small.

Another example of the limits that ideological asymmetry imposes on American foreign policy concerns negotiation tactics. It is easy for the Soviet Union to start a diplomatic campaign with thoroughly unreasonable and outrageous demands that will be gradually toned down in such a way that the outcome will be either no agreement at all—and consequently a Soviet possibility of reopening the matter at any time—or an agreement in which the Soviet Union will have made some gain. It is much more difficult for the United States, given its regime and the vision of world order it tries to promote, to retaliate with equally extreme suggestions. The Soviet Union can ask Western forces to get out of West Berlin. The best the West can do in return is to ask for a plebiscite in West and East Berlin. The Soviet Union can insist on a *troika* in the secretariats of international organizations. The range of United States alternatives goes from a flat "no" to some compromise.

The other limit imposed on the United States comes from geographical differences rather than ideological asymmetry. Even if the diffusion of nuclear weapons made it easier for the United States and the Soviet Union to agree on politically neutral formulas of arms control and disarmament—that is, which would not conceal advantages won by one side—negotiators would still have to cope with the fact that they are not dealing with abstract units but with one land mass and one sea power. Even in the nuclear age of permeable territorial states, geography retains some importance:

the United States needs a minimum of bases and supporters outside the Western Hemisphere in order to deploy its strength and to deter or stop the advances of Communist nations. Even if the contest were not an ideological one that made compromise difficult, geopolitical conditions would make it disadvantageous for the United States to permit too many zones in the world to be neutralized. In a completely disarmed world, such a liability would disappear, but what is in question is not the millennium but how one gets there. Geography restricts the range of concessions the United States can make in arms negotiations; the combination of geographical position and ideological defensive compels it to defend the allies it needs to contain Communist expansion. Once again, freedom of action is limited to a choice of scope and means within a context of necessity.

Geography and ideology combine to make it extremely difficult to translate into action America's intention to pursue a *détente* with the Soviet Union as the best alternative to the risk of war, as well as America's exploitation of the Sino-Soviet dispute. To be "tough" toward the Chinese Communists because they are more bellicose, and gentler toward the Russians because they are becoming more sedate, is a possibly self-defeating policy: the opponent rewarded by this discrimination would find in these rewards not merely a reason for moderation, but also a painless dividend for expansion; if caution brings such a bonus, then not only toughness but also a renunciation of messianism becomes unnecessary for the Soviet Union. If America's aim is to stop being on the defensive, then it cannot pursue a policy aiming merely to make a defensive posture more comfortable. Furthermore, many of the rewards the United States might envisage in order to coax the Russians to behave well must be provided at the expense of America's allies, especially in Europe. This the United States can hardly offer to do.

For a second problem arises from the nature of American alliances. Any alliance restrains the freedom of movement of every partner, included the senior one. Not even Red China could be abandoned by the Soviet Union, should it find itself under attack from the United States. Not even the Soviet Union can sacrifice the interests of East Germany without damaging its own; it was much easier for the isolated Russia of 1939 to reverse its policy than it is now as leader of the socialist camp. Yet an alliance of *autonomous* nations, however unequal in power, introduces even more stringent constraints on the senior partner when he is locked in a bipolar and ideological struggle. The Western alliances are prime examples: the United States may be preponderant, but in almost no place are other national leaders simply puppets manipulated by the United States. In the Soviet camp, the satellites are not autonomous, but China is. The senior partner wants and needs allies; should he, disagreeing with them because they are tiring of the struggle, mistreat them, he would push them out of his camp, unless he were willing to use force against them, as the Soviet Union did in Hungary. It is hard to imagine the United States compelling a reluctant ally by force, unless a case could be made to show that this ally had already become the tool of Communism. The United States could pressure France to consent to German rearmament, but it could not compel her to ratify the European Defense Community or endorse the multilateral nuclear force.[7]

Should the senior partner disagree with his ally because the latter resisted concessions he wanted to make to the common enemy, then the combination of a world struggle and the "nondirective" nature of the alliance gives the weaker partner an almost unassailable position. It is not only in the United Nations that the cold war reverses the traditional hierarchy between the weak and the strong. The blackmail of the weak who appeal to the spirit of the alliance has been one of the most serious restraints on the United States' freedom of movement; the United States can do very little about it, unless the Soviet Union becomes cooperative. To coerce one ally in order to please the enemy is not the best way to keep one's other allies. The United States cannot recognize East Germany—as long as West Germany objects so strenuously that, were the U.S. to dismiss these objections, West German confidence in the alliance would be destroyed. It is false to say that in a bipolar struggle one's ally has "nowhere else to go." Nor can the United States compel Chiang Kai-chek to give up Quemoy and Matsu—as long as the Chinese make it clear that they would interpret any concession as a sign of weakness and an incentive to push harder. Nor can the United States impose its views as to who should govern South Vietnam—if the South Vietnamese Army makes it clear that U.S. interference obstructs the pursuit of the war. Nor could the United States oblige Laotian right-wing forces to stop blocking the formation of a coalition government. If there was anything more startling than the failure of extremely strong U.S. pressures,

[7] See Fred Greene, "The Impact of Military Factors on American Foreign Policy," in Stephen D. Kertesz, ed., *American Diplomacy in a New Era* (South Bend, Ind., 1961), pp. 525–48.

it was the fact that what finally coerced the Laotians was the Communists' use of force. Whether it was in the United States' interest to have the *other* camp provide the means of compelling the Laotian allies of the United States is something else again. Hans Morgenthau has sharply criticized the United States' failure to impose its political will on its allies,[8] but the limits are set by the nature of the competition and the alliances, rather than by deficiencies of will. The major complaint from U.S. allies has not been absence of leadership (except during the final phase of the second Eisenhower Administration).

Often, precisely because of what is at stake in the East-West contest, "it is not wise to scrap alliances which it was unwise to form"[9] or evacuate bases that have lost their military usefulness (unless the nation on whose territory they are asks for their removal). One is bound by one's commitments; one is committed even by one's mistakes. The United States may be free to avoid new and mistaken entanglements in the future, but it is not free to tear out of its scrapbook the political misjudgments of the past. Nor is it free to avoid entanglements altogether. (The mediocrity of SEATO as an instrument of foreign policy has led, not to a United States withdrawal from the defense of Southeast Asia, but to a downgrading of this particular alliance in favor of direct United States involvement.) Once more, freedom of action shrinks to mitigating the bitterness of the unavoidable.

A third set of limits on U.S. foreign policy resembles the previous ones, but they seem less inevitable. I am referring to the restraints the United Nations imposes on United States foreign policy. As in the case of American alliances, the limits result from entanglement, but, whereas the need for alliances is questioned only by utopians, the need to let the United Nations be a major determinant of United States foreign policy is much more debatable. This is not the place to follow the debate in full, but a few statements are in order. First, it is quite impossible for the United States to ignore the United Nations. In the contest between East and West, the allegiance of the "Third World" (so spectacularly represented in the United Nations) is an important stake. Also, the principles of the U.N. Charter reflect a vision of world order that Western nations propose to the rest of the world. In other words, the

[8] Hans J. Morgenthau, in Roy C. Macridis, ed., *Foreign Policy in World Politics* (2nd ed.; Englewood Cliffs, N.J., 1961), pp. 201–24.

[9] Morton Kaplan, *United States Foreign Policy in a Revolutionary Age* (monograph; Princeton Center of International Studies, 1961), p. 20.

United States cannot ignore the United Nations as a forum or as an ideal; nor can the United States permit the Soviet Union to turn it into an instrument of Communist strategy.

Second, it is not at all clear that the United States is obliged to try to use the United Nations as an instrument of its own: if the stake in the conflict becomes a weapon or force on its own merits, its will might well conflict with United States interests or it might become plagued by internal dissensions and institutional weaknesses; to ameliorate these might require of the United States more energy and demand more concessions than the benefits to be derived from such a force would justify. My point is that at various times in the past, the United States has deliberately chosen to enlarge the role of the United Nations as a force in world affairs and that, although the United States' freedom of choice in the future persists here as elsewhere, precedents narrow it according to the same dialectic of commitment observed in alliances. It may have been unwise at times for the U.S. to try to win friends and influence people through the one mechanism in which those friends and people were numerically in command; for in the attempt it put a real, not just a paper, club into their hands. Having done it so often, however, to reverse the policy in the hope of regaining some of the influence already lost may be a sure way to undermine drastically the influence the United States still has.

A final set of limits appears in United States relations with other non-Communist nations—the underdeveloped countries, in particular. It is another consequence of ideological asymmetry, and one for which it would be foolish to blame the United States. Almost by definition, the United States must deal with officialdom. Even when the United States believes that officialdom is corrupt, digs its own grave, and endangers the West's position by throwing reformers into the arms of the Communists, it is officialdom that the United States must convince. This restraint can be traced to liberalism[10] only if one makes it clear that liberalism here means not the Wilsonian view of world politics, but the essence of Western political regimes and Western international law. It is not only the United States that has "failed" to organize parties abroad as instruments of Western interests. To say that the United States must deal with officialdom does not mean that the United States cannot keep in touch with opposition parties, or encourage reformers, or frown on gravediggers in power. Indeed, it may well be that

[10] On this theme, see John Spanier, *American Foreign Policy Since World War II* (New York, 1960).

the United States has been much too shy in all these respects. But even if the United States became a virtuoso in the difficult art of combining diplomatic correctness with subdiplomatic manipulation, there would still remain sharp limits to what a nontotalitarian power can achieve. There is more than a difference of degree between the Central Intelligence Agency and the Communist International.

Given this limitation, one should avoid two mistakes of judgment. When, behind the gates to which America rushed in 1947–48, political developments destroyed or weakened the hold Western nations had kept on Asia and Africa, when change began to shake Latin America as well, Americans complained of having "lost" areas that were never theirs to lose. It is quite as serious a mistake to believe that, because France or Britain has withdrawn from many areas, United States influence will spread more easily there. The limits are set by the international system; the expectations from and disappointments with American "omnipotence" are peculiarly American.

II

The prism through which every nation looks at the outside world has been shaped by its own experience. For a policy-maker, there is as much truth in Eliot's "Hell is ourselves" as in Sartre's "*L'enfer, c'est les autres.*" How the same challenge (say, decolonization) is met by France or Britain tells us much more about the domestic values and political habits of each nation than about the particular external circumstances that distinguish the French from the British problem. Any study of foreign policy that sets goals which cannot be reached so long as the nation does not change its skin and its soul is of limited worth. As in the case of every political community, the limits set by the experience of the United States can be divided into those that derive from the nation's political style and culture and those that result from its system of government.

The political style of the United States has been subjected in recent years to so many searching investigations that one need only restate the familiar.[11] I do not suggest that the elements of this style are immutable; the way in which they have been affected by America's involvement in postwar world affairs has been shown

[11] See, in particular, *Daedalus: The American National Style* (Spring, 1958), and David M. Potter, *People of Plenty* (Chicago, 1954).

often and well.[12] However, there always remains a lag between age-old blinders and reflexes and new (especially external) pressures that make them obsolete. Often, responses that at first might appear to be unprecedented can be shown to be nothing but the application of the old habits of thought and action to a new problem. The "axiomatic" policies analyzed by Ernest May[13] are the instinctive reactions that express the nation's style.

There are three elements in America's experience that are relevant to its foreign policy. The most familiar ingredient is the liberal tradition, well documented by Louis Hartz.[14] It continues to operate in a variety of ways as a filter of American attitudes, which can be summed up as the "sin of transposition," the mistake of projecting into world affairs a vision of public life derived from the experience of the liberal *Rechtsstaat*. What flows from such a vision is the expectancy of ultimate accommodation: even the "realist" school of international politics places in diplomacy and compromise a faith that, given the present international system, might be called *l'espoir des désespérés*, or the last hope of the tough-minded liberal. A liberal community is one in which rifts can be reconciled, or in which the contenders at least entrust to the procedures of government the task of finding a formula for coexistence; diplomacy is supposed to be its international equivalent, and negotiated agreements are to be seen in the same light as laws.

A liberal community is also one in which coercion is most thoroughly concealed behind consensus, so that the use of force is both exceptional and unquestionably aimed at asocial targets. A liberal vision of international affairs suffers from a complete misunderstanding of the role of force in world history. It tends not only to see in the need for military strength a regrettable evil, but also to keep it in a kind of separate compartment and to assign specialists to thinking about it in aseptic isolation. Consequently, there still remains an instinctive inhibition in America's approach to the use of national force. This reticence cannot be explained merely by the obvious dangers of using force in the nuclear age, although it does contribute toward explaining restraint in the years of nu-

[12] See, especially, Robert E. Osgood, *Ideals and Self-Interest in America's Foreign Relations* (Chicago, 1953), and *Limited War* (Chicago, 1957). See also Charles Burton Marshall, *The Limits of Foreign Policy* (New York, 1954).

[13] "The Nature of Foreign Policy: The Calculated vs. the Axiomatic," *Daedalus* (Fall, 1962), pp. 653–67.

[14] Louis Hartz, *The Liberal Tradition in America* (New York, 1955).

clear monopoly. Incessantly, private and official United States disarmament proposals come back to the vision of world government
with a world police force.[15] And since it is clear that the days of
the universal *Rechtsstaat* are not near, American thinking on arms
control is essentially a compromise between a recognition of the
fact that national force is here to stay until then, and the atavistic
desire to avoid having to use the weapons or threaten with them:
if we cannot yet amputate the gangrenous member, let us at least
agree to hide it.

This attitude explains not only the oft-denounced tendency to
fight a "just war" as if it were a community police action to weed
out social pests and eliminate force from history,[16] but also what
I cannot help but call (perhaps because of my own European back-
ground) a lack of maturity in judging other nations' attitudes
toward force. America's caution in handling the Suez crisis in the
summer of 1956, its condemnation of the Anglo-French resort to
force in the fall of 1956, its rebuke to other nations that try to
establish separate deterrents and recover the liberty of diplomatic
action that military power gave them in the past (a liberty they
may well be mistaken in believing is still possible) cannot be accounted for solely by special circumstances of the nuclear age.
Such an attitude leads only too easily to a double standard: one's
own possession and occasional use of force are not objectionable,
since one knows one's own reluctance; other nations' saber-rattling
and gun-boat diplomacies are trigger-happy wickedness. Americans
like to judge others by their actions or capabilities, but to be judged
on their intentions.

The depreciation in a liberal community of the hidden role of
force entails a depreciation of other, more subtle forms of coercion
as well, and a tendency to underrate the elements of struggle that
persist in any political system. The basic tenets of liberal faith
remain the gradual triumph of public opinion, the conciliating and
unifying role of trade and industry, the civilizing and refining of
power through law and legal institutions. All those tenets have left
their mark on the American approach to foreign policy. They do
not operate as absolute obstacles to a more effective approach, but
as blinders that take years and the successive shocks of unfortunate
experiences to remove. The first mental reflex consists in trusting

[15] See, for example, Arthur I. Waskow's suggestions in "Limits of Defense,"
The Atlantic (February, 1962), pp. 80–87.
[16] See below, Chapter 9. See also Robert W. Tucker, *The Just War* (Balti-
more, 1960).

the General Assembly as the expression of world public opinion; in hoping that economic aid will produce social and political progress in stability; in believing that deep conflicts of interest can be transcended through institutional changes (multiplying Peace Observation Committees in the United Nations or consultation committees in NATO); in being convinced that a dictator such as Castro simply cannot be supported by his people and that he is merely a vermin which it is legitimate to destroy by force. Gradually, one learns; but the pattern is always the same—illusions are not so much lost as frustrated. The normal expectation is either of a problem-less peace or of an uninhibited war, yet experience tells us that peace is full of troubles and that war must be limited if the world is to survive. To the liberal, however, experience is a bitter pill.

Louis Hartz has shown that, in America, liberalism and conservatism have tended to merge. From the viewpoint of the limits of American foreign policy, however, the two elements must be kept apart. America's liberalism is not unique: what makes its impact on United States foreign affairs far greater than, say, the impact of similar tenets on British foreign policy is a different experience in past world politics. America's conservatism has unique features, however. Elsewhere, conservatism is above all a philosophy. In the United States, it is a way of life and an approach to action, and both inhibit American foreign policy.

The conservative way of life reflects a domestic experience that is so singular that it amounts to "a severance of communications" between the United States and the outside world.[17] The elements of this experience are well known. A long tradition of equality in affluence has made class struggle *à l'européenne* unnecessary, but it has also made it difficult for Americans to understand and sympathize with such struggles, and it has reduced the possibilities of America's "people of plenty" influencing the underprivileged. The amount of available aid is one thing; the amount of influence, quite another.

The United States has long experience in social and political integration, which its social sciences reflect only too well. In many other countries, there are both evidence of ideological conflict and a discontinuity between society and the political system; integration may or may not be the goal, but it is not the norm. American

[17] See Hoffmann, "L'Amérique incommunicable," *Cahiers de la République* (1959), IV, 90–97; and Jean-Marie Domenach, "Le Modèle américain," *Esprit* (July–August, September, October, 1960), pp. 1219–32; 1360–74; 1520–34.

policy scientists and policy-makers have few answers to the problem of integrating dislocated communities, not only because of the limits on America's capacity for intervening in the domestic affairs of others, but also because of a lack of intellectual familiarity; it is difficult for Americans to understand an ideological mode of argument, unless it be the liberal one that plays conflict down, not up.

Nothing has contributed more to the "severance of communications" than something that is taken to be the very touchstone of conservatism almost anywhere else; the favor shown private interests, especially business interests, because their part in the making of America has on the whole been beneficial. This attitude has weighed on American foreign policy in two ways. Since the United States' experience has been so different from that of Europe, Latin America, or Asia, where private interests (even national ones) have often served only to preserve and increase the privileges of the elite, it has broadened the intellectual gap discussed above. On the other hand, the expansion of U.S. business interests abroad creates a unique problem: no Western government reacts with pleasure to the expropriation of private Western firms by nations that see those firms as instruments of colonial exploitation or obstacles to domestic planning, but the link between those interests and the government is stronger in the United States than in any other country. This is so not because of any "power-elite" conspiracy on populist or Marxist lines, but because of the material importance of those interests abroad and as a result of the national ethos. Here again, we are faced with a flexible limitation, as occasional United States support for "socialistic" governments indicates. Yet, especially in its relations with Latin America, the United States reflex continues to be one of hostility to nationalizations. And, however fast the Executive Branch may learn in this respect, Congress serves as the thermos bottle of American resentment.

It was fashionable not very long ago to ask for a renewal of the American national purpose. Even if America begins to "move again," it is unlikely that the gap between its domestic experience and that of the outside world will be closed. If a "new America" merely strengthens its tradition of equality in plenty, then the gap may even be widened. It is the domestic success of their way of life that makes Americans conservative amid a revolutionary world —and the goal of the new frontier or the great society is certainly not to impair this success in order to make them less so.

The other aspect of American conservatism concerns their approach to the solution of problems, including problems of foreign policy their way of life throws up. It may be called, in Walt W. Rostow's terms, "the operator's way," or it may be termed pragmatism; I would call it the engineering approach. For it is a peculiar kind of pragmatism. It is not steeped in history or psychology, which are sciences (or arts) of the complex and uncertain. It too is reflected in American social sciences, with their passionate search for general laws, their preference for deductive models over inductive generalizations from history, their quest for mathematical formulas that tend to give a reassuring sense of certainty even when they measure the immeasurable.

The engineering approach has three drawbacks that operate as blinders on United States policy-making. First, the drive toward certainty is often carried too far. Either it distorts the importance of those limited areas of policy in which calculable certainty appears to exist (note the enthusiasm for strategy in a nation that is so reluctant to initiate the use of force), or else the quest is carried into areas where there is no certainty. Even military policy is too tricky a matter to be left to IBM machines, however well-fed with variables. In a world in which irrationality exists, the search for a thoroughly rational policy is both a mistake and a delusion. As Aron has written, in the game of international politics, whose objectives are multiple and whose rules are uncertain, there may be *reasonable* politics and *unreasonable* ones, but there cannot be *one rational* conceptualization, least of all when the game itself, because of nuclear weapons, has become unreasonable.[18] The oversimplification and overrating of purely technical but calculable elements over intangible ones are byproducts of a misplaced faith in human engineering.

A second flaw is discontinuity. The engineering approach is a piecemeal approach; one takes up the problems as they come. If game theory reflects the longing for certitude, decision-making theory expresses this other aspect of pragmatism. It strikes me as even more numbing. It concentrates thought and research on the immediate, which is not always the essential. For there is a double price one must pay for waiting until the problems appear: one must repair what one has not prevented—the price of tardiness; then there is the price of retrospective reflection—the remedies one discovers for the future are all too often patterned on the crisis that gave impetus to the search, a crisis not at all certain to be recurrent. Studies of limited war flourished after Korea. It is only now, all of a sudden, that we are paying sufficient attention to "counter-

[18] Aron, *op. cit.*, "Conclusion."

insurgency." The tendency of United States newspapers to explore foreign countries after a crisis has exploded is characteristic. The "discovery" of Africa since 1960 (by the mass media as well as by policy-makers) may be explained in part by the fact that the dark continent had been the preserve of our allies. The late discovery of Latin America after Castro has no similar justification.

Discontinuity also leads to the improvisation of measures, or the accumulation of *ad hoc* researches, that so busily focus on the issue at hand that they neglect the deeper structural causes of the momentary trouble. The tendency to present foreign aid in terms of a shopping list of separate and limited projects obscures the fact that there are few areas of policy in which success requires more time and depends on more prerequisites the donor cannot provide. But there is no better example of an improvisation that fails to answer any of the underlying issues which gave rise to it than the multilateral nuclear force. What was at stake was nothing less than the political and decision-making processes of the alliance—who commands, and toward what goals? What was proposed was a gimmick that, because of its very irrelevance to those issues, proved even more divisive and cumbersome than the issues with which it only pretended to cope.

The third drawback of the engineering approach is America's tendency to support the *status quo*—not out of sympathy with it but because it would take far more time to change it than the emergency allows. Franklin Roosevelt's deal with Darlan and U.S. policy in South Vietnam since 1954 are good examples. Foreign observers often make the mistake of reading an ideological conservatism into such behavior. All that is involved is a kind of scientific conservatism—the engineer who is asked to build a bridge does not start by questioning whether there is a need for it.

Consequently, a sharp contrast appears between the American approach to foreign policy and, say, the style of General de Gaulle. The latter sees policy as a continuous process. He has a *vision* (more or less debatable) of the distant future, of Europe's role in it, of France's rank, etc. He has what one might call middle-range *objectives*, such as the Algerian settlement, the organized political cooperation of Europe, an autonomous French military policy. The *tactics* to be adopted to achieve those objectives depend on the circumstances and are sometimes quite baffling; but the objectives are relentlessly pursued. In the case of United States policy, the observer often has the feeling that there is an enormous gap between the vague, over-all vision of a world consonant with United

States values and interests, and the daily tactical maneuvers. From time to time, a grand announcement seems to mark a milestone: at best, it is a program, such as Lend Lease or the Marshall Plan, which sets a definite objective and can become the object of a quasi-military campaign; at worst, it is an empty gesture—and, as Hedley Bull has observed, a policy of gestures is the opposite of international politics.[19] Sometimes, it is something in between: a "grand design" described in ringing terms, ambitious enough to raise hopes but too vague to be able to fulfill them.

Too often, United States policy gives the impression that it is formulated by men who worry about what to do tomorrow and who also know what they would like the world to be at the end of its political history. Their ideals have little operational (though high inspirational) value; their operational concepts are of excessively short-range value. Thus, in the recent Atlantic disarray, we were presented both with an ideal of interdependence, followed by no policy measures except in the realm of trade (where they amounted to a response to European initiatives), and with the instrumentality of the MLF, hardly conceived as an application of the dumbbell image of Atlantic partnership. To take each issue "on its merits" may not be the best way of doing it justice; "problem-solving" may be the worst approach to the solution of problems, although it may be the most drastic method of discovering how intractable they are.

The last element in the American experience is separate from United States liberalism and conservatism, although it has accentuated their impact on the American approach to foreign policy. I refer to the unique position of the United States in world affairs before World War II. The United States was not a major power in the game; but it was not a stake either. Usually, it was not deeply involved; but when it wanted to act on the world stage, its geographic position and its power allowed it to respond to challenges in what Hans Morgenthau has called "unequivocal acts" depending on the United States alone.[20] Two attitudes have resulted from such a happy history. One is impatience—a lack of understanding of the virtue of time,[21] a perpetual fear of the

[19] Hedley Bull, *The Control of the Arms Race* (2nd ed; New York, 1965), p. 80.

[20] Hans J. Morgenthau, *The Purpose of American Politics* (New York, 1960), p. 130.

[21] See Dean Acheson's remarks on John F. Kennedy's speech about Algeria in 1957, *Power and Diplomacy* (Cambridge, Mass., 1958), pp. 122 ff.

fragility and instability of certain situations which makes many Americans want to destroy them right away because they may be undermined in the long run (for instance, West Germany's links to the West), or which makes them precipitate the very dangers they purport to forestall, by rushing in with dishes that whet the appetite they are supposed to subdue (for instance, Germany's nuclear appetite). American liberalism and American conservatism are equally marked by this impatience: it reinforces the liberal desire to reach the Erewhon of reconciliation as soon as possible and also the conservative tendency to plan piecemeal solutions to be enforced by brushing aside all human obstacles. The other attitude is the familiar faith in American omnipotence. When impatience and the illusion of omnipotence coincide, the result is a relentless drive to rearm Germany in 1950–51 or a Cuban invasion in 1961 or a Dominican landing in 1965.

United States liberalism hampers American foreign policy because it sees the world in colors rosier than those the world actually displays. United States conservatism limits American foreign policy because it makes the world look infinitely less complex than it is. The heritage of America's sheltered past weighs on its foreign policy because it really amounts to wishing the world away whenever its imperfections and complications become too blatant. It can be argued that the Korean War, or the handling of the Congo crisis or, even more, the sophisticated use of power in the 1962 Cuban crisis indicates how much United States policy-makers have learned. However, public opinion has shown alarming signs of impatience and of a continuing belief in omnipotence,[22] and the policy-makers are caught between what they know of the outside world and their fears of domestic reactions.

For there are other handicaps still—the obstacles provided by the political system. This is not the place to discuss to what extent a democratic system restricts the freedom of action of foreign-policy-makers. (Indeed, at such a level of generality, the subject is not of great interest.) But three characteristics of United States democracy curtail this freedom in important ways.

A first one has already been mentioned: the amorphous, brooding omnipresence of public opinion in the democratic sky. Some

[22] The recent spate of books, movements, marches, etc., for "peace" or "victory" indicates that the pattern has not changed: uncertainty breeds frustration; both extremes react to it as if it were in the power of the United States alone to restore world harmony or to crush the enemy. On the left, impatience activates the liberal's horror of weapons; on the right, impatience strengthens the "engineering" enthusiasm for strategy as a political panacea.

very different generalizations about public opinion in democracies seem to be valid. First, it is quite malleable and responsive to strong leadership; in this respect, it provides opportunities rather than restraints. Second, democratic leaders tend to overestimate the conservatism of public opinion and to exaggerate the gap between what they would like to do and what they believe the public will accept—be it a leap into supranationality, or a retreat from empire, or the recognition of Red China. Third, even with strong leadership, whenever the gap between traditional expectations and present experience widens, so that feelings of frustration or humiliation spring from it, public opinion tends to be not a mere wind to which leaders would be wise to bend, but a real twister. It destroys the leaders when they are blamed for disappointments, rarely of their own making; then, it continues to inhibit the formulation of foreign policy long after the tornado has vanished. What happened in the United States in the last years of Acheson's tenure and in the early years of Dulles' has been well documented. When such a hurricane develops, it becomes impossible for policymakers to pursue the objectives that ought to be pursued, and necessary to state objectives that obviously cannot be achieved.

A second characteristic is the presidential system. The fact that the Chief Executive is elected by universal suffrage and that he normally converses not with the nation's representatives but with the public that elects him is of considerable importance to the formulation and presentation of American foreign policy. A parliamentary premier addresses the nation and converses with parliament. The President converses with the public and addresses Congress. The advantages are different in each case. In the former, the more or less brute reactions of public opinion are filtered through parliament, but when parliament, as under the French Fourth Republic, expresses only too articulately the divisions of the nation, foreign policy may be paralyzed. At any rate, the premium is on moderation, the stress on continuity. The American system reinforces (and has to a large extent engendered) the flaws of the American style; here the emphasis is on the dramatic and the new. Even though opportunities for undiluted leadership are greater in a system in which the link between the Executive and the people is direct, inevitably much of the leader's effort goes into creating an image instead of defining the substance. The more intractable the external limits imposed by the international system are, the more frantic is the attempt to make shifts in tone, switches in style, and changes in personality pass for revolutions in policy.

The temptation would be less irresistible if the trend of the political system did not slope in that very direction.

The habit of expecting dramatic events perpetuates not only the panting rhythm of United States policy-making but the illusion of omnipotence and national impatience as well; consequently, the lag between public reflexes and external realities persists. The leader's hunch that public opinion remains sluggishly far behind him, therefore, is justified; and whenever the public realizes that the image mirrors nothing and that the new plan is a gimmick, a crisis of frustration assails foreign policy. It is a vicious circle. As such, it encourages the tendency to lead not with rational argument (too easily dismissed as an academic exercise that passes above the voters' heads) but through inspirational exhortation. Persuasion through ritual formulas and the invocation of national (or party) clichés is easier than persuasion through demonstration, which other systems of leadership often require. Not only does the necessary adjustment of the political culture to a revolutionary world thus get slowed down, but this style of leadership also produces an insidious self-intoxication of the leaders. It is usually in books about politics rather than in politics itself that leaders are cynical enough to realize that what they say is trash. Parliamentary leaders may be cynical, but they are rarely humble. Presidents are sometimes modest men, but hardly ever cynics.

The stress on image and innovation appears as a compensation, and often as a pitiful cover, for a third feature of American's political system: the dispersion of governmental power. It makes the definition of a substantive policy an ordeal that would have tried the patience of Penelope, and rapid innovation is an outcome so unlikely that it appears only in major emergencies. New teams of men come to Washington full of long repressed convictions about how to make foreign policy "right," or overflowing with ideas about how to make foreign policy sophisticated. Their emotions and their ideas soon get caught in the "thorns and branches and twigs of the governmental tree."[23] As a result, continuity in the substance of policies is preserved, but discontinuity in handling issues is not eliminated.

It was not in the United States that Parkinson's Law was conceived, but the United States Government shows three forms of it: there is the fragmentation of power that the separation between

[23] George F. Kennan, "America's Administrative Response to World Problems," *Daedalus* (Spring, 1958), p. 16.

the Presidency and Congress entails; there is the dispersion that results from the increasing importance of the House of Representatives in the control of foreign policy; there is the mushrooming of executive agencies that insist on participating in the definition of foreign policy—sometimes on an equal footing with the State Department, often on behalf of particular domestic interest groups in their constituency. If one also takes into account the proliferation of experts who work as consultants for all those institutions, and the press (which is both a sounding board for the various organs and a power of its own), one gets an awe-inspiring picture of government by interagency and inter-branch compacts, government by leaks and subcontracts.

The search for a consensus is one of the more damaging by-products of such fragmentation. It involves an erosion of substance and the wearing out of initiatives, ideas, and people. It has its advantages—what one might call, with a backward glance at the Republicans who came to power in 1952, after twenty years in opposition, the taming of the wild. But the disadvantages have also become apparent. Not only is innovation made difficult—after all, the constraints of the international system do not allow much of it—but the concern for middle-range objectives, half-way between distant dreams and daily diligence, is corroded. Even the margins of choice that the external system and the domestic culture still provide are interpreted restrictively. There have been recent examples of the taming of the shrewd.

As a result, the domestic system operates best when a sharp crisis pins its back to the wall, when the margin of choice appears narrowest, when the choice is only between the certainty of disaster through inaction and the recognition of the necessity of risks: what was true in 1947 was manifest again in the Cuban crisis of October, 1962. When the alternatives are less blinding, the trouble is protracted: *vide* Vietnam.

Another by-product affects less directly the substance of policy and more obviously its presentation: the necessity for speaking different languages to the different "publics," such as the electorate, the Congress, foreign nations, and foreign dignitaries in the United Nations. The resulting confusion may not impair the judgment of the policy-maker, who is usually aware of which is substance and which is wrapping. Yet, by increasing at times the suspiciousness of Congress and the reluctance of other nations to accept U.S. policies, such a wealth of communications may result in no communication at all, for it is likely that the various listeners will compare notes at some point. The dilemma in which the policy-maker finds himself is embarrassing: if he tries for a consensus among the various publics, the policy he formulates may well be so pale as to be ineffective; if he attempts to push a more daring one but cannot sell it to all under the same cover, he may find no buyers.

Both the search for consensus and the concern for presentation heighten the tendency to discuss issues in terms of personalities. The more fragmented the system of power, the more the political universe becomes a stock market of reputations and influence. The merits on which problems are tackled become the merits of the men engaged in policy-making, and those men represent not so much ideas as tangible bits and pieces of power.

III

How much freedom of action United States foreign policy effectively retains cannot be determined merely by tracing the main restraints and their degree of intractability. The problem can be formulated as follows: given the limits set by the present international system and by its own nature, what should the United States try to achieve? Although it is true that no policy ought to aim at what it can obviously neither formulate nor accomplish, nevertheless, as we have seen, many of the constraints and compulsions are not totally immovable or irresistible. Thus, there is a fundamental problem of direction: what is the range within which it is legitimate to define goals and means? Before we examine the main alternatives, however, we must see why such a definition has proved so difficult, for it is obviously a task that has been going on continuously. It has been complicated not just because of the formidable series of restraints I have listed (in a way, the less freedom they allow, the easier the task should be), but because of certain new dilemmas of policy-making; what has been called the crisis of perplexity[24] is a crisis of complexity.

The problem of the choice of policy in the United States today is radically novel for two reasons. First, there is the contrast between the foreign-policy problems faced by a major power in a system such as the nineteenth-century one and those of a major power today. Before 1914, the stakes of the game were limited to such issues as the conquest of a territory or the acquisition of advantages for one's traders and businessmen; with economic activi-

[24] Morgenthau, *op. cit.*, p. 143.

ties largely in the hands of private citizens, the dimensions of the balance of power were essentially military; so were the underpinnings of international order. Law and a universal system of trade and payments followed the armies or fleets of the big powers. Consequently, the instruments of action these powers needed were the diplomat and the soldier. Yet, although the stakes were limited and the means well defined, freedom of choice was considerable in the use of these means and in the pursuit of the objectives.

Today, the situation is reversed. The stake is formidable. In a sense, it is no less than the possibility of continuing the game and establishing a new kind of international order, after the collapse of the old one. The dimensions of international equilibrium have multiplied. The invention of nuclear weapons so complicates the military balance that one can now distinguish a strategic balance (the balance of terror, properly speaking), a tactical one (the balance of conventional forces), and what one could call the balance of subversion: guerrilla wars, which erupt both because of political conditions and because of a much lower risk of escalation. In addition, international politics must cope with economic development, with the promotion of social and political stability (or conformity), and with propaganda and cultural activities (so rich in political fall-out). Consequently, the task of the major power— obliged as in the past to placate feuding allies or to remain friendly with two reciprocal enemies—has become more demanding, for the performance of age-old functions now entails much more extended and intense initiative. The means that major powers have to employ in order to shape the world's future go far beyond the soldier and the diplomat. The technical-assistance expert, the Fulbright lecturer, the Peace Corps volunteer, the labor-union organizer, or the agent of the CIA may be just as important. Yet, although the keyboard has many more notes, the tunes the performer can play are fewer.

In the second place, there are many indications of a reversal of the old relations between large and small powers. Before 1914, a small power had not only narrower interests and more limited means than had a big state, but also on the whole much less freedom of action. The tune was played by the members of the Concert, and the lesser states had to dance to it. Today, to revert to an earlier metaphor, the super-power is an albatross, but the smaller nations are seagulls.

The super-power cannot abruptly change direction without undoing past laborious work, and, in the case of the United States, the complexity of its own political system contributes to continuity. A smaller nation has much more freedom; especially if it is a new and underdeveloped one, it can practice a kind of blackmail of weakness, and it can choose between various ways of sheltering itself from the cold war—from nonalignment to refuge under the umbrella of one of the contenders. The very fact that its political system is often a rather rudimentary machine at the disposal of a charismatic leader facilitates reversals and fluctuations. Any revolutionary period puts the lesser units of world politics (small princes in the days of the wars of religion or the new states of today) in a position in which they enjoy far more attention and influence than their actual power would justify, precisely because military power becomes only one factor among many.

As a result, the position of the United States is highly uncomfortable. Both the United States and the Soviet Union find themselves engaged in a game whose results are even more uncertain than those in past international politics. Their greater military potency condemns them to military quasi-chastity. The new dimensions of international politics are the most difficult to control. On the other hand, the United States is at a disadvantage in this enterprise—because of its traditional craving for certainty, because it has no official doctrine that assures that the uncertainties of the present must lead to a predetermined future, and because the normal tendency of statesmen who find themselves on the defensive, having to fight on a variety of fronts not of their own choosing, is to apply familiar rules of strategy that were effective in the past. If the rational is all too often the familiar, it is because the familiar seems the most rational; but the result is frustration.

That result is disappointing, first, because the old rules do not fit. One rule is to deal with the challenge of Communist power not quite in the way the United States dealt with other challenges in the past (what Charles Burton Marshall calls the quantitative view of power—the elimination of someone's evil power by nullifying his capacity—has been made suicidal by nuclear war), but in the way that comes closest to it. As Robert Tucker has shown, the doctrine of massive retaliation was a peacetime extension of the classical American doctrine of war. As its credibility decreases, the United States does refine and revise its approach. But its policy remains fundamentally a military one. It tends to treat in military terms problems that are not always military; whenever it is thus misapplied, it fails. For instance, guerrilla wars are indeed "prima facie evidence" of political and economic failure—evidence of a defeat on the nonmilitary front.[25] Similarly, the tendency to see Communism in military terms has led the United States to insist on painfully won and relatively meaningless Pan American resolutions condemning Communism, even though the main problem in Latin America at present is neither conventional war nor guerrilla war nor Soviet bases, but economic and social unrest that favors indigenous Communism: to concentrate on the irrelevant actually serves the enemy. Furthermore, even if an essentially military strategy succeeds in the only thing one can expect from it (the military containment of the adversary, as has been the case in Europe, the Middle East, and around Formosa), it nevertheless breeds frustration if opinion mistakenly sees it not simply as one policy among many but as a panacea. Containment and deterrence simply cannot solve the world's problems, but because they reflect traditional U.S. responses to international conflict, they have fed expectations they alone cannot satisfy.

Another set of misleading guidelines has been applied to policy in underdeveloped countries. The granting of all kinds of aid for all sorts of projects, with the expectation of progress, domestic stability, and international good behavior could not but be frustrated, for reasons mentioned before. In order to have a chance of producing all the beneficial results hoped for, the United States would have to do what no liberal nation can do, and what indeed the Communists themselves can do only when they are masters of a country—rule it and reform it through and through.

Resort to the familiar has been disappointing for a second reason. The guidelines not only turned out to be erroneous but were also to a considerable extent mutually exclusive forms of action. The very need to move on all the new fronts at once has led the United States to resort simultaneously to contradictory principles that in the past could be applied more or less effectively but at least seriatim. Occasionally, contradictory policies converge at one point: trouble for the United States. Raymond Aron has referred to the way in which both the militant (and military) anti-Communist approach, as exemplified by alliances with undeveloped countries (or by Punta del Este), and the pro-neutralist policy advocated by many liberals give to the underdeveloped nations, committed and uncommitted alike, an excessive hold on United States

[25] See Walt W. Rostow, *The United States in the World Arena* (New York, 1960), p. 323.

policy.[26] America's attitude toward underdeveloped nations has been schizophrenic, showing an excessive emphasis on military assistance and a fondness for neutralism that demoralizes those leaders who have chosen to side with the West. America's policy toward the Soviet Union has been torn between a grand strategy of military situations of strength (often oversold as a way of putting enough pressure on the walls of the Russian Jericho to make them tumble) and an addiction to negotiating for negotiation's sake, which fails to take into account that when there is little on which to negotiate seriously, all that comes out of endless meetings is an inflation of propaganda and a deflation of vain hopes.

There is another form of contradiction. To put it bluntly, it comes from the desire to have one's cake and eat it too. United States policy on Europe provides a choice example. Since the cold war requires Western military strength and since the development of the new nations requires Western economic strength, the United States has consistently promoted the creation of a Western European community of nations, even at the cost of a split between the "ins" (the six) and the "outs" (Great Britain). But the United States has also wanted the new European entity to discriminate as little as possible against nonmembers, so as not to disrupt world trade and not to worsen the plight of producers of primary products in Latin America or in the British-speaking parts of Africa. This is more difficult to achieve. Even more difficult is the reconciliation between America's desire that Europe should be more than an economic market with very loose common policies and America's hope that Great Britain will be able to join. Far more troublesome still is America's wish that the new Europe—economically booming, thanks largely to the United States, and encouraged by it to find a voice of its own—abstain from challenging United States leadership in the formulation of Atlantic military and external policies. Pygmalion should not expect that, once the statue has come to life, it will stay fixed on its pedestal. Strength does not let itself be sliced easily into a social-economic sector (good) and an external one (bad or off-limits).

Thus, plunged in a revolutionary world, the United States has tried to gain (or regain) control. It has succeeded whenever it did well what it *had* to do, but it has found the going rough. We must now turn to the future, and try to see what are the margins of

[26] "Reflections on American Diplomacy," *Daedalus* (Fall, 1962), pp. 717–32.

choice within which United States policy-makers can escape from the dilemmas that I have described.

IV

The *directions* to be envisaged do not include two objectives which would be consonant with various domestic reflexes but which are, so to speak, outside the terms of the international competition. The United States cannot act as if the competition between East and West had disappeared, or as if "victory" in traditional terms were possible without a holocaust. This does not at all mean that the present system condemns the United States to take it as a life sentence; it means that political defeat and military destruction are not legitimate ways of changing the system. There remain other ways, in the two main areas of policy-making.

A first area is the military competition with Communist states —a competition that runs the gamut from the nuclear deterrence of central war to guerrilla warfare in Southeast Asia, from the preparation of military budgets to the merry-go-round of disarmament negotiations. This is an area where choice is extremely limited but not altogether eliminated. It is not up to the United States or to the West to make the Soviet military threat disappear;[27] but the United States can nevertheless affect the competition, in three different ways.

In the first place, there is a problem of *geographical scope*: does the United States choose to resist wherever military pressure is applied—especially in those "gray areas" where the Soviets, the Chinese, and their allies, through subversive warfare, are capable of infiltrating and corroding allies of the United States whose political and economic weakness has opened the way to Communist enterprises? The alternatives are unpleasant, since the battlefield is of the enemy's own choosing, but once the battle begins, they cannot be avoided. If the United States decides to fight, then, since it is not in the best position for waging antiguerrilla warfare so far from home and so near the Russians and the Chinese, the danger of escalation becomes serious. The point may come when only the threat of an upward leap in the American commitment will deter

[27] This does not mean I believe in the Soviet threat of a surprise nuclear attack. It has been argued, however, that the Soviet "failure" to produce as many missiles as U.S. officials feared proves that Soviet intentions were misjudged. All it really shows is that, given the nuclear stalemate (as long as it lasts), the main fronts of the competition will be in less apocalyptic areas. It does not mean that there is no Soviet military threat.

the Communists from further increments of "liberation" warfare. Or else the United States may decide that the stake is not worth such a risk, and that it is better to cut bait (even if this means, say, giving up Laos under a face-saving device that fools only those who want to be fooled). Although defeat in most of the gray areas would amount to a setback but not a catastrophe, the political repercussions at home and on other United States alliances might be disastrous.

Precisely because the choice is so unpleasant, it is obviously in the interest of the United States to avoid having to make it. Whenever the United States has contracted such an alliance, its only hope of escaping from the dilemma consists in promoting political reform and social progress to save its ally from the dry rot that incites "liberation wars." A military alliance in those areas obliges the United States to take full responsibility for domestic developments, if it wants to prevent actual military engagement. But we know that such a responsibility is most difficult for the United States to carry out. Since Communist conquest of those areas is less likely when reformist forces have no reason to equate the politicians in power with the United States (and the Soviets or Chinese with emancipation), the idea of any future military alliance in these areas ought to be abandoned. Meanwhile, as regards those alliances which have been concluded in the past (often for excellent geographical reasons), there is no escape from almost equally bitter choices.

Next, there is a question of *strategic doctrine*. "Massive retaliation" is thoroughly discredited as a means of deterring "subconventional" wars, and it becomes increasingly less plausible for the deterrence of conventional wars. The United States has literally no choice but to increase its conventional forces and its capacity to fight those "subconventional" wars it considers worth fighting. However, there remains one area of choice. It is certain that a holocaust would result from either an escalation leading to the use of nuclear weapons or a first-strike strategy applied after it had failed to deter an attack on vital stakes such as Europe. In order to prevent such disasters, should the United States adopt a doctrine clearly designed to avoid resort to tactical and strategic nuclear weapons? On the other hand, one may fear that such a doctrine would encourage the Soviet Union to multiply "liberation" and conventional wars without having to worry about nuclear retaliation; and it might compel other nations that feel threatened by the Soviets to develop their own nuclear deterrents as a substitute for the American one. Moreover, in a world of nuclear weapons, any war, however limited at first, may well escalate, despite the initial doctrine. Should the United States, therefore, maintain its nuclear arsenal not only larger than a minimum deterrence strategy would require, but also diversified enough to have nuclear weapons available to deter and to fight different types of war? The less "irrational" the doctrine, the less unlikely deliberate wars become: a rational strategy tends to be one that assumes that wars can remain rational instruments of policy. The more "irrational" the doctrine, the more disastrous the consequences, should the enemy fail to take the threat seriously. The adoption of either doctrine entails a continuation of the arms race, so long as no negotiated agreements are forthcoming. But the *nature* of the arms race depends on the choice of doctrine.

A third choice remains: it concerns the *intensity* of the military competition. To do away with the competition, at least in the near future, is beyond the reach of the United States—unless the spread of nuclear weapons creates such perils to peace that the Soviet Union and the United States would at last overcome the asymmetries and obstacles to negotiated arms control and disarmament—i.e., agree to give up, at least in part, their freedom to use or threaten to use weapons. This is not impossible; but such a reconciliation of enemies, brought about by a greater threat, does not seem at hand. In the meantime, the United States has two alternatives: either to take unilateral measures of arms control in the hope of making the nuclear age less irrational and of eliciting parallel measures of restraint from the Soviet Union; or to refuse to reassure the enemy, to increase pressure on him, to oblige him to devote more resources to the unproductive arms race, and to force him into concessions. The former policy has been chiefly followed, as shown by an impressive series of restraints: United States opposition to nuclear diffusion, United States "punishment" of the British and French at Suez, United States caution in military clashes with the East, United States moderation after the Soviet withdrawal of missiles from Cuba, and United States reliance on the United Nations for acts of "international neutralization."

Once again, it must be made clear that each one of these policies has disadvantages and advantages. A policy of unilateral restraints moderates but also perpetuates, civilizes but also rationalizes, the competition; indeed, the more it succeeds in slowing down nuclear diffusion, the less it incites the two supreme contenders to get out of the "comfortable" world in which each believes that it can retain its own arms, and have also a cautious adversary. The other policy creates extreme dangers but may well bring nearer the day when the world (to use Aron's terms) must give up the traditional power game so as not to give up its life.

As to the issues of strategic doctrine and intensity of competition, the United States' choice will be determined to a large extent by developments beyond its control, such as the speed of China's military growth and her political behavior. But the political style and system of the United States will also be of great importance: the weight of the liberal tradition; the engineering approach—with its stress on rationality; the fragmentation of power—with its built-in caution—all converge toward a deliberate choice of the first policy in each of those two issues. Should the result of such a choice be a multiplication of small wars and the frustration of hopes for negotiated restraints, then the old reflexes of impatience, crusading zeal, nostalgia for the axiomatic, and "unequivocal" response might provoke upsets. Thus, whatever the choice, the risks will remain great and the margins of freedom narrow as long as the military competition persists. Since traditional "victory" and a leap into the millennium are equally impossible, the best the United States can strive for is a gradual change in the rules and basic elements of the game—the end of bipolarity and ideological conflict. But this cannot be achieved by *direct* action in the East-West conflict. It may result from the continuation of an over-all military stalemate, from developments within the Communist area or from events in the non-Communist parts of the world. Certainly, American actions designed to encourage a gradual weakening of ties between the Soviet Union and the states of Eastern Europe through trade and cultural contacts with the latter, for instance, can contribute to change. But the limitations on United States manuevers are sharp: for reasons mentioned before, the United States must avoid consolidating the Soviet Union and East Germany.

In the other main area of our concern—U.S. foreign policy in the non-Communist world—the United States faces so many different problems that it is impossible to discuss them here in detail. Whether one looks at the prospects in Latin America, the problems in Africa, or the relations among partners of the would-be North Atlantic community, the issues seem to have one point in common: they require a choice between what I would call (with no pretense at impartiality) the frustrations of preponderance versus the ambition for modesty.

What is at stake is how best to promote, in the non-Communist world, the values on which most Americans agree—a pluralist world of states that will solve their disputes peacefully, cooperate in order to promote economic development, and avoid disrupting their neighbors' affairs. In other words, what is at stake is the best method for trying to *moderate* the international system, for reintroducing as much limitation of the ends and means as is compatible with the likely continuation of the East-West conflict (at least, until the effects of moderation reach it too) and with the invention of nuclear weapons.

Now, there are two "ideal-types" of possible policies. At one extreme, there is a *maximalist* policy. It would have the United States intervene as forcefully and with as rich a range of instruments as possible in order to promote its objectives; yet it would try to preserve for the United States as much control of the direction as possible—in particular, to maintain United States preponderance in the North Atlantic Community and its position as the linchpin of the Pan American system. At the other extreme, there is a *minimalist* policy. It could be summed up as trusting pluralism. Such a policy would try to limit the scope and instruments of United States intervention to those areas and methods least likely to prove frustrating; yet it would argue that all the energy that did not go into manipulating others and trying to maintain U.S. preponderance should go into the definition of common policies on matters of common interest.

Like all ideal-types, those two are exaggerations. Still, whether we envisage the Alliance for Progress or the development of NATO's military policies, we find that the actual alternatives come fairly close to those extremes. (Of course, they are often presented otherwise.) I would like to give my reasons for suggesting the more modest formula. A first reason is the necessity to avoid the disappointments of overcommitment. In underdeveloped countries, the effects of technical and economic aid are difficult to chart. It is not within the possibilities of a power such as the United States to ram through the social and political reforms without which such aid risks being wasted. Wherever local leaders are indifferent to such reforms, it is hard for the United States to persuade the ruling classes to enforce the changes themselves. For, although the United States presents the reforms as a calculated risk that can stave off the far greater likelihood of unrest, local elites tend to see in the reforms the most immediate threat to their position, and in potential unrest, a distant cloud. Consequently, if the United States limits its commitment to the kind of aid that, given the special circumstances of each country, is most likely to produce good results, it could avoid the Charybdis of total indifference, all too easily exploited by the Communists, and the Scylla of identification with often calamitous elites, even more beneficial to the Communists. The fact that, in a country like Brazil, reformist movements push neutralist or third-force foreign policies should be a warning. The United States is not equipped to manipulate satellites: either it must tie its chances to the local rulers (a risk that worked for obvious reasons in Western Europe better than anywhere else), or it must try to take over, as it has been edging toward in South Vietnam; but this is hardly what it does best.

A second reason for a more modest approach is the increasing complexity of the world the United States must deal with. The greater the number of states, the more refined the approach will have to be; the more successful the attempt at turning those states into genuine nations, the more diversity will have to be taken into account. Again, the United States is ill equipped to control events in countries it ill knows and in which its own concerns, world-wide and world-shaking as they may seem at home, are likely to appear irrelevant or parochial.

Thirdly, should the United States succeed in promoting its objectives, then the nations it will have helped to grow will undoubtedly desire to weigh more heavily in international affairs. This is precisely what has happened in Europe. American warnings of the perils of nationalism have little chance of deterring others, as long as they sound less like an invitation to join in a great and somewhat undefined *auto da fé* of sovereignty than as a grumbling protest against rising challenges to American power.

Fourth, resignation to not being able to control—resignation to what I have called the uncertainties of roulette—has its rewards: if the ball does not always stop on the number on which the United States gambles, it is even less likely to stop at the Communist number, unless American involvement has boosted Communist chances. In the short run, the Soviet Union and Red China have the advantages of better means for intervention and the asset of a philosophy that pretends to provide a master key to development. United States efforts amount to a disparate set of keys, many of which fail to fit or work at all. Yet in the long run, the

Soviet Union and the Red Chinese risk stumbling over the determination of most nations' leaders to be not only agents of economic growth but also champions of national independence. If it is this ambition that proves to be the bane of Soviet efforts, then it is in the interest of the United States to respect it.

Any attempt to intervene too much and to preserve a preponderance resulting from the temporary collapse of Europe, one that developed at a time when there were half as many states, is bound to founder on the limits set by the international system and to exacerbate domestic frustrations. Yet it is also clear that a pluralistic world of sovereign states, prey to the disease of nuclear diffusion, is not a reassuring prospect—hence the necessary talk about all kinds of partnership. Here we must, however, sound a note of caution: the idea is a good one, but its realization should not be spoiled (once again) by impatience or traces of the illusion of omnipotence. Let us look at NATO, the main achievement so far of the Atlantic nations. There are three very different kinds of joint "rational" military policies conceivable. Rationality can be interpreted in the light of United States interests: a likely outcome would be an increase in European conventional forces, and a United States monopoly of the nuclear deterrent. Then there is the rationality of the alliance as a whole, which leads to the advocacy of a joint nuclear deterrent. Finally, there is the rationality that is a compromise between the first two and the separate interests of the main partners—along the lines of an attempt at coordinating as well as possible an acceptable common policy. The trouble with ideas of partnership is that what they often conceal is a nostalgia for a rationality of the first type; or else they leap forward to a rationality of the second type, which is still a premature abstraction from separate state realities that have not converged enough. At best, it could be achieved only after a rational policy of the third type has been hammered out.[28]

To try to work now toward partnership of the third type strikes me as essential. It is not a spectacular enterprise, but grand institutional schemes are worthless when there are no common policies for them to carry out, as the history of the United Nations demonstrates. The interests that states consider most vital are those that are not only most difficult for another to control or manipu-

---

[28] These points are more fully covered in Hoffmann, "Discord in Community," in Francis O. Wilcox and H. Field Haviland, Jr., eds., *The Atlantic Community* (New York, 1963), pp. 3–31; and "Europe's Identity Crisis," *Daedalus* (Fall, 1964), pp. 1244–97.

late but also most difficult to transcend through supranational or majority rule. However, they are also the interests most important to reconcile, lest they disrupt attempts to build world order. Thus, though less exciting than the Pan American meetings that discuss the Alliance for Progress, negotiations to stabilize the prices of primary products would probably contribute far more to the link between the Latins and the Colossus of the North.

The United States, for reasons we have seen, is used to going it alone or doing it alone, either in isolation or through organizations it dominates. To continue thus may be instinctive, but it is mistaken, for it is an attempt at doing more than can be done, and it achieves less than it could achieve. It incites others to try to do it also and leads to domestic disappointments and international tension. A policy more modest in its pretensions, but less self-indulgent, requires that America's *esprit de géométrie* be tempered by much more *esprit de finesse*—that she get into the painful habit of working with, rather than through or without, others. But this is, after all, what involvement in world affairs requires. If it means gradually transcending the limits of domestic traditions, does it not imply that what is true of others is true of the United States as well: that the decisive keys to the success of a foreign policy are in the hands of its makers?

EIGHT

TERROR IN THEORY AND PRACTICE

T HE ADVENT of the nuclear age has raised these questions: how great a revolution in international relations have the new weapons effected? Does the magnitude of the danger inherent in nuclear weapons add to the traditional imperative of prudence a moral imperative of "respect for others"? Has the germ of a universal conscience appeared at the dawn of universal history? Or, since we continue to live in a world of separate states, how can one expect the imperative of prudence to restrain and harness the countless causes of conflict that mark an international system in which force is still an agent of change and states still find its use occasionally advantageous? Will even the most elaborate strategy of prudence guarantee the preservation of a modicum of moderation, or avoid a holocaust if it fails?

All these questions have been discussed in American strategic literature; they have also received a provisional reply in the history of the postwar world. Writers have either stressed or exemplified the apparently insoluble dilemmas of the balance of terror; the facts, until now, have shown that mankind can live with those dilemmas. Whether the facts will continue to show this is, of course, another matter.

The Realm of Thought

The intellectual reaction to the new nuclear weapons has been quite ambiguous. Men have talked about their living in a radically new phase of history, in which war can no longer be "the continuation of politics by other means," but on the other hand, they have indulged in the familiar and only semi-conscious procedure of reducing the new to the known, of fitting the new into well-established modes of thought, instead of thinking it out afresh. America's strategic doctrine—developed at a time when the United States had a monopoly on the means of mass destruction, perfected at a time when the United States still enjoyed considerable superiority in the capacity of inflicting intolerable damage—stressed "massive retaliation." As a way of deterring war, it shrewdly exploited what was new; as a way of waging war, it merely continued a tradition. It is not surprising that writers of American strategic literature have often discussed the new age by discussing this doctrine. This dual scrutiny has taken place at three levels of theory: philosophy, policy science, and empirical theory.

I

Robert Tucker's book *The Just War*[1] belongs to the realm of political philosophy. His purpose is to submit America's original deterrence strategy to the test, not of pragmatic considerations (credibility, efficiency) but of moral ones. Pitilessly, he shows the extent to which this doctrine, apparently developed for the circumstances of a revolutionary new age, merely adapted America's traditional aspirations and impulses concerning the use of force to the universe of thermonuclear terror. Tucker's book is one of many that denounce the American style of absolutism, moralism, and perfectionism in international relations. (His position is particularly close to Arnold Wolfers' in this regard.) Tucker finds in the doctrine of massive retaliation what his predecessors had already found in America's prewar utopias concerning progress through international organization, or in the methods with which Americans

[1] New York, 1960.

waged World War II: the conviction that whoever first resorts to
force is evil, no matter what the reasons for his initiative; and the
conviction that just war is defensive war, whether it is a war of self-
defense or one of collective defense sanctioned by international
organization. Tucker then attempts to demonstrate all the weaknesses of this approach. He finds two basic illusions: first, there is
the tendency to equate the international milieu with domestic civil
society, a tendency that leads to evil results, for the freedom an
individual has to defend himself is subordinated to the control of
the state, whereas the state's self-defense takes place without control and without limits other than those set by the state itself. The
second illusion consists in a refusal to believe that a state can be
forced to resort to violence—a way of thinking that stems from
America's sheltered historical experience. Here, Tucker denounces
the rationalization of American plenty, which has allowed the
United States to reach its objectives in a less brutal fashion than
other nations have sometimes been obliged to use.

Even more serious are the ambiguities of American doctrine,
whether traditional or "new." It indignantly rejects preventive war;
but Tucker shows that preventive war can be defensive in all regards (that of cause, or of purpose) except as regards the *initiation*
of force, i.e., the excessively formalistic criterion of "defensive" to
which American doctrine clings. He also shows that a war which is
defensive as regards the initiation of force may be objectionable for
the same reason that the notion of preventive war was in the past:
either the state, in order to protect its interests, will interpret legitimate self-defense broadly (for instance, by assimilating a threatening
subversion to direct aggression) and thus make of its doctrine a justifying ideology marred by hypocrisy; or else, in order to follow a
restrictive interpretation, it will run the risk of leaving essential interests without protection.

What Tucker criticizes most vigorously however, are the moral
consequences of America's doctrine in the present age—the view
that, since America's resort to force cannot be anything but defensive, the ethical problem is thereby deemed solved and all other
problems raised by war have become merely technical. Against
such good conscience, Tucker vehemently protests. Insofar as both
ends and means are concerned, he demonstrates that America's
doctrine is not at all defensive. Of course, since the circumstances
in which force is used are "just"—i.e., the initiative came from
the enemy—the purpose of using it is also automatically held to be
"just"; but aims such as unconditional surrender, the re-education

of the aggressor, and the elimination of the future use of force are not at all defensive. The same is true of means: Americans have in the past waged war without inhibition, and the doctrine of massive retaliation suggested that even limited attacks should be met by thermonuclear reprisals. (Moreover, in the original version of the doctrine, the truly defensive weapons that would be used in retaliation against an enemy attack were those that hit not the enemy's striking force or its bases but its population in its cities; they were defensive before the war, because they did not incite the enemy to strike first, since they did not threaten his striking force; but they became violently *offensive* after the war started.) Tucker compares this postwar doctrine and the doctrine of the Kellogg-Briand pact: in both cases, the purpose is to prevent war; in both cases, if war breaks out, no limitation is any longer considered; indeed, to define limitations in advance would be to compromise the practical efficiency and moral purity of the threat.

Tucker shows how altogether unpolitical such a conception is, because it deliberately sacrifices the maintenance of a minimum of order among states (even during the struggle), because its success —its effective deterrence of any aggression—presupposes a Western will never to yield and always to consider that any enemy move challenges vital interests and principles (thus justifying eventual resort to thermonuclear force), finally because even if it succeeded completely, it would create nothing better than an international society based on pure force, in which rivals would still confront one another and peace would depend only on the threat of annihilation. Thus, Tucker views America's first postwar doctrine as a testimony to the desire to recapture lost security through the traditional methods of unlimited war. He condemns it because he believes that the moral and political implications of America's classical conception, which this doctrine perpetuates, are even less acceptable in the atomic age than before.

Going from Tucker's book to Herman Kahn's huge work *On Thermonuclear War*[2] means changing climates in a most brutal way. Instead of an anguished conscience subtly analyzing moral dilemmas, we confront a specialist of nuclear strategy who considers a thoroughly and even at times cheerfully amoral universe, who has spent years studying all the data and all the technical problems of wars to come. The explosive power of his enormous and slightly disorganized accumulation of thoughts and proposals

[2] Princeton, 1961.

is such that the controversies provoked by its publication dealt with the tone and manner of its presentation at least as much as with its substance. (Indeed, humanitarian misgivings, commonplace statements about the horrors of nuclear war, and considerations of the moral and political context of the cold war are of no concern to the author.) He has looked thermonuclear war in the face and he has not been blinded: this is enough to expose him to the charge of being an accomplice of evil. It is true that his black humor is not always in good taste, and some of the implications that flow quite naturally from his analysis seem somewhat like provocations. The reader who has worked his way through Kahn's three "lectures," twelve chapters, five appendixes, and numerous charts has good reason to feel somewhat annihilated.

Herman Kahn's intention is thoroughly revolutionary. Whereas Tucker stresses the originality of the nuclear age and challenges what he sees as a mere warmed-up old strategy, Kahn challenges the notion of a new era in international affairs and recommends a new strategy. America's postwar doctrine is questionable to him neither for moral reasons nor only because its credibility decreased as Russia's destructive power increased. As Tucker remarks, the doctrine of massive retaliation did outlive the circumstances in which it appeared (America's monopoly of nuclear power) because it was thought that, even in the age of the balance of terror, the risk of an American resort to weapons of mass destruction, *despite* the damage the United States would then suffer in retaliation, remained great enough to prevent the Soviet Union from large-scale aggression. This reasoning has been particularly dear to champions of the so-called minimum or limited deterrence strategy, according to whom the United States could maintain *adequate* deterrence even if she concentrated only on "counter-city" forces instead of "counter-force" arsenals—a task that requires fewer, less precise, and less costly weapons. The enemy would therefore have no interest in using his own thermonuclear weapons, since the balance of terror ensured either that those weapons remained unused or that their use led to the mutual suicide of the two adversaries, the chance of such suicide being enough to discourage them.

This is the theory that Kahn attacks. According to him, the concept of "mutual homicide" is quite inaccurate. "When one examines the possible effects of thermonuclear war carefully, one notices that there are . . . many postwar states that should be distinguished"[3]—hence, a chart of "tragic but distinguishable post-

[3] Kahn, *op. cit.*, p. 19.

war states": they vary from 2 million dead and one year required for American's economic recovery to 160 million dead and 100 years. Kahn's thesis is that survival is possible: all depends on the preparation the nation undertakes before the war and the strategy it uses during the war. With adequate preparation, including, if needed, the total evacuation of city populations to protected shelters, a country like the United States could recover from even the complete destruction of its urban centers. On this point, Kahn produces analyses that are detailed, highly unsavory, and probably over-optimistic. But the crucial consequence of his theory is that if thermonuclear war does not necessarily mean annihilation, then it must again be envisaged as a strategic and political possibility and not as the homicidal and final spasm that follows the failure of deterrence. So long as states are what they have always been—competing wills, so long as their leaders do not yet possess those terrifying weapons literally capable of destroying the earth (christened by Herman Kahn with the picturesque names of "Doomsday Machines and Doomsday-in-a-hurry Machines"), there is a strong chance that war will indeed break out. It is, therefore, the state's duty: (1) to provide itself with a strategic arsenal capable not only of preventing war but of waging it and ending it in "reasonable" conditions; (2) to protect itself in such a way that if it is attacked it can nevertheless keep fighting—which requires both strong air and civil defenses and a strong capacity for recovery. Kahn's argument is that since we are still far from the certainty of inevitable collective suicide in the case of war, then war remains possible, and, since it is, the state must see to it that war still has a meaning: it is up to the state to act so that it can recuperate from an attack and fight in order to obtain a compromise peace, or so that by striking first it prevents its foe from wounding it severely or even from striking at all.

Kahn, who does not indulge in pure theory, thus rediscovers Rousseau's argument: the differences between states stimulate competition, and competition leads to wars; asymmetry is the fuel of conflict. It is precisely on this point that Kahn criticizes the thesis of minimum deterrence, for it presupposes that America's thermonuclear forces, after having been attacked by the Soviet Union, would still be able to inflict losses on the assailant such that the prospect of this retaliation would be enough to deter him from any attack. Now, if measures are not taken to protect America's retaliatory force (dispersal, underground placement, placement in submarines, etc.), it may well happen that America's force could be damaged so heavily that what losses it could still inflict would be bearable to the enemy and would be out of proportion with the advantages the enemy gained by striking first. The thesis of minimum deterrence forgets the asymmetry that follows from the considerable advantage that thermonuclear weapons give to the side that strikes first. As for the possibility of making America's retaliatory force so invulnerable that this advantage would be wiped out for her opponent and the model of mutual destruction be real, Kahn remains rather skeptical; moreover, even if that force survived an attack relatively well, it would still have to strike an enemy that would be fully alerted and far less vulnerable (since its urban centers contain a much smaller percentage of its total population than ours).

Most of Kahn's book is devoted to his examination, from every angle, of the strategic problems raised by the postulate that war is still possible. He reviews the kinds of forces he deems indispensable, the objectives the enemies may have (here he re-emphasizes the lack of symmetry between assailant and victim), the types of possible wars (through surprise attack, miscalculation, a serious crisis, etc.). Nothing demonstrates the interest and audacity of his central thesis—that new weapons have effected no mutation in international relations—better than his third part, entitled "From World War I to World War VIII," in which he discusses both past world wars from the viewpoint of political and military strategy, shows what would have happened if war had broken out in 1951 and 1956, given the forces in existence, and finally "assumes" world wars in 1961, 1965, 1969, 1973, and analyzes their elements. One of the main effects of that somewhat terrifying demonstration is a chart of "historical prototypes" of the problems he thinks the world will have to face in the next fifteen years; there are no less than ten types of possible crises, among which we find those that marked the pre-1914 period, new Munichs, new ultimatums to Hacha (1939), new bombings of Rotterdam, and new Pearl Harbors. Kahn uses this chart as an argument against minimum deterrence, which, he maintains, could not all by itself help one to face so many different possibilities. As for the strategy, or, rather, strategies, that Herman Kahn advocates, I will come to them later, but one can guess that it is miles away from the holy simplicity of massive retaliation; yet if Kahn finds that doctrine too elementary, he certainly does not do so for the same moral and humanitarian reasons as Tucker.

To move on to Thomas Schelling's book *The Strategy of Conflict*[4] is to change climates once again. Instead of a painful search for unattainable values, instead of a somewhat exuberant quest for strategic efficiency, we find the aseptic, clear, cool universe of pure theory. This theory is inspired by practical problems: on many points, Schelling's abstract discussions confirm Kahn's *ad hoc* arguments; one of his chapters (as well as an appendix) deals with very concrete problems (measures against surprise attacks, the use of nuclear weapons in limited wars); but his analysis is done in the light of a strategic theory which, while fragmentary, is highly suggestive.

What Schelling (an economist who has moved from the strategy of firms to that of states) is trying to promote is a "reorientation of game theory." Various students of international relations have shown interest in game theory because it is not open to the criticisms addressed to mathematical models derived from physics[5]; it tries to prescribe the rational behavior of competing actors who attempt to occupy the most advantageous positions so as to achieve the maximum gain. Its point of departure is two postulates that correspond to the very essence of political phenomena: the importance of competition to behavior, and the importance of interdependence in strategy. It therefore would seem that such an effort would have the dual normative capacity required for adequate theory: the capacity to explore not what happens in reality but what ought to happen in ideal circumstances, and the capacity to forecast how the players ought to behave in given circumstances if they wanted to win. Until now, game theory has not been able to fulfill either task—because of weaknesses that Schelling reviews.

The main flaw is that game theory has dealt only with zero-sum games, i.e., games of pure conflict in which my gain is your loss. Most concrete situations in international relations, however, are mixed games in which conflicting and common interests are involved—hence, a whole range of differences. In games of pure conflict, there is only the barest minimum of interdependence: the players refrain from communicating. In mixed games, communication between the players is essential. In zero-sum games, the basic postulate is symmetry. In non-zero-sum games and in reality, the value systems are rarely identical, the players cannot use exactly the same tactics, nor is the same information available to them. In

---

4 Cambridge, Mass., 1960.
5 See Anatol Rapoport's *Fights, Games and Debates* (Ann Arbor, 1960) and *Strategy and Conscience* (New York, 1964).

zero-sum games, the level of abstraction is very high: the mathematical structure of the game is all one needs to know. In reality, tactics are largely determined by various empirical data, various symbols, various signals: the rules of the game can be discerned only if these details are incorporated into the game. In zero-sum games, the rules do not change during the game; in other games and in reality, one of the stakes is the working-out of such rules by trial and error.

Another flaw concerns the preferences of the players. In the current state of game theory, one presupposes that each player has a preference scale that remains coherent and constant throughout the game. But it is easy to prove that there is no coherence where the players are "collective" players (committees, states, alliances), and also that it may be rational to revise the scale of preferences if new information is received during the game. Therefore, game theory applies only to a marginal and paradoxical case: pure conflict with limited stakes, i.e., the characteristic conflicts of moderate, balance-of-power, international systems.

Schelling tries to stretch game theory so as to work in the theories of mixed strategy and especially of deterrence. He tries to answer questions such as, what partners' value scales make a deterrent threat plausible? What kinds of communications are needed? What kinds of rationality must the partner whom one tries to deter exhibit? To what extent is trust required? What is the value of different sorts of threats? To what extent is the game affected by the strategy of a third player? The scope of these investigations exceeds the question of military deterrence; Schelling wants to elaborate the theory of any "formalized structure of behavior"—etiquette, chivalry, diplomacy, law (mainly criminal law) —for, in all those cases, as in military strategy, there are interdependent decisions made by partners whose interests are partly conflicting and partly shared.

Among the studies Schelling makes, three have considerable theoretical and practical interest. First, he analyzes strategic bargaining as the art of committing oneself irreversibly so as to limit one's freedom of maneuver—an apparent weakness that is really a source of strength, since it tends to oblige the adversary to compromise. Consequently, the strength of the irreversible threat is not weakened by the possibility that its execution could harm the threatener more than the threatened; also, it may be advantageous to give up the initiative and oblige the other side to choose between failure and disaster; finally, it may be advantageous to delegate the initiative to a third power, whose commitment is more obvious or more credible.

Schelling discusses a second type of effective threat: when the player cannot resort to the strategy of commitment, he can still use a threat that leaves something to chance. Thus, John Foster Dulles' kind of brinkmanship is effective when the final outcome does not depend entirely on the threatener; for instance, a threat of fighting a limited war to resist local aggression creates, in the present state of the world, a risk of general war that is quite capable of deterring one's opponent. (Schelling interprets in this way America's strategy at Quemoy and the presence of American forces in Europe.) Consequently, the player has an interest, not in keeping war carefully limited between sharply defined boundaries, but in preserving a moderate risk of general war. (Kahn is of the same opinion.)

Thirdly, Schelling's analysis of tacit bargaining shows that the outcome is determined by the partners' need to coordinate their strategies in order to achieve a common gain. The two essential aspects to the problem are: how are those strategies coordinated, and around what points? Schelling stresses the importance of salient points that are easy to recognize and qualitatively distinguishable, so that each side may calculate that the other side will choose such a point as its goal or as its meeting place: in a limited war, borders such as the 38th Parallel in Korea constitute a boundary that the "partners" tacitly accept; another example is resort to conventional weapons only, since the difference between them and nuclear weapons is one of those essential qualitative differences, even though some nuclear weapons are weaker than some conventional ones.

The method of this extended theory of strategy differs from "pure" game theory, since the outcome of mixed games depends on how the partners coordinate their decisions, whereas a game of pure conflict is a succession of unilateral moves. A theory of mixed games inevitably entails an empirical element: the context of the game, the salient points, the players' skill—all are decisive. Generalizations must be based on experimental research, and mathematical analysis is not enough. The purpose remains mathematical formulation, but it will come only much later. Experimentation is indispensable for the formulation and validation of hypotheses on such points as the relations between the structure of the game and its unfolding, or the advantages or disadvantages of communications. (Experience shows that a partner may derive benefits from his ignorance, if the other one *knows* that he is ignorant.) For the time being, due to a lack of sufficient experimentation, we are still far from a full-fledged theory of mixed strategy, and one may wonder to what extent mathematical formulation will be possible. Even for the theory of pure conflict, one must undertake a formidable number of numerical operations, and the theory of mixed strategy takes us away from the algebra-type game toward the simulation-type game. However, we see how strong an impulse deterrence has given to theoretical research.

II

We also see this: Schelling presents the theory of mixed strategy as a particularly appropriate framework for international relations, and Kahn draws from this theory a number of practical consequences. Both men (Kahn more explicitly than Schelling) deny that nuclear weapons have brought about a change in kind in the relations among the playing states: there are only new complications and new risks. But is the theory of mixed strategy really an appropriate framework? In the light of Kahn's and Schelling's works, I would like to try to answer. It seems to me that game theory runs into two kinds of trouble, which correspond to the two meanings of the word normative: the explanation of the essence of a phenomenon, and guidance for action.

The essence of international relations differs from that of games, even mixed games. International relations are the interaction of two elements: decisions and what Pierre Renouvin and J.-B. Duroselle call the "deep forces."[6] Strategic theory neglects the latter and therefore should at any rate be combined with a historical sociology that would try to explain why things often happen quite differently from what the schemes of game theory have led one to expect. Even decisions raise questions that game theory does not yet solve: the question of intransitive or incoherent preferences, and the question of the influence of personalities; Raymond Aron has noted that decisions "could have been different with a different man in the same situation or with the same man in another mood."[7] Finally, the interaction between "deep forces" and decisions creates problems not accounted for by strategic theory: decisions are to some extent shaped by the international system, by national philosophies or ideologies, or even by this intangible,

[6] *Introduction à l'Histoire des Relations Internationales* (Paris, 1964).
[7] *Dimensions de la Conscience Historique* (Paris, 1961), p. 271.

exasperating, but undeniable element—national character. (In a particularly bloody form of mixed strategy—driving—the decisions of a French driver are profoundly different from an American driver's.) In other words, there is no such thing as national behavior in the abstract; game theory, even reoriented toward experimentation, remains excessively abstract.

This is precisely why, in the second place, it may prove to be a highly dangerous guide for action. There are two possibilities: either the theory of mixed strategy will become diversified enough to cover the multiple types of competition that make up international affairs and that have different rules precisely because the stakes differ radically and because the proportions of conflict to cooperation entailed by the partners' interdependence vary; in this case, the theory of mixed strategy would indeed become the theory of international relations, but we are still infinitely far from it, for the reason I have just given. Or else we are faced with a tendency to reduce international relations to the strategy of deterrence, and the flaws I have listed above call the practical effects of such a development into serious question.

To begin with, there is a basic conceptual uncertainty. As Raymond Aron argues, international relations is a series of competitive acts, with loose rules, moving toward ill-determined goals over a period of time—hence the impact of changes on strategies and the role of accidents. As soon as one moves away from the limiting case of pure conflict, games are capable of receiving either a multiplicity of solutions or none at all: the quest for rational behavior ends either in doubt or in fragile certainties. This is what Kahn's and Schelling's studies prove—for instance, through contradicting each other. In his discussion of mutual fear of surprise attack, Schelling states that the old practice of hostages is one guarantee against such attacks and that each of the present contenders holds the opponent's population as a hostage; a large-scale program of civil defense, which would shelter the population, would also destabilize the system and increase the risk of war. Kahn, on the contrary, is the passionate champion of shelters and of evacuations in emergencies; for as long as the population is exposed, the government risks not being able to resist enemy threats and provocations—and knowing that, the enemy will be incited to be daring. Similarly, concerning the "rationality of irrationality," the strategy of unbreakable commitments whose value Schelling stresses, Kahn, while acknowledging that it may give the advantage to whoever commits himself first, shows that it may become catastrophic if one's opponent, instead of backing down, dares to go ahead, precisely, perhaps, because he does not find the irrevocability of one's commitment credible.

Time introduces uncertainty too. Kahn recognizes that measures that are rational in the short run may clash with some that are rational in the middle range, and both kinds may clash with measures that are rational for the long run. Thus, as of 1961, it might have been rational to defend Formosa with nuclear weapons; the spread of nuclear weapons would be rational in the middle range (Kahn thought that by 1965 they could play a credible triggering role toward America's thermonuclear force, thus strengthening deterrence); but both possibilities have bad long-term implications. (1975 might be a disastrous year if the world had gotten into the habit of using nuclear weapons and if each state had missiles.)

A third kind of uncertainty is due not to time but to space, as it were. The theory of mixed strategy barely allows us to predict (within the limits we have seen) what the rational behavior of two opponents ought to be. As the diffusion of nuclear weapons undermines or even destroys bipolarity, not only will the likelihood of rational behavior decrease (which would affect, if not the theory itself, at least its practical relevance), but it will become almost impossible to define the rational behavior of the many interdependent players, linked by ties of varying hostility and sympathy.

The last kind of uncertainty is not the least: the uncertainty that has been created in the minds of various critics by one of the few certainties resulting from the works discussed here (and from many other American works), at the cost of some internal contradictions. Schelling and Kahn assert that competing states in the atomic age have a common interest in survival, i.e., in preventing the contest from reaching the stage of mutual homicide; they consider that competition, and the distrust it breeds, rules out disarmament, but they believe that arms control is possible. Ultimate hope and faith thus suddenly reappear in the rough, tough universe of cold-war strategy, under the guise of unilateral or agreed-on measures that would reflect the mixed character of strategy, half-way between a panting arms race and disarmament. The postulate would be the inevitable permanence of deterrence because of the competition, the goal would be to lower the risk of war, the means would be the reduction of the "first-strike" advantage, the prevention of accidental war, and the limitation of damage if war comes.

Those prospects for stabilization are terribly conditional. To begin with, there is a technological difficulty: what is the right moment for stabilizing this or that part of the arms race? As weapons systems become more complicated, nations hesitate to accept early limitations, since they hope for major benefits from those weapons' development. (This was the lesson of the Soviet and American resumption of nuclear tests after the 1958 moratorium.) Moreover, stabilization on one point may incite one side to try a break-through on another.

Politically, this assurance that arms control could be an effective solution rests on two debatable assumptions. One's optimism about arms control would be much more conditional if the arms-control theories did not assume a nuclear duopoly. Kahn reasons only about the two super-powers. And even within the cold-war contest, the assumption of a duopoly is inadequate: the super-powers find it difficult to act as if they had more in common with each other than with their respective allies (who fear being discriminated against as non-nuclear powers), and thus they have to concentrate on areas where they can move more freely—at the cost of avoiding certain measures, such as a ban on the "first use" of nuclear weapons (out of fear that they might provoke alliance tensions and encourage proliferation), and at the cost of having only a limited impact on third parties. On the other hand, were the Soviet-American rivalry to cease being the main problem, arms-control agreements between the super-powers, while easier to effect, would also be less essential: the effects on third parties would be dubious, unless the two ex-rivals went as far as creating a duopoly of constraints on dissenters—a perfectly unlikely prospect unless political settlements have accompanied arms control or the spread of nuclear weapons became very swift. Moreover, third parties could undermine world peace on their own; even now, a nuclear war could break out without the participation of at least one major nuclear power.

Next, the basically correct assumption that the main rivals share a common interest is flawed in three serious ways. First, while this common interest in controlling arms does exist, to isolate it would mean to divorce arms from politics: with political issues unresolved and "controlled" armaments in place, there is a risk that in an acute crisis the arms-control agreements would be the first to go; this fear has acted as a dampener on negotiations (for instance, again, on the ban on the first use of nuclear weapons: such a treaty would commit the United States to prefer defeat in Europe to escalation). Also, technical arms-control solutions take on different meanings depending on the political context: a non-nuclear zone has one meaning if it covers an area in which there is no great-power confrontation, and a very different one if the zone is Central Europe, where a mere removal of nuclear weapons may increase instability. Moreover, arms-control agreements would require, in most cases, inspection: the ratio of inspection to stability achieved may well appear excessive if there is neither political improvement nor disarmament.

Here we reach the second flaw: although the common interest exists, the two partners' positions and calculations are asymmetrical. And yet theorists of arms control often seem to assume symmetry, exactly as in the kind of game theory Schelling criticized or the minimum-deterrence theory Kahn attacked. For the partners to agree on arms control, one requires a delicate and difficult mixture of conflict and cooperation, trust and distrust: so much rivalry and suspicion that deterrence cannot be abandoned, yet enough awareness of the common interest to make each opponent willing to reassure his foe about his peaceful intentions and even to guarantee the security of his foe's striking force. Such a scheme presupposes opponents who talk the same language and translate correctly the information they receive, and it presupposes that both are equally convinced of the need to give up resort not only to wars (other than limited) but even to "brinkmanship," without however, the giving up of arms. A world of this kind would require almost identical military systems, similar political, geographical, and strategic conditions in both camps, and the same political evaluation of events. Kahn himself, commenting on the conference on the suspension of nuclear tests, deplores the bad effects of asymmetry: the Soviet Union, he wrote, would probably accept an inspection scheme that provided the United States with no military information about Soviet secrets, and the United States would accept a scheme that allowed it to detect at least some of Russia's clandestine nuclear experiments. "Unfortunately, every proposal to date either gives us bonus intelligence about the Soviets or seems to give them real opportunities for cheating."[8] The U.S. and the U.S.S.R. have a common interest in opposing the proliferation of nuclear arms, but the U.S.S.R. includes in its definition of "proliferation" the United States' mere granting of access to

[8] Kahn, *op. cit.*, p. 245.

nuclear knowledge and decisions to Germany, whereas America's interest in NATO, which may require such an arrangement, leads to a definition that excludes it. Does the Soviet Union have an interest in giving up the advantage it gains by the fact that vivid fears exist in America of a sudden enemy attack? Or the advantage that the politically offensive power gains from the uncertainty its foe experiences with respect to the forces that may be used against him? It is in the United States, not in the Soviet Union, that citizens, students, academics can multiply speeches and petitions describing nuclear war in doomsday tones and warning their government not to brandish it as a threat. From the Soviet viewpoint, arms control compounds the disadvantages of the arms race (the preservation of the opponent's forces and the constant need not to let him get too far ahead) with those of disarmament (inspection) without providing the advantages of either—dismantling the foe's roadblocks (particularly his foreign bases, whose elimination the Soviet Union has tied to its acceptance of control posts) in disarmament or the free use of credible threats in the arms race.

Thirdly, although common interests exist, the two super-powers do not necessarily share an interest in having them solemnly enshrined in explicit agreements. Here, we find the special weakness that international law betrays in revolutionary periods or in systems whose relative moderation is due not (as in balance-of-power systems) to deep "organic" or structural factors, but to the introduction into deeply troubled structural elements of a technological innovation that imposes prudence on each player rather than a sense of society on all. Reciprocity of interests, the usual basis of international law, may be present, but it is too delicate, too subject to self-centered interpretations by statesmen who do not want to tie their hands, to serve as the foundation of treaties. Each side wants to preserve as much freedom of movement as possible in the manipulation of the common interests. This explains why "reciprocal interaction," i.e., arms control through unilateral measures, have been and remain more likely than formal agreements; such measures show simultaneously the seriousness of concern for self-restraint and the persistence of the claim to self-help.

Thus, between deterrence, which both sides practice, and general war, which they both shun, there can be arms control but also room for threat and maneuver. If arms remain an instrument of policy, the Soviet Union, which has always followed Clausewitz on this point, is unlikely to subscribe to their neutralization. Does one not find at the bottom of America's arms-control theory that impulse which Tucker denounced—the drive to ban force from history while keeping for oneself enough force to punish one's adversary if he does not consent to it? In Schelling's scheme, the weapons to be strengthened and protected, both to reassure the opponent in peacetime and to be able to hit him if war breaks out anyhow, are precisely those that are aimed at the population, i.e., the most cruel ones but those least capable of inciting the foe to strike first. Technically ingenious, the notion of negotiated arms control suffers from its basically apolitical conception, from a tendency to see in international affairs primarily strategic relations: it is a dream or an act of faith in a purely military rationality made by scientists, engineers, or mathematicians aseptically fascinated by weapons, and by liberals who have trouble integrating force and politics or understanding that an opponent's *Weltanschauung* may be thoroughly different from one's own. Even Schelling recognizes that if arms control results in the proliferation of small wars (or, one might add, of nuclear weapons), stabilization agreements will not survive such shocks.

The basic conceptual weakness that mars the theory of mixed strategy as a guide for action is not the only one; there is also a moral-political peril. Kahn's work gives a striking example of it. He recognizes that in 99 per cent of peacetime calculations, nonmilitary factors of deterrence are decisive, but that it would be disastrous to forget the remaining 1 per cent. The result of this reasoning is that the marginal case controls the rest, due to the very logic of competition: since one should not confuse the odious and the impossible, one must prevent the odious from becoming possible—a danger that will loom as long as every "legitimate risk," every "legitimate circumstance," has not been taken into account: "Insofar as the international political situation involves opposition against a living, thinking enemy, if you leave yourself open to any particular form of attack, you encourage that form."[9] Thus, Kahn's preferred strategy is that of the "full panoply." Since a thermonuclear force of "Type I" (for retaliation against direct attack) suffers from the defects mentioned above (vulnerability, low credibility in case of enemy provocation without attack, insufficiency in case of a "catalytic" general war or a general war produced by escalation), one needs more. One also needs a force of Type II, capable of striking, not the cities, but the nuclear forces of the foe, i.e., a first-strike force that will deter him from extreme provocations (against Berlin, in form of an ultimatum or even in form of an attack on a European ally of the U.S.). Such a force could also, should war

9 *Ibid.*, p. 643.

break out nevertheless, destroy many of the enemy's forces, thus exploiting the first-strike advantage in a nuclear war. Since the possession of a Type-II force by a state gives its foe a reason to pre-empt, he must be deterred through maximum protection of the Type-I force.[10] Since a first strike is likely to leave part of the enemy force intact, one must try to limit the damage his retaliation will cause by means of a vast shelter program and active defense against his remaining planes and missiles. Such a Type-I force is useless in limited wars, and, since using a Type-II force in them would be absurd (the main role of a first-strike force in such cases is to deter the foe from enlarging the war, lest he subject himself to a first strike), one also needs Type-III forces—conventional forces capable of waging limited wars.

Uncertainties pile up and oblige the strategist to ask for ever greater efforts. There are technical uncertainties: insofar as each side tries to make his retaliatory force invulnerable—that is, to approach more closely the model of mutual homicide in case of nuclear war—the likelihood of limited wars and the need for Type-III forces increase; but insofar as efforts to protect one's retaliatory force do not wipe out the advantage of a first strike, the need for a Type-II force remains. There are uncertainties about rational behavior: insofar as one could make an opponent back down from an extreme provocation, by alerting one's first-strike force and by sheltering one's population, thereby making it clear that one won't back down oneself (a perfectly reasonable way to behave), one would also expose oneself to the danger that the foe might think one was going to attack him preventively, and thus to the danger of being attacked preemptively by him (which makes the whole thing appear less reasonable already). The solution is not to give up the Type-II force but to have a Type-I force strong enough to deter him.[11] Kahn's leitmotiv is: "we need more of . . ." everything: we must be prepared against every kind of war and prepared to wage any kind should deterrence fail.[12] Kahn condemns the world to the "burrow" Kafka describes in his nightmarish story, a burrow dug by an animal in quest of peace and security. Constant noises of mysterious origin keep the poor beast rushing in perpetual anguish in whatever direction the knocking seems to come from. This is the fate to which atomic insecurity and political competition reduce us. What makes it particularly ironic is that Kahn assures us that this formidable panoply should be used only after

10 *Ibid.*, pp. 204–5.
11 *Ibid.*, pp. 143–44, 214 ff., 648.
12 *Ibid.*, pp. 271, 273, 274, 277, 279, 301–4, 548, 643 ff.

nonmilitary methods of deterrence have failed, and on the other hand that even with such a panoply at our disposal, we could not afford to relax our vigilance: without a Type-II force, we would be as badly off as France and Britain between 1936 and 1940, when they were exposed to all provocations, condemned to the defensive by the Maginot Line strategy, and finally forced into war at the least favorable moment; but even with a full panoply, we would merely revert to the pre-1914 situation. . . .

Such suggestions, followed by such effects, make the mind rebel and look for flaws in the reasoning. Does not the analysis suffer from excessive pessimism, *and* excessive optimism? It is too dark; it ends in a vision of a war-obsessed society made up of men who have gotten the habit of crawling into shelters. Maybe this vision has the same defects as the massive-retaliation dogma and the traditional just-war concept denounced by Tucker: it is once again an analysis that treats as decisive the circumstances, but not the causes, of the conflicts, that discusses strategic problems as technical ones, quite apart from political objectives, and that prescribes that war ought to be waged according to the sole criterion of efficiency and that peace ought to depend solely on force, equated with justice. Since the days of America's innocence and of her nuclear monopoly have passed, the intensification and the complications of the peril have rendered the vision less simple and the doctrine less rigid—not less abstract or less formalistic.

Kahn's reasoning is also too optimistic. It supposes that crises and wars can be managed under coolly rational rules, not only by the leaders, but by whole populations. It supposes that the opponent will usually be lucid, reasonable, and clever enough to understand the "signals" received from the other side: he will know, for instance, that an evacuation is not a prelude to aggression, or that, if the United States systematically studies all the ways to "cheat" an inspection mechanism, it is in order to oblige the opponent to accept rigorous supervision, not in order to cheat.[13] The prescriptions that flow from this reasoning may be like self-fulfilling prophecies—a risk due to familiar flaws: the tendency to re-introduce symmetry in the hope that, in a game in which signals exchanged by the players are crucial, they will be correctly interpreted; an apolitical conception that allows one to reduce the most impassioned experience in politics—modern war—to a rational game; a good conscience, convinced that since America will use force only defensively, even if the deterrence measures adopted (such as alerting a first-strike force in a crisis) are ambiguous, the opponent will

[13] *Ibid.*, p. 454.

have no excuse if he interprets them wrongly. The outcome is a strange mix of symmetry and asymmetry: one has no doubt about one's own intentions, and one expects the enemy to take them as his guide, but one bases one's own strategy on the more or less provocative nature of measures taken by the enemy rather than on *his* intentions, which are deemed too uncertain.

III

Must we then condemn Kahn and the theory of strategy, by applying Tucker's criticisms to them? The answer is not easy. Since absolute security is beyond reach as long as the competition lasts, the doctrine of the "full panoply" provides the chance to make war less destructive than in the elementary doctrine attacked by Tucker, even (or specially) in the form of a "minimum deterrence" aimed at cities. It also provides a chance to avoid peacetime provocations à la Hitler, or Pearl Harbors, otherwise still tempting. But on the other hand, the price one pays for this opportunity is a kind of militarization of life, and the goals of the doctrine—preventing war or total destruction in war—would be reached, paradoxically, only if men behaved much more rationally than in the past, since the new weapons are so formidable. Because international relations have not fundamentally changed, war remains possible. Because weapons have changed, one hopes that the right kind of strategy will help men to avoid doomsday. But precisely because those weapons are what they are, and because the competition has rarely been more fierce, such a strategy seems like a dress-rehearsal for doomsday. Not Kahn, but international relations are responsible for such absurdity; they create the vision of a nuclear garrison state, watching out for the perils from behind its electronic defenses, moving or burying its "absolute" weapons so as to remove them from the enemy's reach, and thus behaving so as to force the enemy to behave in the same way.

Even Tucker cannot find a way out. He notes that at present, in the nuclear age, the only defensive war is one which disarms the foe, i.e., preventive war; a defensive war in the classical sense—retaliation against an attack—would be pure vengeance against populations. Due to their consequences, neither kind of war can any longer be deemed just. At times, Tucker suggests that in this world which has created the new weapons, nothing can justify resort to arms; at times, it is only blind and unrestrained resort to arms that he attacks.[14] At the end, he lays a curse on technology, which does not

---

[14] The present situation is an inexhaustible source of paradoxes. Among those who think that nuclear war would mean joint suicide, some—in favor

make men evil but creates conditions in which it becomes more and more difficult to be good. He fears that technology may encourage men, if they do not change, to look for "radical solutions," at the same time as it deprives them of the time they would need to correct miscalculations. But technology also risks bringing them to less elementary solutions, like Kahn's, and saving them from terror only by condemning them to the burrow. In the long run, it risks precipitating them from the burrow into terror.

Insofar as the military contest is but one aspect of today's competition, Schelling's and Kahn's mode of reasoning and Tucker's despair may be equally dangerous. But, paradoxically, theories of strategy that are not very good at distinguishing between military and nonmilitary forms of the contest, or even at prescribing a rational kind of behavior for the military aspects, are still necessary as long as war is a possibility—in other words, as long as there are states and weapons. One understands why the moralist rebels against the time bomb of the present international system. From the viewpoint of action, there are only acts of faith: in the instinct of survival and the contagiousness of trust on the part of all kinds of pacifists, in the need for perfect preparation (and the *deus ex machina* of arms control) on the part of strategic theorists, in the efficacy of mixing the logic of strategic theory and the requirements of other aspects of the competition on the part of statesmen. On the level of science, the idea of a theory of rational behavior in a competition with multiple dimensions and unlimited stakes may remain delusory. On the level of statecraft, only the future will tell us whether the statesmen's gambles are wiser than the pacifists' bets and strategists' warnings.

The Realm of Action

I

The past tells us a great deal already. Where moralists fear to tread, where theorists multiply schemes and scenarios, governments

of minimum deterrence—are both optimistic, insofar as they deem man sufficiently transformed by the new weapons to avoid war thanks to such a strategy, and pessimistic since they do not deem man sufficiently transformed to disarm. Others, the apostles of disarmament, are pessimistic, insofar as they deem men too much like what they were in the past in order not to kill each other if they keep their weapons, but optimistic since they hope men are changed enough to be willing to give up their weapons.

have to adopt strategies. And never have the contrasts between
theory and reality been more striking. Theory itself, as I have indicated, has been divided. Some, horrified by the vision of life in the
burrow as well as by the prospect of nuclear death, have argued, in
tones varying from despair to invective, that attempts by governments to tame, to "normalize, conventionalize, and 'nationalize'"
the nuclear monster were tragically wrong, and that the states'
duty was to stop the game in order to get off.[15] Others, convinced
that states are captives of the game, spend treasures of ingenuity
trying precisely to tame the monster so as to permit the game to go
on. Governments are indeed the prisoners of the competition; they
behave like the characters in Ionesco's play who keep a corpse in
the backroom which suddenly starts to grow fantastically, and who
do not know "how to get rid of it." They could not help noticing
that the solutions offered by strategic theorists were both contradictory *en bloc* and full of pitfalls in detail. Intellectuals have
stressed the imperatives of conscience or the dictates of strategy.
Governments, with uneasy consciences, have experienced the oft-
discussed paradoxes of strategy in the nuclear age.

On the one hand, there are paradoxes of conflicting objectives:

1. There is an inevitable tension between the difficult task of
coping with the weapons (the enemy's, one's allies', and one's
own) and the equally necessary task of dealing with the political
issues. The nuclear age blurs the distinction between peace and
war by turning peace into a permanent exercise both in preventing
war and in getting ready for it; this will be the case even if the
"relationship of major tension" changed or subsided, as long as
nuclear weapons remain around. Consequently, strategy becomes
a peacetime occupation of the first order of magnitude; once a
subordinate, or a junior colleague of true "policy" during peacetime, it has become a full associate and often tends to become
master. Indeed, the blurring of the line between war and peace
introduces into peacetime a characteristic feature of total war: the
frequent subordination of political to military considerations. On
both sides, it is clear that strategic imperatives (however diverse)
have had a paralyzing grip on policy. Paradoxically enough—by
contrast, say, with what happened in the summer of 1914—the
results have been mixed, rather than wholly disastrous. Insofar as
the chief rivals are concerned, there have been occasional fiascoes
due to the subordination of politics to strategic considerations—

[15] Hans J. Morgenthau, "The Four Paradoxes of Nuclear Strategy," *American Political Science Review*, LVIII, No. I (March, 1964), 35.

Cuba for the Soviet Union, Vietnam for the United States—but on the whole, the supreme imperative of peace has put a muzzle on each of the barking dogs: strategy, while comparable to total war in its demands, aims to avoid it, and policy is hampered by the competition of the rivals and by the very success of deterrence strategy, which results in denials rather than positive achievements. Consequently, the world is full of frozen "situations of crisis" around which the adversaries crawl in slow motion—not only in Germany and Berlin, Quemoy and Matsu, but in Suez, Cyprus, and Kashmir. The interest each antagonist has in a strategy that enhances his political fortunes and in a policy that assures his "prevalence" has blocked disarmament and arms-control negotiations as well as the settlement of divisive issues, but the interest each has in a strategy of deterrence and in a policy that minimizes losses has allowed for stalemate and symbolic measures of *détente*. Secondly, however, the muzzling of the rivals has increased tensions among allies: strategically, the lesser members of each camp rebel against the caution of the leader's strategy; politically, they rebel against the subordination of their interests to the leader's. As a result, the chief rivals are faced with a serious problem: what kind of a politico-strategic mix should they concoct? If it is one that stresses competition and hostility, they may improve relations within their respective camps, but at the cost of dangers for and a militarization of peace. If it aims at a *rapprochement* in the interest of peace, they risk a further deterioration of political relations with their allies and a possible deterioration of their strategic position in the competition.

2. Strategy itself tries to pursue three objectives that are not particularly easy to reconcile. The first one is the deterrence of major wars, in an age when such a war would no longer be the continuation of politics by other means. The second one is the limitation of war, should deterrence fail. The third one is victory, since the competition persists. What makes the attempt at reconciling those goals so much more difficult than in the past (when nations often tried to plan in all three directions) is the fact that deterrence today is based on a threat whose execution would be a disaster, insofar as a stage of "peril parity" has been reached between the main antagonists. The traditional continuity between deterrence and the use of force exists no more. Whereas we live in "neither war nor peace," we are afraid of a radical discontinuity; if deterrence should fail, the panacea would become the incinerator. Hence the "dialogue of the deaf" among strategists; the deterrers pin all

their hopes on the success of deterrence; if it works, peace will be assured; given the consequences of failure, we must do all we can to make it work. The pessimists stress the possibility and the effects of failure, and conclude that we must find something better, that we must get away from nuclear weapons altogether. At present, nations with nuclear weapons are faced with a divorce between peacetime strategy—designed to support one's policy while deterring the opponent from major war—and wartime strategy. For the strategy best calculated to deter, i.e., to preserve peace, may well be the most disastrous if deterrence failed and war broke out. This would be the case either if one's strategy of deterrence relied on a threat of automatic nuclear retaliation, in which case there would be no possibility of reaching the goal of limiting the damage, *or* if one's strategy of deterrence entailed a network of guarantees (to the antagonist) against surprise attack, of measures designed to preserve channels of communication with him, of restraints excluding certain zones from the arms race—since carrying out such a strategy in wartime would thwart the goal of victory.

The dilemma is serious: to announce in peacetime a strategy designed for use after the failure of deterrence will provoke shrieks of anxiety. If its emphasis is on victory, it will look as if it destabilized an already shaky system, gave the opponent an incentive to pre-empt, and anyhow lacked credibility—three ways of weakening its deterrent force. If its emphasis is on damage-limiting, it will look implausible, should it consist of avoiding the enemy's cities at a time when his military installations are invulnerable; or only too plausible, should it consist of postponing as long as possible the resort to nuclear weapons against a non-nuclear attack; or again dangerously destabilizing and giving a new twist to the race, should it consist of a shelter program—three ways again of weakening deterrence, as well as of encouraging the spread of nuclear weapons. Of course, it is theoretically possible to rely on one strategy for deterrence and on another one for use, but this would complicate planning by turning the state into the burrow, and weaken deterrence by making it clearly look like a bluff. Moreover (to make things even more complex), since there are two possible objectives for a war strategy and not merely one, there are dangers of contradiction here also: a damage-limiting strategy that relies on conventional forces or on a nuclear counter-force strategy or on "off-limits" zones (such as outer space) makes victory rather difficult.

On the other hand, there are paradoxes of uncertainty that affect deterrence.

1. The deterrence of major wars is made problematic not only by the contradiction of the two objectives in case deterrence fails, but also because of the simultaneous existence of two opposing facts about the so-called balance of terror. The first is a trend toward stability, i.e., toward the certainty of mutual destruction, or at least intolerable damage, or, again, "a situation in which neither side is tempted to strike first"[16] for that very reason. But there are also reasons to question how stable this stability is,[17] two of which are particularly important: the continuing advantage of whoever strikes first (invulnerability being a relative notion) and the chance of a technological break-through that will alter the military situation. In other words, stability is a probability, but not a certainty. Three sets of problems result for the major nuclear powers. First, the kind of deterrence strategy adopted will differ depending on whether the emphasis is put on stability or on "delicacy." If the former, then deterrence by means of the threat of using nuclear weapons will be reserved to "central war," i.e., to retaliation against a nuclear attack: it will be deterrence through the *certainty* of retaliation. If the emphasis is put on delicacy, that is, on the remaining elements of *uncertainty*, then the temptation to deter non-nuclear attacks by a threat of a nuclear strike will be great—a temptation to resort to a not-wholly-incredible threat so as to exploit the opponent's own doubts about the wisdom of provocations. This latter strategy is not "irrational" so long as (a) a nuclear first strike, despite the consequences for the party who makes it, seems congruent with the stakes, and the devastations it would inflict on the enemy out of proportion with the gain he seeks; (b) the abandonment of such a threat in favor of a purely non-nuclear deterrent strategy could give to the enemy both an incentive to move ahead and a chance to make a gain, if the conventional forces appear insufficient to save the threatened positions; and (c) even the use of conventional methods does not wipe out the peril of escalation in any case. Thus the choice is a delicate one. But, secondly, any attempt to obviate the choice by adopting both strategies runs into other contradictions. It is contradictory to try to make thermonuclear war impossible by making its cost prohibitive to the party who initiates it (thus allowing small non-nuclear wars) *and* to make limited wars as well as thermonuclear wars impossible by rendering the threat of a nuclear initiative possible. For

[16] Raymond Aron, *The Great Debate* (New York, 1965), p. 34.
[17] See Albert Wohlstetter, "The Delicate Balance of Terror," *Foreign Affairs*, January, 1959.

instance, stability requires that nations take measures to arm themselves against surprise attack, but such measures destroy the advantage of the first strike and thus weaken the plausibility of the threat. Inversely, a shelter program would increase this plausibility by increasing the capacity to survive retaliation, but it would weaken the kind of deterrence that relies on the certainty of intolerable reprisals. Thirdly, it is not always easy to know whether a given move tends to increase the stability or the delicacy of the system, or whether it provides the kind of deterrence it promises. Thus, the spread of nuclear weapons within an alliance can be considered both as a reinforcement of stability, insofar as it thwarts an enemy hope of destroying the whole alliance's thermonuclear arsenal in one fell swoop, and as a contribution to instability. Measures designed to reinforce the credibility of a first-strike nuclear threat against an enemy's non-nuclear attack—such as the acquisition of a small independent nuclear capacity, or the reinforcement of conventional forces so as to raise the "atomic threshold" to a convincing level—can easily be criticized as in fact weakening the threat, because of the incomparability of the damages to the threatener and the threatened in the first case, because of the possibility of seeing in the move a kind of atomic disengagement in the other. A measure designed to reinforce stability may also have the opposite effect: too perfect a signal system against surprise attack could increase the chance of accidental war, whereas too elaborate a network of guarantees to the opponent against surprise attack could tempt him into multiplying provocations.

2. Finally, there is what one might call uncertainty, not about the facts of the balance of terror, but about the behavior of others. Here, we must deal with the difficulty of defining a "rational" strategy of deterrence. Granted that one's object is to avoid large-scale war and defeat, is the best method a strategy of so-called rationality or one of irrationality? The difficulty of providing an answer comes from uncertainty about facts and also from uncertainty about behavior. On the one hand, if the balance of terror is stable, a strategy of irrationality would be a total bluff, since the enemy would have no fear of it; if the balance is delicate, it could make sense, for it would exploit the opponent's fear of destruction. On the other hand, the choice also depends on whether the opponent is more likely to be deterred by a huge threat that may appear to him to be somewhat of a bluff (given the threatener's own reluctance to carry it out) or by a threat more strictly tailored to the case at hand, yet less frightening. Each side must assess not

only the other side's fundamental inclination but the other side's assessment of his rival. Schelling, we saw, has shown that in games of mixed strategy with limited stakes, an apparently "irrational" behavior can be "rational," in the sense of helping the user of such tactics to reach his goals, precisely because the opponent must include in his own calculations the possibility that his rival may be foolish enough to bring the house down on both. This is even more relevant when the stakes are infinite; apparently irrational behavior may succeed, apparently rational behavior (in the classical sense of moderate) may be mistaken.

As a result, nuclear powers are faced with a highly uncertain choice. A rational strategy of deterrence is a wager on stability and is based on the belief that it is foolish to expose oneself to the humiliation-or-holocaust dilemma in every crisis—the opponent would not assume that one really means it. Thus, such a strategy would entail a careful gradation of threats, a careful hierarchy of commitments, and a consideration of each case on the merits. But the danger lies in the encouragement it gives to a multiplication of small tests, some of which might get out of hand in a world in which third parties tend to complicate such tests and in which the temptation to escalate one's way out of stalemate or defeat may be strong.

An irrational strategy is a wager on delicacy and on the strength of the adversary's residual fear of the threatener's willingness to carry out a disproportionate threat. It resembles a minefield; it entails attaching a nuclear menace to every crisis, and a liberal resort to commitments and threats. It may succeed thereby in averting both nuclear wars and more limited confrontations (there have been no military tests over Berlin), but it can never afford to fail.

An attempt to mix the two strategies may well cumulate the disadvantages of both, provide an incentive to miscalculation, and require what we called earlier a full panoply. It may be worth noting that the term "irrationality" implies a debatable value judgment; for such a strategy, marked by a disproportion between the means invoked and the immediate stake, may be well suited to the ultimate stake—the over-all containment of the adversary—whereas the so-called rational strategy, whose means are proportional to the stake of a given crisis, may be unsuited to this ultimate stake.

In coping with those paradoxes, the various powers have made very different choices. This is not the place to review them in detail—especially since they are well known—but it is useful to point out how each of the major beasts has chosen to behave in the burrow and how its behavior keeps the beast in anguish.

1. The evolutions of American doctrine have been frequent, sometimes puzzling. If we stop to ponder only the so-called Mc-Namara doctrine, with its emphasis on "pauses" and "thresholds," its reversal of the "sword-and-shield" distinction, its priority to a conventional build-up in Europe, we cannot but conclude that it is based primarily on a blend of military considerations and only accessorily concerned with political ones.[18] To be sure, it has a basis in political reality: given the nature of the cold war, it is not unreasonable to believe that the offensive power might use some of its enormous supply of conventional forces in Europe; nor is it unreasonable to believe that in so striking, it would abstain from nuclear weapons in order to keep a chance of preserving its own "sanctuary," especially considering American superiority in nuclear weapons and delivery systems. On this basis, however, different strategies can be elaborated (and have been proposed). The Mc-Namara strategy (*a*) relies for deterrence on conventional forces and on a *postponed* residual threat of a nuclear initiative—that is, it relegates this menace to being a threat to deter a continuation of the enemy's offensive after an initial, conventional phase; and (*b*) selects, should deterrence fail, essentially a damage-limiting strategy. Now, this doctrine is open both to strategic and to political criticisms. Strategically, the stress on a damage-limiting strategy of use seems to detract from its deterrent power by "suggest[ing] to a potential aggressor that hostility could remain confined."[19] Moreover, the deterrent plausibility of the doctrine might be further weakened by an inherent contradiction: if the threat to use nuclear weapons is considered important enough to remain in the doctrine, though postponed, then why not emphasize it rather than the conventional forces? Nor is the damage-limiting capacity of this strategy, should deterrence fail, entirely clear. If the threat is felt to be too implausible to be brandished right away, and plausible only if its execution would come in time of dire need but not before (i.e., if the enemy keeps pushing), does this not create a strong incentive for the enemy to resort to nuclear weapons right away? Furthermore, to wait until one's own forces have been overwhelmed so as to give the enemy the "option" to pursue (or not), means both to delay the use of the weapons until the local situation has evolved in the enemy's favor (i.e., to keep on one's own side and

[18] See Henry Kissinger, *The Troubled Partnership* (New York, 1965).
[19] Aron, *op. cit.*, p. 175.

not at all on the enemy's the burden of deciding whether the stake is worth the perils of escalation) *and* to make the decision to use nuclear weapons only when it may well be too late to achieve anything but destruction through such a measure.

As for the political weaknesses of the doctrine, they are of three kinds. With respect to the adversary, the doctrine is overly "rational"; it substitutes an abstract chess player for the real opponent; it assumes that the deterrent power of a threat of nuclear initiative has declined because of "peril parity," but it does not take into account the fact that in the "game" as it is actually played, the existence of such a threat backed by tangible evidence of commitment means that one has decided that *defending* the stake is worth the maximum and therefore puts on the opponent the burden of deciding whether *acquiring* it is worth as much to him. There is good evidence that the "nuclear teeth" of the tiger frighten this particular foe: to act as if one's teeth had been sawed off simply because the foe has atomic teeth too, when it is up to the latter to take or not to take the initiative that would sink one's even sharper teeth into his skin, is a mistake of "overrationality" that needlessly reverses the responsibilities and burdens. Secondly, with respect to its conception of war, the doctrine shows an extraordinarily high degree of hope in the capacity to control nuclear war and limit nuclear "exchanges." To be sure, nobody knows how a nuclear war will be fought; but if recent major wars are any indication, the means and passions involved will not be easy to restrain or restrict. Indeed, what they teach us is that the very prospect of being unable to limit the war is at least as likely a deterrent as the schemes of graduated war games. With respect to the allies, finally, the authors of the doctrine failed to realize that what appears as "damage-limiting" from the viewpoint of the whole alliance would be seen by these allies both as "damage-concentrating" on them, and as increasing the chances for devastation to the very extent to which the deterrent value of the doctrine was reduced.

Not all of these flaws, fortunately, have been put to the test: the doctrine has not, so far, failed to deter—the likely reason for this being not its own virtues but the other side's own intentions and assessments, to which we shall shortly come. However, some of its flaws have clearly emerged. Its political blindness concerning the allies has had unfortunate consequences: it has encouraged precisely what it was supposed to discourage, given its proclaimed need for centralized control—i.e., independent deterrents whose role and use contradict its requirements. It has also encouraged attempts by other allies to gain greater access to decision-making, so as to be able to deflect American strategy from its course. Militarily, it has failed to solve one problem within its own purview, one outside. The decision to deter and, if need be, stop a Soviet military advance primarily with conventional forces supposes that those forces now be adequate; yet the magical (and debatable) figure of thirty divisions has not been reached. The emphasis on the conventional–nuclear war range has left the United States open to challenge on the one front not covered by the doctrine: that of "subconventional" war. The record of the past twenty years shows that the U.S. has succeeded in containing its foes when counter-insurgency methods were sufficient to crush a rebellion deprived of outside support or lacking a political cause (Greece, the Philippines), when it was able to match the conventional forces thrown into battle by its enemies (Korea), or when a genuine *risk* or a credible *threat* of escalation to the nuclear level has existed (Europe, Formosa, Quemoy on the one hand; Berlin, Cuba in 1962 on the other). This suggests the necessity to keep vital commitments under the nuclear umbrella. The United States has failed when counterinsurgency has proven ineffective and major escalation unwise (Vietnam)—which suggests the need for carefully considering the political underbrush before making commitments that could lead to brushfire wars. And the United States has run into difficulties with some of its allies when it suggested that the nuclear stalemate obliged it to revise its strategy. In this last respect, its plight has been the mirror image of that of the U.S.S.R.

2. Nevertheless, Soviet strategy offers a very different picture, and a paradox (again). Here is a strategy that represents a much better blend of military and political considerations; yet, whereas the flaws of the American doctrine are largely latent, those of the Soviet's have been grievously exposed. Soviet strategy can be explained by the Soviet Union's political objective: to expand Soviet influence and power without taking the risk of endangering the home base. The main obstacle has not been the possibility of an American surprise attack: whereas U.S. strategy has often equated Soviet intentions with Soviet capabilities, the Soviet Union has not made that assimilation and has seemed reasonably convinced that the U.S. would not resort to such a move, despite its capacity to do so, unless pushed too hard. (This does not mean, of course, that the Soviets have not *talked* as if the danger existed.) The real obstacle has been America's superiority in nuclear weapons—the capacity of the U.S., if pushed too hard, to inflict devastating dam-

age on the Soviet Union through either an (unlikely) surprise attack, a nuclear initiative following a Soviet non-nuclear move, or retaliation against a Soviet nuclear strike. Consequently, the problem for the Soviet Union could be redefined as follows: to find a way of expanding Soviet influence without provoking the enemy into using his one element of superior strength. This imbalance has, on the whole, condemned the Soviet Union to a "minimum-deterrence" strategy. The Soviet way of expanding had to be non-nuclear.

The U.S.S.R.'s solution was grounded on two considerations. The first one was that despite the growing Soviet capacity to retaliate against the United States and because of America's stronger nuclear power, the U.S. was not unlikely to devastate the Soviet Union should the latter move into an area of vital interest to it—hence, an imperative of abstention from such moves. To be sure, we find here a rather amusing assessment of American behavior by the Soviet Union. The Soviet Union has acted as if the United States' constant reminder of "peril parity," of the folly of using nuclear weapons, etc., could not be taken seriously—i.e., she has refused to accept as likely behavior the official U.S. policy of downgrading the nuclear deterrent, whereas the United States has refused to accept as likely behavior the U.S.S.R.'s abstention from provocations in areas covered by U.S. nuclear commitments! This symmetry conceals one important asymmetry, however: the Soviet Union's refusal to accept American policy at face value was based on a rather correct interpretation of past American behavior (cf. Tucker), whereas the American interpretation of Soviet intentions was based on an American calculation of what a rational player would do in the Soviet Union's position rather than on a study of actual Soviet behavior—which, in Europe at least, has followed this first imperative closely.

Secondly, abstention from deliberate provocations was not enough, because it was neither a recipe for expansion nor a guarantee against eventual American provocations. Expansion was still to be sought, but at the level of what I would call sub-provocations —brandishing the threat of force for political reasons (demoralizing the weakest parts of the enemy's camp through rocket-rattling) or actual resorting to limited force in such a way as not to provoke vital interests of the U.S. (indirect military action [Korea], the promotion of subversion, and direct recourse to nonmilitary piecemeal advances or to *faits accomplis* [Prague, the Berlin wall]). Now, in order to protect such advances as well as to deter (unlikely) U.S. offensive moves, the Soviet Union has threatened that any limited war will almost necessarily escalate. This threat has been termed surprising, given the fact that the Soviet Union's superiority in conventional forces gave Russia an advantage in limited wars, whereas American nuclear superiority gave the U.S. an advantage in escalated wars.[20] And yet the Soviet doctrine made sense insofar as (a) it implicitly assumed that the Soviet Union could not use its conventional forces to great advantage, given the intolerable risk of American nuclear reaction, whereas (b) the threat of escalation could deter the United States from starting a limited operation to counteract Soviet advances, despite its nuclear superiority. This calculation was based on two considerations. First, these advances could be made so as never to give the U.S. the urge to reply, as it were, "Well, let's have it out then!" —i.e., so as never to give the U.S. the urge to take the Soviet Union at its word. The Soviet move would appear either too small to justify a U.S. nuclear reaction or so small that even a limited countermove could be deterred by the Soviet threat of escalation (it would be up to the U.S. to decide whether it wants to risk destruction); or else, in case of a *fait accompli*, the Soviet Union could count on the disproportion between the stake it had already gained and a nuclear holocaust. (This coincides admirably with the Soviets' tendency to "play the defensive": the threat of nuclear war is made only in order to "protect" what one "has.") Second, despite America's superior capacity, its urge to exploit its advantage would be kept in check by Soviet threats of escalation unless strongly provoked, because of the very fear of nuclear war that the United States exhibits.

Nevertheless, this strategy, so well adapted to America's actual behavior (rather than to her proclaimed intentions), has run headlong into one blind alley and a stone wall. The stone wall was, of course, in Cuba. (Every commentator has had his own version of the Cuban affair: here is mine.) The second Soviet imperative—to seek expansions via sub-provocations—while wisely based on an assessment of American anxieties, had nevertheless two weaknesses. One Achilles' heel was that if the Soviet advance was less than "marginal," the American fear of starting a nuclear war would be overcome by the American fear of losing a vital stake. The success of Soviet strategy thus depended on rightly labelling Soviet moves: a wall in Berlin is one thing; missiles in Cuba are—so it turned out—quite another. There was an element of gamble involved, since the distinction between situations of type I (provocations to

[20] *Ibid.*

be avoided so as not to awaken the tiger) and situations of type II (advances to be risked because the tiger would be restrained by the threat of escalation) was highly uncertain. The second Achilles' heel was that the Soviet threat of escalation, given Soviet nuclear inferiority, was to a certain extent a bluff. The Soviet attempt to put missiles into Cuba was precisely an effort to turn the bluff into a plausible threat: with offensive missiles close to the United States, it was no longer only Western Europe that was a Soviet hostage (a situation whose deterrent value on the United States seemed to be in decline, given the McNamara doctrine), nor was it American cities (which could already be hit by the Soviet Union's retaliatory force in the U.S.S.R.): it was the American nuclear arsenal itself. Thus, for the Soviet Union, the move in Cuba was intended to put teeth into the Soviet strategy of threatening nuclear war, (i.e., to give the Soviet Union a first-strike capacity), and it was a gamble at applying that very doctrine in the case at hand: the installation of the missiles was to be the *fait accompli*, the (now plausible) threat of escalation was to discourage an American reaction.

Something went wrong. The United States discovered the plot before the planned dénouement occurred, and the Soviet Union found itself rudely thrown from situation II back to situation I. The *fait accompli* was no longer the Soviet *coup* but the U.S. blockade: it was up to the Soviet Union to decide whether to start climbing up the ladder of escalation; the shoe was on the wrong foot. As for Soviet inaction in Berlin, where so many expected Russia to "open a second front," here too they would have had to shoot first, and with their nuclear bluff exposed (and good evidence that, given the strength of American commitments, Berlin, like Cuba, could be counted as belonging to the realm of situation I), abstention was required.[21] (The American success here, incidently, highlights the unreality of the McNamara doctrine: the Cuban "game" was played by the Soviet Union not as a succession of separate, cool, chess moves, but as a bewildering crisis.)

As for the blind alley, it has been the relative failure of the Soviet Union to break the circle of containment. In Europe, since "situation I" obtained, Soviet gains have had to be peripheral indeed: Prague was Communized and Hungary reclaimed, but subversion failed in Greece and West Berlin is still free—a testimony to the neutralization of a conventional Soviet advantage by America's nuclear force. Soviet attempts to gain influence in Africa have

[21] See Arnold Horelick, "The Cuban Missile Crisis," *World Politics*, XVI, No. 3 (April, 1964), 363–89.

been foiled by and large without the overt use of American force (i.e., situation II was never relevant)—hence, Soviet indignation at the U.N. and lassitude toward the new nations. Only Cuba has been a gain of sorts, for reasons totally independent of Soviet moves—and then the U.S.S.R. failed to turn the island into a Soviet base. Vietnam is an asset, but an ambiguous one: the U.S.S.R. is obviously torn between applying to it the logic of "situation II" (preventing an American enlargement of the war by threatening at least limited escalation) and being trapped in an area that the Sino-Soviet competition makes as murky for itself as the disintegration of South Vietnam makes it for the United States. Such a deadlock, on the one hand, and the noticeable Soviet de-emphasis of nuclear escalation in situations of type II[22] ever since Cuba, on the other, have had an obvious result: restlessness has shaken the former Soviet bloc. Paradoxically enough, the United States applies a doctrine of graduated response to the one area in which the Soviets still fear massive retaliation, and the Soviet Union's only alternative is to "leap" into areas in which its own past threat of escalation is not very plausible, and in which an American graduated response can often be to America's advantage.

America's record has been largely one of strategic success, although part of the price is an increasing loss of control over allies (or neutrals), which feel less threatened by war. The Soviet record indicates a corresponding loss of control; only here it is due not to success in containment but to failure in expansion. As a result, a reshuffling of Soviet policy has taken place, along with the revision of strategy: the original vision is still proclaimed intact; but, among the objectives, survival, safety, and peace have become preponderant, and a spectacular switch from coercive to primarily noncoercive competition has occurred. The row with China, due to this face-lifting of Soviet policy, reinforces Soviet prudence in turn; for if the new Soviet strategy is more cautious toward local wars in which the Soviet Union or its close allies could be involved, the Soviet willingness to support such wars in areas where the Chinese would be the direct beneficiaries is even smaller.

3. The dilemmas experienced by the super-powers have encouraged other states to complicate the balance of terror even further. The decision of the lesser powers that have decided to "go nuclear"

---

[22] See Thomas Wolfe, *Soviet Strategy at the Crossroads* (Cambridge, Mass., 1964): escalation of local wars is presented only as a possibility (with a fairly high atomic threshold); support to national liberation wars is upheld, but unspecified.

shows a triumph of political over military considerations. For the military arguments in favor of small deterrents, while far from negligible, are equally far from being decisive. It has been shown again and again that small deterrent forces, which are vulnerable on the ground, increase the nation's susceptibility to blackmail as much as they may help to deter an opponent from provocation. It has been shown that the main guarantee against provocations remains the threat of the senior partner's much less vulnerable force, despite that partner's growing reluctance to brandish the threat. It has been shown that the acquisition of independent nuclear power by lesser allies in the hope of influencing their senior partner's strategy and triggering his force in case of an attack on their own may well have the opposite effect—to weaken the willingness of the senior partner to risk his life. But political considerations have been decisive: a nuclear capacity is a symbol of power, and the psychological effects—on rank and on prestige—are at least as valuable as the debatable net increase in strength. Moreover, since solidarity of the super-powers against nuclear war has not yet replaced their competition, the secondary nuclear powers have felt that the acquisition of such a capacity was not likely all by itself to dissolve the alliance or the necessary solidarity against a threat from the other camp.

Here again, however, dangers have appeared. The costs of the nuclear programs are prohibitive, hold back the possible development of other forms of power, and above all seem to condemn the states in question to an all-or-nothing strategy which, in turn, puts buoyancy and plausibility back into an enemy's policy of small, marginal moves backed by the threat of escalation; they would even give some justification to an enemy's larger non-nuclear move (daring the smaller nuclear power to commit suicide) if that gamble were not made too dangerous by the existence of a senior protector. Also, proliferation of nuclear forces creates problems for world stability that cannot fail to complicate even the "proliferator's" life. Thus, an acrimonious debate rages within each ex-camp. The senior partners fear an apocalypse and resent small nuclear forces that might make it more likely, if deterrence fails. Their challengers are more optimistic about the possibility of avoiding a global apocalypse, thanks to the nuclear stalemate "on top"; they defend small nuclear forces on the grounds that they make Armageddon less likely (by complicating an aggressor's calculations) and are capable of deterring an opponent even from minor crises (by threatening to turn them into Armageddon). They are, that is, both more afraid than the super-powers of such crises (minor for the latter, not for the former), and less dubious about a nuclear deterrence of these crises.

Thus, these separate strategic calculations have shown how difficult life in the nuclear age can be. All the choices, even the most closely reasoned, have their weaknesses, their dead ends, their perils. And yet—world peace has been preserved.

II

We must move now from the level of the units to the system itself, so as to examine how life under the balance of terror has been preserved: how an international system that exhibits most of the symptoms of past revolutionary systems—heterogeneity, immoderate ends and means—has nevertheless succeeded in remaining *relatively* moderate. How have the dilemmas of the various actors resulted in a *relatively* peaceful play?

The conflicts that have rocked the world have been far less apocalyptic than the power rivalries and ideological hostilities implied: the one element of moderation in the system resides precisely in the area of force.

1. Thermonuclear weapons have not been used, and the thermonuclear threat has not been used for offensive purposes. (The United States has brandished it for the defense of various parts of the *status quo*, the Soviet Union has rattled its rockets in order to protect Egypt at Suez, Cuba, or—rather belatedly during the Quemoy crisis—China.) This restraint verges on the magical.

2. In the military clashes that have taken place:

a) The two chief opponents—the U.S. and the U.S.S.R.—have avoided direct military engagements. In cases of direct confrontations, they have remained below the threshold of force: through a convergent groping for limits, as during the Berlin blockade, through self-restraint on both sides, as during the protracted Berlin crisis of 1958–62, or through a hasty retreat when the heat became too great, as in Cuba in October, 1962. Or else, the super-powers have chosen to fight by proxy: the North Korean army and the Chinese "volunteers" acted as cushions for the Soviet Union in the Korean war; the North Vietnamese play this role for both Russia and China today; the various rebels served as proxies for the Soviet Union in Greece, the Philippines, Laos, Vietnam.

b) In the wars of independence fought by colonized peoples against their European masters, violence almost never reached the level of inter-state war; despite incidents such as the French bombing of Sakhiet in Tunisia in 1958, the main repercussions of outside support to the rebels have been strained diplomatic relations.

c) In each camp, the senior partner has disciplined its allies: the United States stopped Britain and France at Suez, and took measures to put right-wing Laotians as well as Chiang on a leash; the Soviet Union has put pressure on the Chinese and the Pathet-Lao in Laos.

d) In conflicts among or within nations of the Third World, the U.N. has resorted to "international neutralization"—i.e., neither collective security (too dangerous if aimed at a large power, too disproportionate against a lesser one) nor big-power intervention (precisely because of the peril of escalation), but the dispatching of an international constabulary to fight fire with water instead of fire (Kashmir; the Middle East in 1948, 1956, 1958; the Congo; the Yemen; West Irian; Cyprus).

3. Tacit measures of arms control have served to guarantee or support these kinds of restraints. The test ban and the superpowers' refusal to favor the spread of nuclear weapons, the strategy of communications among opponents, even the relative prudence each side has shown in dealing with coercive moves taken by the other in its tacitly accepted zone of preponderance—all these have played such a role.

None of this means that force has disappeared as the distinguishing feature of international relations. There have been shocks between the blocs, if not between the chief rivals; within each camp, force has been used to prevent a member from defecting or to oblige him to submit to the camp's orthodoxy; civil wars have been exploited by the main rivals; the conflicts of decolonization have been particularly bloody, and the sequels of decolonization often equally violent; even the U.N. has resorted to force in Korea and Katanga. However, within those obvious limits, the present system can be called reasonably moderate, at least in means. As a result of such moderation, a system that was originally rigid shows signs of flexibility—the ability to absorb changes in important elements of the system without major violence, and a loosening of alignments. Thus, the system now shows some features common to past multipolar balance-of-power systems.

Such stability must be explained. Recently, Kenneth Waltz has attributed it to a bipolarity[23] in which the poles are states, not

[23] "The Stability of a Bipolar World," *Daedalus* (Summer, 1964), pp. 883–909.

blocs: their contest excludes peripheries (it includes the whole planet), it is sweeping in extension and in intensity, it breeds recurrent (yet managed) crises. The trouble with this view is that there is no reason why such a competition should lead to peace rather than war. Even if one accepts the distinction between a bloc and a single power, one has the precedent of the Peloponnesian War to make one doubt the stabilizing virtue of bipolar systems. Moreover, the present "poles" are or have been at least partly blocs, with complications resulting both in the management of one's allies and the coaxing of one's satellites. In my opinion, whatever stability has been achieved is due to the exceptional convergence of two independent forces: bipolarity (normally a factor of instability) and the increasing costs in the use of force—costs that not only oblige the poles to prudence, but also give to bipolarity a meaning far different from what it had in the past, because the difficulty the superpowers experience in using precisely what makes them so far superior to all the others signifies that the achievements of their power are far from proportional to their material capabilities. There are only two powers if the "minute of truth"—general war—comes; but the increased costs of force postpone this minute and thus lower the productivity of the two nuclear states' power in comparison to that of lesser states.[24]

As an instrument of national policy, force has, beyond two limits at the extreme ends of the spectrum, ceased to pay. Conventional (or nuclear) force is either powerless or unprofitable against the determined opposition of a population backed by outside support. Nuclear war is suicidal, and conflicts that could "go nuclear" are consequently handled with considerable restraint. Historically, this restraint has already survived two phases: during the first (ca. 1945–55), the United States handled its monopoly of nuclear weapons or of the effective means of delivery with prudence, due to the Soviet "hostages" in Europe and Asia and to the nature of America's own vision and policy. In the second phase (since 1955), peril parity has prevented central wars and also inhibited or limited wars against the allies of a super-power when the super-power is clearly committed.

Analytically, the nuclear restraint operates in two different fashions: through deterrence (I am prevented from using nuclear

---

[24] I intend to analyze these aspects of the new system (the transformation of power and the frustrations of bipolarity) in greater detail in a forthcoming book based on lectures given in the spring of 1965 at the Council on Foreign Relations.

force because I am afraid of the consequences of the nuclear force you have threatened to deliver) and through self-deterrence (I refrain from using nuclear force against you, even though you cannot retaliate against me in this way). Self-deterrence is due either to a conviction that nuclear means are disproportionate to the stakes involved, or to a belief that they are inadequate (for instance, in revolutionary wars)—a conviction and belief reinforced by the fear of what a violation of the nuclear restraints now would mean in the future. Self-deterrence is relatively easy to endure when one can legitimately hope to stop the enemy at lower levels of violence; but it has existed even when this prospect was unlikely, because of the fear of the psycho-political repercussions of resort to nuclear weapons, and of the non-nuclear damages the enemy could inflict. It is on the United States' self-deterrence that the Chinese count, as they have made clear in their acrimonious exchanges with the Soviet Union—whereas the latter, in order to justify her prudence, has stressed mutual deterrence.

Intellectually, nuclear restraint has strengthened American and Soviet inhibitions about the role of force. (Whether Hitler, who was not so inhibited, would have been thus impressed is a different story.) The United States has been tempted to use all-out force only when directly provoked and when the resort to force could be justified by constructive purposes; so far, no direct attack has occurred, and no constructive purposes can easily survive nuclear war. As for the Communists, even though their ideology emphasizes struggle and victory, war as such has been presented as an imperialist necessity rather than a Communist duty. There is no disagreement in the "Socialist camp" about the need for caution; there is disagreement about how seriously the opponent's nuclear weapons must be "respected" in order to avoid world war—the Chinese refusing to revise their ideological priorities (perhaps because they have had no operational nuclear weapons so far), and the Soviet Union considering the nuclear danger important enough to make it the number-one enemy.

The major consequence of the nuclear revolution has been the transformation of the role of force in contests among states—what Aron has called the substitution of crises for wars. In past revolutionary international systems, the tests of wills involved large-scale violence, i.e., a final (although not necessarily initial) proportionality of achievements to military capabilities; in past balance-of-power systems, this proportionality could serve as a deterrent to the use of force, but, given the uncertainties of such deterrence, it could also serve to determine the outcome of struggles that took place in any event. Today, as in balance-of-power systems, there is some use of force, but the relation between capabilities and the outcome is often indirect.

In the tests that have highlighted the evolution of the "relationship of major tension" between East and West, the super-powers seem to have been guided by two principles—simple to enunciate, but complicated in their application: "Act so as to avoid giving the opponent an opportunity to pose a credible threat of dangerous escalation, but, also, act so as to pose such a threat to him if he moves too far." Each side's formidable nuclear potential plays primarily a double *negative* role in international politics, then: it thwarts the other side's achievements, but it also curtails its own. As in balance-of-power systems, the restraints accepted by or imposed on a great power consist in the equal or superior force of its rival(s); what is new is the nature of that force. Whereas disturbances in the balance of power led only to limited wars, disturbances today would, if they involved nuclear weapons, easily lead to disaster. Therefore, the restraints observed today are considerably greater than in balance-of-power systems: a contender is less willing to gamble on the chance that his rival(s) will not really try to stop him.

In working out those principles, the chief contenders have relied primarily on "bargaining techniques" that conform to Schelling's analysis:

1. *Initiative*: It is important for *me* to be able to throw on *you* the responsibility of forcing *me* to escalate dangerously; I must seize the ominous initiative that puts on you the onus of making the fateful move that will oblige me to resort to a perhaps fatal response. On the whole, it is easier for the defensive power to play this game, but a skillful offensive player can play it too, through the technique of *faits accomplis* in particular.

2. *Commitment*: This is the act that manifests that your move will bear the burden of setting off my response; i.e., the initiative as described above is best made clear and solemn by a commitment. The actor must choose where to place his commitments, to what he ought to commit himself (how far he is prepared to escalate in response to an enemy move), whether to "fractionate" his commitment or, on the contrary, to keep it indivisible (so as not to go through separate calculations for each fraction), whether to make it specific or leave it vague. The answers are largely determined by the value of the stake: if it is high, the chances are that the com-

mitment will be made well in advance of a crisis and that it will be an undivided commitment, to a high degree of peril if necessary; if the stake is low, the commitment will be gradual and graduated —the escalation ladder will have many more rungs and will take longer to climb.

3. *Threat*: One's commitment is to the use, or greater use, of force in order to prevent enemy provocations or moves or the continuation of provocations or moves. The main problem here is one of plausibility: one commits oneself so as to make the threat plausible, but does not an inherently implausible threat devalue one's commitment? A small threat may be plausible, but not threatening enough to deter. A large threat, which explicitly refers to the possibility of total destruction or leaves the holocaust to chance, has considerable force, despite its surface implausibility. This is due to the nature of the statesman's calculation: "Due to the threat that buttresses your commitment, I may be destroyed if I move, even though you will be destroyed too; if I am right in assuming that you are bluffing, my move will bring a gain of x; if I am wrong, I am dead. Therefore, I had better not move." Since self-interest remains at the heart of this calculation, the "small chance of total destruction"[25] is not likely to be risked: the unlikeliness of the apocalypse is overshadowed by its horror. This implies that the decisive factor in the calculations during a crisis is not the ratio of my opponent's nuclear forces to my own, but the fact that my move may bring intolerable havoc upon me; one can be deterred by a force capable of less destruction than one could oneself inflict—even by a small force whose capacity of destruction still considerably exceeds the value one puts on the stake involved. In other words, this kind of a threat remains efficient even though the threatener might suffer more than the threatened, since the responsibility for initiation rests with the threatened. At the root of the strategic "great debate," one finds the question of how far this reasoning can be applied. Are we in possession of a miracle pill that loses its potency after a point, and where is this point? Does it work equally well against all opponents?

In the tests that have occurred so far:

1. Force has been most conspicuous where the stakes were minor, the commitments gradual, the threats limited; there has been no resort to force between the contenders in places like Berlin, Cuba (1962), Formosa, or Hungary. The super-powers'

25 Thornton Read, "Military Policy in a Changing Political Context" (Princeton Policy Memorandum No. 31), p. 16.

overwhelming capacity to destroy has been the condition for reducing crises to tests of wills or tests of limited force, but it has not been the yardstick for the outcome of the tests. In Korea and Vietnam, the total force ratios have certainly had little to do with the military results. Power has been used in often unlimited threats of punishment, used considerably to deny, but used only in a limited way to punish. The main achievement of power has been denial.

2. The outcome of these crises has been determined by the interaction of a variety of factors: the availability or not of a "full panoply" of force to give plausibility to threats (if one is missing a first-strike nuclear capacity, this prevents one from posing the still efficient threat of total destruction; if one is weak at the conventional or subconventional level, it obliges one to rely exclusively on this threat and thus weakens one's credibility); margin for maneuver (smallest when the stake is greatest and the commitment firmest); the statesmen's will; and their skill (first, the art of appearing to be the most willing to carry out threats—which might be called the art of prevailing, in which bluff and will are inextricably mixed—and, later, the art of restraint, for, once one has safeguarded one's own commitment, it is necessary not to challenge one's opponent's basic commitment to saving face or preserving his security; otherwise, the statesman's calculation [as demonstrated above] would be invalidated). In other words, with the increase in the damages force can wreak, psychological elements of statecraft become more important—which would justify psychologists' and social psychologists' repeated criticisms of "defense theorists" or "strategic thinking" only if such critics were able to develop concepts and insights appropriate to statesmanship in international relations.

The tests that have marked other kinds of tension (and that are by definition less dangerous for international stability) have followed a variety of patterns.

1. Some have been traditional in their nature and outcome. The results of several tests have been pretty much determined by the ratio of forces aligned on each side. These were sometimes tests of will that did not become tests of force precisely because the disproportion between the respective forces was too great: here I refer precisely to those instances of "international neutralization" in which the pressure of both super-powers, or one super-power supported by many other nations, has put an end to a violent conflict among smaller powers (Holland and Indonesia, the Middle East

in 1948, West Irian). As in balance-of-power systems, these events show the determination of the strong not to let the weak rock the boat through inter-state violence or civil disorders with major international complications. Or else, the tests' outcome was predictably uneven simply because of the disproportionate force (Tibet, Hungary). Or else, there were violent tests that appeared uncertain at the start but that ended either because one side reached its limited objectives (the Sino-Indian war) or because the process of international neutralization was launched in order to stop the bloodshed (the Arab-Israeli conflict).

On the other hand, there have been numerous insurrectionary movements aimed at expelling a much stronger, alien power. Many of these movements have succeeded despite this disproportion, due to an asymmetry in tactics that often favors insurgents when the political conditions support them.

2. Other tests have been quite original. Here I refer to crises between a super-power and a smaller power that, by wisely avoiding the resort to violence altogether, had not exposed itself to a disproportionate test of force. This is the area with a certain amount of "equalization of power": the super-powers still have advantages, in the use of minor forms of their coercive power and their power to reward, but the bulk of their coercive power is for all intents and purposes neutralized, partly by self-deterrence, partly by their competition (each one fears that its use of major force against a lesser power could be exploited by its rival or serve as a dangerous precedent); their remaining assets can be balanced by some small states' defensive capacity. Here again, achievements are not proportional to capabilities: giants can be stalemated not only by giants but by pygmies also—hence the survival of Tito, or Castro.

I refer also to those instances of international neutralization clearly aimed at keeping the super-powers from confronting each other directly over a crisis within a state or among states (Suez, Congo, the Middle East in 1958, Cyprus). The role the U.N. plays here reflects not only the super-powers' consensus against allowing third parties to disturb peace, but also their incapacity to act together formally—due to their competition, the small powers' fear of being dragged into their contests, their occasional agreement to restrict the scope of their confrontation, and the need for an international authority that they cannot provide. The U.N. thus appears as a face-saving device for the great, and both a buffer and a spring-board for the small.

As a result of these various tests, the old discontinuity between war and peacetime diplomacy (which uses coercive power primarily as a reserve) has been replaced by a new dichotomy: at one end of the spectrum, we find a proliferation of "sub-wars," either civil or insurrectionary wars, or minor resorts to force in which the larger powers do not, or only barely, join; the classical descriptions of war do not apply to them either because one is dealing with revolutions or because the limits that obtain are due less to a voluntary or balance-of-power enforced restriction of the *ends* than to a careful management of *means* at the service of broad, long-term ends that one still hopes to attain, but piecemeal. At the other extreme, there is the super-powers' direct confrontation and their permanent game of "chicken," which relies primarily on threats. The area of greatest confusion is in between the two: where the perils of the game of chicken compound the dangers of an existing violent conflict—i.e., when the super-powers become involved in and through third parties. Competition between the United States and the Soviet Union tends to move toward precisely that area, since there, the game of chicken, involving apparently smaller stakes and commitments, seems less risky than in an area of direct confrontation, where the proximity to nuclear fire is too great. If force is to be used, it seems likely that only the lesser forms of coercion will be displayed. This move away from direct confrontation (in Berlin, in Germany, or in outer space) into the "gray areas" not only explains the confusion of simultaneous *détente* and entanglement, but also weakens every one of the conditions of bipolar stability on which the arguments advanced by Kenneth Waltz rely.

The question thus raised is that of the limits of the relative moderation shown by the present system. Some limits are set by tests of will involving the chief rivals, in which the restraints observed so far would collapse; these are *disturbances* that would get out of control. Other limits are seen in the *conditions* of dangerous instability (capable of leading to serious disturbances) that paradoxically arise from the very moderation observed so far.

The tests of wills involving the chief contenders have been kept until now within the bounds of prudence. But any game in which the players use self-help in the definition of prudence has its dangers: the present state of international relations is a system of trials that brook no major errors. By major errors I mean not errors leading to limited wars—as in the balance-of-power systems, the number of times that force is used is no criterion of instability —but errors leading to the risk of a major explosion. What could provoke it?

1. Uncertainties concerning the initiative. There are many situations that are far from clear-cut, in which each side feels it can impose on the other the idea that it exercises what I have called the ominous initiative. This is likely to occur in revolutionary subwars, where the rebels and their supporters consider the *fait accompli* of the rebellion to be the real "ominous initiative" that places the burden of escalation on the opponents, whereas the defensive acts as if its own determination to protect the *status quo ante* against "attempts at change through force" was the crucial initiative (Vietnam). It can also occur when there is uncertainty about one side's initial commitment.

2. Uncertainties concerning commitments. These are particularly dangerous, as the Korean War and Cuban missile crisis showed. (In Korea, first the Soviet Union was mistaken about the United States' commitment, then the United States made a mistake about China's.) They are likely to occur when two limited commitments are in opposition at the start of a test, but when the stakes rise during the test. The danger comes not only from the tendency to climb up the escalation ladder, but also from the fact that the limitations the contenders observe may actually benefit the side that is weakest at high levels of force, and thus tempt the loser to jump to those levels, the initial smallness of its commitment being gradually changed by pressure toward victory. Again, this is particularly true of subversive wars.

There is another type of case, in which one side's attack or provocation raises the stake so much that it creates the defender's commitment *ex post facto*. The situation on the offensive side is thereby suddenly transformed; the offense might have been deterred by a commitment *ex ante* and is now faced with a reversal of initiative: the responsibility for the fateful move is now his, and he must decide *after* the act whether this act is a commitment, and what level of risk it is worth. This commitment *ex post facto* by the defensive side describes America's role in Korea in June, 1950, and China's role five months later, as well as America's tactic in Cuba after the Soviet missiles were discovered. In Korea, both sides decided that they were committed, but only to a limited level of risk; in Cuba, the Soviet Union decided that the risk was too great and scrapped the move.

The danger that comes from uncertainties about commitment is considerably increased by third parties: if they are not formally associated with any of the chief contenders, the danger of miscalculation by the offensive side is increased whenever he does not expect them to be protected by his rival; or, third parties may try to force one of the rivals to commit himself to their protection—an attempt to play a triggering function, either by resorting to deliberate attack, which would force the protector to support them and thereby create two foes for the other side (North Vietnam attempting to implicate the U.S.S.R. in the fall and winter of 1965) or by maneuvering so as to be attacked by an offensive side that mistakenly doubts the protector will support the attacked party (North Korea succeeding in implicating China in October, 1950).

3. Mistakes in the manipulation of threats. First, a strategy relying on graduated threats may fail to deter, and may even encourage, limited moves whose development may involuntarily lead to the "quantum jump"—the sudden escalation to high levels when a change in the value of the stake has occurred through gradual escalation or sudden full commitment. Secondly, whereas the strategy of the small threat may not, if it fails, keep to small threats, the strategy of the large threat may not deter any more. There is for one thing the case where the reasoning presented above ("If I move, I may expose his bluff; but if he wasn't bluffing, I'll be dead") fails to stop a move because the party involved did not believe that the reasoning applied. He thinks, "I can push, since he can't do much harm to me"; yet a disaster follows. This may happen if a large nuclear power pressures a small nuclear power, thinking that the prospect of annihilation will deter the latter from striking first, especially since it could inflict only limited damage; if the smaller power, in desperation, carries out its threat, catastrophe might result. Also, if a large nuclear power pressures a small power (nuclear or not) that it believes to be isolated, and if this move provides the small power with a protector, the initiative here too suddenly reverses: the offensive side has put itself in a situation where it may now be faced with a major threat. It could retreat, but then there is a danger of slipping into another type of situation: when the reasoning applies but no longer deters because the side to which it applies is beyond rational calculation. This is the case of the small nuclear power under acute provocation, which feels that its choice is only between two forms of death and prefers the form that allows for simultaneous revenge. It is also the case, not at the beginning of a test or series of tests, but

at the end, of the large nuclear power to which no avenue of honorable retreat is left. The real danger in direct confrontations is not the cool, preventive first strike but the final, desperate first strike. A third kind of error in the manipulation of threats is provided by what might be called the irrelevant threat: in situations of revolutionary war, either graduated or large-scale threats of escalation by a major power that finds itself supporting the losing side may fail to have any impact on the local military situation precisely because of the essential differences between those wars, even supported from the outside, and conventional wars such as Korea. An attempt to equate them only increases the over-all peril in a particularly insidious way. What characterizes revolutionary wars is that they are close to zero-sum games: negotiated settlements that do more than provide a fig leaf to cover the defeat of one side are rare; compromise solutions (Laos, Cyprus, Congo) are unstable; and it is difficult to induce the winning side to negotiate (Vietnam in 1954 and now). When such wars are not "branched on" the relationship of major tension, they have fortunately had only a small impact on world stability, because of the external restraints observed (the protection of "sanctuaries" in particular). But Vietnam shows that when they do become tied to the dominant conflict, they may become the Achilles' heel of nuclear restraint. As long as the stakes are low (Laos in 1962) or as long as the East-West balance is not at stake (Cyprus), the common interests of outside powers (the United States and the Soviet Union, Greece and Turkey) can be brought to bear on the local situation so as to return it to the category of mixed games. But when the local game is played for high stakes in the East-West balance, resort to threats that do not affect the local military situation and carry escalation into the sanctuaries entails two dangers: that of giving to the *broader* game, played by all the powers involved in the outcome of the *local* battle, the character of a zero-sum game (instead of the opposite); and that of forcing the party whose threats and moves have failed to improve the local situation into the most uncomfortable choice of all: between further escalation —without any guaranteed local impact, but with the aim of proving his commitment (thus turning a local revolutionary war into a classical inter-state conflict, but one partaking of the intensely hostile feelings of revolutionary wars)—and major humiliation.

It is easy to see that, by itself, bipolarity offers no life insurance to the world. Even if the two nuclear super-powers preserve and increase their margin of superiority, the world they must operate in is a minefield. One peril is, as we have seen, that of the confrontation that goes out of control because of mistakes and miscalculations induced by third parties: although their own power to destroy is infinitesimal by comparison, their power to obstruct and play havoc is great. So far, the supreme function of the super-states' nuclear power has been to *deny*; one may worry about the lesser states' capacity to maneuver and *do* mischief. Since bipolarity does not mean a division of the world into two empires, the combination of rivalry at the top and fragmentation below provides for infinite possibilities of crisis. The other peril is that of revolutionary wars: not only do they offer all the uncertainties about initiative, threat, and commitment listed above, but the world is ripe and rotten with opportunities for rebellions: one of the rival powers sees in revolutions its best chances for advance (despite a split in its camp); the other is singularly ill equipped by tradition and training to deal with them; and such intervention by the super-powers creates the situation of confrontation with third-party involvement in the most dangerous circumstances.[26] Revolutionary wars, so hard to wage coolly, and crises with third-party involvement are conflicts in which the conditions for successful "tension-management," i.e., the continuing exchange of signals and messages and the persistence of bargaining in the midst of contest, may well be destroyed. When there are too many parties sending signals and too many receiving them, too many passions and too many self-centered calculations, the signals become distorted, messages are lost, and bargaining turns into mutual pigheadedness.

The tests between the chief contenders carry important risks, since the Doomsday machine does not yet exist that would insure obliteration each time a power made a move previously defined as unacceptable by the rival. Calculations in uncertainty continue. So far, the uncertainties of nuclear war have kept all players at a very low level of risk, reckoning that the gains from dangerous moves were outweighed by the possibility of disaster or that the improbability of disaster was outweighed by its size. But the uncertainties in crisis control persist—insofar as both the level and the outcome

---

[26] It is therefore doubly imperative—for purely selfish reasons as well as for reasons of world order—that the United States avoid military commitments that could lead her to fight revolutionary wars in politically unfavorable circumstances. Contrary to what a mechanical view of containment sometimes seems to imply, the most effective as well as least destabilizing way of containing a rival in areas open to successful revolutionary wars is to refrain from military commitments—to refuse to turn the area into a zone of contest that one will either lose or win only at considerable peril for peace.

are concerned. There is the basic uncertainty beyond all calculation—the "residual threat of total war"—which explains our shaky moderation, and there are uncertainties in the calculations that statesmen continue to make in order to achieve their goals, from which the threats to stability come.

The second set of dangers for stability is provided not by crises but by situations that grow out of the present conditions of the use of force and that favor in turn the outbreak of crises.

1. As in balance-of-power systems, which frustrated the great powers by preventing most of them from gaining their objectives, the frustration of the super-powers by deterrence may lead to situations in which their reasonableness is sorely tried; it may lead them to look for opportunities to exploit whatever superiority they possess over each other.

2. The increasing difficulty of using force on a large scale magnifies a tendency that also existed in balance-of-power systems in which great powers stalemated each other and disciplined the small: the freezing of unhealthy or artificial situations which, so to speak, cry for a solution that theoretically force could provide but for reasons of elementary prudence should not, and which diplomacy without force cannot affect (the Middle East, Kashmir, Malaysia and Indonesia, Cyprus). Such situations are, of course, breeding grounds for further crises.

3. An original element is represented by the following fact: the difficulty the super-powers experience, because of self-deterrence and competition, in resorting to violence in order to discipline lesser states (unless in their immediate bailiwick, and unless these states have exposed themselves to such violence by having used it themselves, through war or in revolution) encourages small states to commit a variety of destabilizing acts—short of the outright use of force (Nasser nationalizing Suez), helping or fomenting subversion (Sukarno, Greece in Cyprus), or developing their own nuclear forces.

Why, if the possession of a nuclear force decreases the productivity of the possessor's power, should states nevertheless want it? In part, as we saw, because "politics as usual" continues: since the super-powers have not given up the weapons, since the ultimate power of life and death remains in the hands of the owners of nuclear weapons, their acquisition is a normal goal of any challenger of the hierarchy. Moreover, the nuclear stalemate has given some of the super-powers' ex-protégés an incentive to steal fire from heaven: on the one hand, their protectors seem less willing to risk nuclear destruction to protect others, so that those who feel that their safety requires that the escalation ladder have only few rungs are tempted to build their own, next to the super-power's overly graduated one; on the other hand, the stalemate gives the super-powers' challengers a sense of relative security that allows them to weave an atomic headscarf (supposedly required because of holes in the nuclear umbrella) right under the protection of the umbrella they challenge. Finally, nuclear power is tempting because of its negative productivity: it may not help one obtain what one covets, but it helps one keep what one has, it gives one the supreme power of denying one's foe a gain at one's expense. Those who have had nuclear power have waged war on other people's territory; they have not had to suffer it on their own—like Vietnam or Korea, Cuba or Egypt. It may not increase one's own capacity to use force (on the contrary), but it protects one against the others' use of force.

Thus, through the proliferation of nuclear weapons, the present nuclear stalemate and bipolarity may carry the seeds of their own destruction. For even if the two nuclear "poles" of today remain infinitely stronger than any new ones, the kinds of crises and the management of crises may be drastically changed. Proliferation undermines the conditions of stability listed by Waltz—absence of peripheries, concentration of perils, clarity of national interests. Proliferation is not automatic—the decision to develop nuclear weapons depends on technical possibilities, domestic predispositions, and a nation's foreign policy. (The latter will lead to proliferation if its leaders are determined not to remain behind another state that has nuclear weapons, or if it possesses a combination of a sense of threat, a fear of not being otherwise sufficiently protected, and a calculation that the acquisition of the weapons will not decrease the nation's security or the security of a close friend.) But it has proved difficult to stop: it may, indeed, be too late to "save bipolarity." Bipolarity could only be preserved in two ways. One is a return in intense Soviet-American competition, which would remove from frightened or tense allies the incentive to push their own nuclear efforts, and would increase the fear of conflagration among nonaligned powers. But we would then return to a world in which the outcome of any test could be determined, not by the ratio of respective fears or hesitations about the use of force, but by the ratio of the respective forces: the price of bipolarity would be supreme instability and peril. The other way is the passage from *détente* to *rapprochement* to genuine condominium—the collusion of the super-powers against the loss of power, a return to Roosevelt's "big policeman" notion. But for quite a while, it seems, the logic of competition rules this possibility out: the very superiority of the super-powers over everyone else keeps them in contest, and their dependents or rivals would see to this; by the time the United States or Soviet Union might reflect about the advantages of a condominium and about the size of the threat to their power, their capacity to snuff out challengers' forces or prevent further proliferation without peril to peace might have diminished.

The spread of nuclear weapons does not automatically mean disaster. One must distinguish among the possessors. Much depends on the foreign-policy context (do the weapons serve a defensive vision and strategy, or a revisionist or revolutionary vision and strategy?); on the degree of tension in the local situation (the greatest danger is where the acquisition of nuclear weapons by one state may give it the temptation to exterminate its enemy through a first strike, or give the enemy the temptation to pre-empt through conventional means before the nuclear striking force is operational); on the connection between the local situation and the relationship of major tension (on the whole, the acquisition of nuclear weapons by an ally of a super-power should provide the new owner with no incentive to aggressiveness, for even if the "triggering" function operates, its consequences would still be fatal for the possessor of the small force). Paradoxically, then, the greatest danger of the nuclear weapons being used would come when there is no direct connection to the main contest, or when the connection has become uncertain (as might be the case for China's force if the Soviet-Chinese split should continue), or when there is such a tie but when the small nuclear power plays badly and tries to use its force to trigger its senior ally's force to defend very minor interests, or at least interests that are decidedly minor for the senior ally.

The likely implications of the spread of nuclear weapons for the international system are a democratization of the life-and-death power now monopolized by the super-states, and an extension of the uses of coercive power short of war—the power to deny and the limited power to punish exerted under the nuclear umbrella. Neither would be stabilizing, for even if the spread of nuclear weapons is accompanied by a spread of unwillingness to use them, this unwillingness would be badly tested by the many tensions left without resolution because of the danger of resorting to force; an extended use of the lesser forms of coercion would raise the temperature further.

The main problems would be the super-powers'; their superiority might persist, but their roles could become much more difficult to play. One of their roles is that of powers with a common interest in preserving peace. Until now, they have succeeded in imposing it on lesser powers without too much trouble. This would no longer be the case. A small nuclear power determined to blackmail or to attack a non-nuclear state could, despite its own inferiority, play the game of chicken with the super-powers if the latter tried to stop the attack, for it could throw on them the responsibility for escalation—thus raising the risks and costs of peacekeeping far above what they have been in the past. (Even though it could not devastate the super-powers' home territories, it might use or threaten to use tactical nuclear weapons against any force of outside intervention.) The super-powers might thus be obliged to choose the task of universal policeman—giving a joint guarantee to all potential victims of nuclear blackmail, an advance commitment to use force for their protection—in a world in which, however, their capacity to achieve their goals without using force might still be as inhibited as it is today. They would thus oscillate between relative impotence at low levels of risk, and omnipotence at very high levels—not a happy prospect. The other possibility is for them to reduce their policing to those areas where they can bring their power to bear without resort to force—i.e., to isolate local conflicts caused by intractable smaller states in order to save the rest of the world from escalation. The cost here would be fragmentation of the world into local jungles—not a happy or stabilizing prospect. Since both courses of action are full of disadvantages, a way out might be found through resort to international organizations on which the policing responsibility would be thrown; but since that policing might involve the use of force, one would have to solve first all the problems that arise from attempts to establish international military forces capable of deterring and punishing.[27]

Another role played by the super-powers is that of rivals in a contest. Until now, they have deterred each other from direct attack against each other or each other's main allies, and from the nuclear blackmailing of third parties. Here also, things might get more difficult. Mutual deterrence would become more uncertain

[27] See Hoffmann, "Erewhon or Lilliput," in Lincoln Bloomfield *et al.*, *International Military Forces* (Boston, 1964).

if super-power A had to deter its rival B not from attacking or blackmailing C, but from supporting a small nuclear power D which tries to attack or blackmail a non-nuclear power E that A wants to protect: escalation in intensity would be accompanied by escalation in extension. There would therefore be the risk of a scramble for guarantees—by non-nuclear powers, in order to be protected by a super-power against threatening nuclear neighbors; by small nuclear powers, in order to be protected by a super-power against being deterred from their course by the other super-power. The result would be extreme instability: if a super-power declined to give its guarantee, so as not to get involved, it could easily promote the disintegration of its own camp and the triumph of its rival; if it granted the guarantee, then the whole world could become like the present relation between the United States and Europe or between the U.S.S.R. and Cuba, in which the guarantor has some doubts about carrying out the guarantee and the guaranteed has some doubts about the value of the protector's commitment—with results that promote proliferation.

Finally, the choice between the two roles may become more difficult. Total competition would be a recipe either for destruction or for an increase in the irrelevance of super-powers in a world populated by ascending rivals. Total solidarity is unlikely, because it would require that each super-power consider the nuclear problem independently of political advantages and disadvantages to itself (for instance, obliging the United States to side against Great Britain should the latter use or threaten to use nuclear power against, say, Indonesia, or obliging the Soviet Union to side against China should the latter blackmail Japan).

Thus, prediction is very risky: how the super-powers will behave will depend on the circumstances. As long as Chinese nuclear power is small, the U.S. may well choose to guarantee China's neighbors in the Far East, thus counting on China's unwillingness to risk destruction. But should an American (not necessarily nuclear) involvement with China lead to a reassertion of Soviet-Chinese solidarity, America's own unwillingness to risk destruction would reintroduce uncertainty in the value of the guarantees. The result might then be either proliferation of nuclear weapons in the rest of Asia, or (given China's position) massive Asian tributes and concessions to China in order to divert her wrath. If the danger is the Middle East, where the super-powers' rivalry continues to make joint guarantees or a jointly enforced prohibition on nuclear weapons unlikely, the most likely outcome is a local jungle—

i.e., an explosion that could bring in outside intervention, but only *after* a local explosion. None of this confirms C. P. Snow's prediction about a holocaust, but it shows how much more difficult the management of crises might be. Life would be simple if the possession of nuclear weapons were a straightforward factor of wisdom and restraint, or a guarantee of folly. In the latter case, a bipolar nuclear system would be just as bad as any other nuclear international system; in the former, diffusion of nuclear weapons would not matter. The trouble is, of course, that the enlightenment those weapons bring to their owners is fragile and conditional. The problem of world order is therefore enormous in a world in which policing-through-force is perhaps suicidal, and policing-without-force less and less likely to be effective. Order rests on the continuing plausibility of a threat whose execution is distasteful to all.[28]

III

We may now try to answer the question raised at the beginning of this essay: how much does the present system differ from past ones? It is dominated by both the need for force and the fear of force, and this is unique. (Balance-of-power systems knew the fear of unilateral use of force, rather than of force in general.) All powers, all camps, all ideologies, all rebels need force—and therefore all bans on force are hedged. The fear, in a way, has fed the need—in the forms of nuclear proliferation, frozen crises, or the new international legitimacy that supports subversive violence in colonial cases, partly as a safety valve. But the fear of force has kept nuclear war away. Thus, insofar as force is concerned, we witness a dialectic of the old and the new: the increase in the costs of force has deprived it of much of its usual role in history; but the difficulty of shaping a future without resorting to violence makes

[28] I recognize that this discussion of the proliferation of nuclear weapons is "alarmist." "The worst is not sure," says the proverb. Indeed, one can conceive of a joint super-power move to put an end to proliferation by force after a local nuclear crisis set off by a small nuclear power—a kind of "mutation at the brink"—or of local nuclear conflicts from which the super-powers would disengage themselves and which would thus not lead to a major disturbance. My points, however, are: the best (or second best) is as unsure as the worst; occasional joint policing is more likely than permanent joint policing; and occasional small nuclear conflicts could threaten over-all stability—not merely because super-power disentanglement is not always possible, but also because the resort to nuclear weapons by small states without apocalyptic effects could weaken the super-powers' own partly magical taboo on the use or aggressive threat of use of those weapons.

men think again about "safe ways" of using force, and the old habit of competing to acquire those very means that are today so hard to use rationally continues, in the hope that their acquisition would perpetuate the troubled sleep of terror.

All past international systems have been hierarchical. The present one has two faces—I hesitate to call them "real" and "apparent," since in a world where "real" power is more a nemesis than a reservoir, appearances become reality. One is the face of power in traditional terms of usable material assets: here, there is bipolarity and a hierarchy more stringent than ever. The other face is that of the very "polycentrism" due to the super-powers' relative impotence: a measure of equalization results both from the smaller states' capacity to promote fairly daring policies (as long, at least, as they refrain from the outright use of force) and from the super-powers' inability to impose their views on other nations (due partly to their rivalry, partly to the impossibility of using all their might in such cases). This second face, which is new, is good insofar as any kind of reduction of the force differential between the lions and the lesser breeds is a prerequisite to the transformation of the jungle into a society, but it is bad insofar as the multiplication of beasts on the loose is no guarantee of security and responsibility.

All past international systems have followed the model of the "state of war." Today, there is evidence of new state behavior in an otherwise traditional structure. States are still stopped by power imbalances and stalemates, and the United States deliberately acts to checkmate and to overpower its rivals' expansion, as Great Britain did in the past. But the fact that the deterring force is nuclear increases the unwillingness of the deterrer to use it, and the unwillingness of the deterred to test it. Whereas yesterday the state's imperative of self-enhancement operated against *external* forces that restrained it but rarely threatened the state's survival, today this imperative must compromise with an equally essential, "internalized" imperative of survival.

The originality of this situation is not sufficient by itself, however, to replace fragmentation with consensus, the absence of central power with central power: my need to take your survival into account does not mean willingness to accommodate you. Each state goes on seeing the world through its own glasses, each one wants to survive "best." So far, the main achievement has been the compression of force to low levels: there has been restrained competition, not community. So far, terror has been less terrifying in practice than either in the theory of inevitable hell, or in the theory of necessary burrows. But unless the risks entailed by the proliferation of nuclear weapons and the paradoxes of our present "stability" have a sobering effect on all, and if, on the contrary, the so-far successful management of terror lulls statesmen into complacency, then all the "great debates" might well end in the *Götterdämmerung* of a mismanaged confrontation.

NINE

THE SOUND AND THE FURY: THE SOCIAL SCIENTIST VERSUS WAR IN HISTORY

REVOLUTIONS MAY NOT BE "among the most recent of all major political data," but wars are indeed "among the oldest phenomena of the recorded past."[1] Crucial as revolutions have been in the life of most nations, they appear nevertheless like exceptional developments, avalanches that suddenly bury the road on which the travelers are moving. Wars, on the other hand, have blasted open many roads, and they have been constant companions to the travelers. Revolutions interrupt and transform the domestic polity; wars transform but also define the international milieu. Revolutions tear up the fabric of domestic law and order and inflict occasional wounds on the body politic. Wars are the seamless web and ceaseless wound in international relations.

Whoever studies the causes of war—as seen by political thinkers or revealed by history—and the place of war in international systems and foreign policy comes to contradictory conclusions, none of which is comforting. On the one hand, men's thoughts and

---

[1] Hannah Arendt, *On Revolution* (New York, 1963), p. 1.

actions prove that war is (or has been) a fire that almost anything (or any combination of things) can ignite and feed. Countless biological, psychological, material, and political factors can provoke war; countless elements of the international system, countless choices of foreign-policy goals and technological means can shape its contours. In all societies, conflicts break out because of scarcity—material often, psychological always. The world is not a world of plenty, it never appeases all fears, meets all needs, fulfills all desires. Even if goods became suddenly abundant and well distributed, power would remain a rare commodity, and mutual understanding would still be as unevenly distributed as common sense, Descartes notwithstanding. Among nations, conflict turns into war almost inevitably. For the contest between groups that feel themselves intensely different from one another and whose highest loyalty is to themselves prepares the ground for violence, and war is there to serve as an available method of action and outlet of passion, as an instrument in the calculation of gains, a carrier of the dreams and delusions of the great, the fears and faiths of the many. Scarcity and inequities in a fragmented world make war appear obvious. How many goals could never have been even sought if leaders and nations had not been able to use force? The game of power—part bluff, part blows—has always presupposed that the player could at some point use his power coercively.

On the other hand, if such is the fundamental cause of *war*, it is too general to serve as the explanation of *wars*. War has this air of fatality, but the study of the concrete causes of specific *wars* shows that this or that war was hardly inevitable, that it broke out only because someone behaved in a way that could have been different or prevented, or that it could have happened at another time, or with different effects. In a sense, every war could be called a miscarriage of diplomacy, as Aron called World War I, or an unnecessary war, as Churchill called World War II.

This contradiction has led students of war and history to ask three different but related questions. One is the question of freedom versus necessity: what margin of choice, what impact on events do men have in history? Are they merely the pawns of forces beyond their control? If so, are those forces compelling laws comparable to the laws of physics—*necessitá*—or are they the random manifestation of *fortuna*? Secondly, is there to be found in the historical record of wars what the French call a *sens*—a direction or pattern, and a meaning,—a way of making a particularly frequent, destructive, and cataclysmic form of human behavior intelligible, not merely by accounting for its causes, but also by finding in its unfolding and in its effects a logic, a convincing or compelling force that saves it from being mere sound and fury? (Were we to conclude that men are the tools of *necessitá*, we could perhaps find, not the ultimate *why* for those laws of destiny, but some principle of order comparable to that which governs the movements of planets; were we to conclude either that men are the victims of *fortuna* or that they are free agents, we might well find neither pattern nor meaning in their behavior.) Finally, what do the social scientist's methods contribute to the discussion of these problems? Are his tools helpful in coping with largely philosophical issues? The social scientist's daily work—the empirical study of social events—cannot but provoke such questions, unless social science dwindles to a mere compilation of small investigations, a mere sniffing of the ground with never as much as a glance at the sky. But does the social scientist have anything to contribute to the discussion of these problems? To be sure, any abstract answer to questions of philosophy runs the risk of being illusory, but perhaps the social scientist is condemned by the very nature of his work to stick to the ground, to see the distant sky but never to explore it, to raise questions but never to be able to answer them. What is at issue here is not only the famous gap between *is* and *ought*, but another gap between two kinds of *is*—one that can be empirically examined, and one that may well not.

II

One man has tried to answer these three questions—Tolstoy, in *War and Peace*. His starting point was, not the contradiction at the level of whole societies—between inevitable war and contingent wars—but the contradiction in the experience of the individual, between the evidence of necessity and the evidence of freedom. The evidence of necessity he demonstrates throughout the novel—when he shows the insignificance of the acts of minor individuals caught in the war, and in his frequent charges that the will and power of statesmen and generals are self-delusions, that the leaders' impact on events is remote and minute, that neither great men nor ideas nor rationally determined goals have the force to move peoples and shape history. Yet, there is also the indestructible consciousness of freedom, experienced by all men, and the notion of good and evil—moral responsibility—which comes from this awareness. Like Rousseau and Kant, Tolstoy has chosen to show in war the annihilation of man's freedom by history; but, where Rousseau insures the triumph of man's freedom by abolishing history, where Kant resorts to a philosophy of history in which Nature's hidden plan leads man to the realization of freedom and to peace, Tolstoy remains torn by the contradiction and incapable of finding a satisfactory resolution.

There are two attempts, not at resolution, but at accommodation. The first[2] is the opposition between individual life and gregarious "swarm-life"—between inner freedom, the freedom of will and action insofar as the actor alone is concerned, on the one hand, and the diminishment of freedom whenever our acts are tied to others, a diminishment tantamount to disappearance when the tie is that of great historical cataclysms such as wars, on the other. Here, Tolstoy proposes a kind of objective criterion: the magnitude of our connections with others. His second attempt[3] deals exclusively with the latter mode of being—man's life in history, man's behavior with others. Our study of history shows that both freedom and necessity operate, that every act *appears* partly free and partly determined. The key word here is "appears." The proportion of freedom or determinism depends *on the point of view*: the act appears more free if its link with the outside world appears not very close, if its distance in time is not very great, if its causes seem obscure; the act appears more determined if the ties in space, time, and causality appear clearly to us. Man's actions in history cannot be seen as totally free, for we cannot imagine man out of space, time, and causality. But man's actions cannot appear entirely determined, because we do not *know* the infinite number of conditions in space, the infinite period of historical duration, the infinite series of causes. The criterion here becomes much more subjective: acts *appear* free because we do not know the laws that govern men. Freedom is a vital force that we experience in our consciousness—a force comparable to weight or chemical affinity; but man acting in history is subject to laws, just as planets are, and his freedom cannot suspend those laws any more than celestial bodies can. The more distant man's actions are from the observer, the more visible are the laws.

Tolstoy's second answer thus seems to be: if we only knew the laws of history, we would recognize that freedom of action in history is an illusion—comparable to the illusion that the earth is

---

[2] *War and Peace*, tr. by Louise and Aylmer Maude (London, 1922–23), Book IX, chap. 1.

[3] *Ibid.*, second epilogue.

immobile. But he does not mean to say that empirical knowledge will provide the answer. Indeed, his novel is a long and telling attack on the methods of the social sciences insofar as they are concerned with causes. In terms comparable to Bergson's, as Sir Isaiah Berlin has said,[4] he shows the vanity of causal analysis: there are too many facts for it to be able to grasp them all; history is a flow that such analysis interrupts arbitrarily, and the causes thus discovered are always either tautological or ridiculously unequal to the events they supposedly explain. What the historian (or social scientist) should try to discover instead is laws comparable to those of physics; laws that tell us *how*, and give up *why*. Tolstoy's final answer to our three questions is: man's freedom-in-history is an illusion despite what our conscience says; there is a still undiscovered order in history, which is the order of necessity and whose meaning cannot be sought in causal terms (any more than it would make sense to ask, what is the meaning of the planets' movements); social sciences are useless unless they turn from the search for causes to the search for laws.

Berlin's analysis notwithstanding, there is fatalism and mysticism in such a vision. We are told that there is a pattern in history that we will discover only if we cease asking why. This assertion that man's actions in society are ruled by laws of necessity that are knowable yet not understandable is a philosophy. Its merit is to make us realize that every so-called scientific approach to the study of man and history is based on *a priori* assumptions. An approach that treats men as if they were planets, and societies as constellations, and that tries to define the peculiar laws of motion of the social universe is certainly plausible. Indeed, it has been followed by many contemporary social scientists. Tolstoy's advantage over them is that he was explicit about the underlying assumption of this approach—that these laws do not describe how man behaves in consequence of his own drives, interests, or ideas, but how man is moved by forces beyond his comprehension; they are not laws of manmade history, but laws of man's rape by history.

The approach I have advocated in these essays is of a different kind. It refuses to prejudge the issue of freedom *vs.* necessity; finding evidence of both, like Tolstoy, it avoids declaring in advance that the former is an illusion. Moreover, it believes that in human affairs necessity itself is of man's own *making*, although history may well be governed by forces beyond man's *control*. For there is a difference between a necessity imposed from without—by God,

[4] *The Hedgehog and the Fox* (New York, 1963).

Providence, Destiny, or Nature—capable of being recognized but destined to be revered (or detested) without comprehension, and a necessity due to man's moves without mastery, and a necessity that results from statistical regularities of human behavior, or from the capricious interplay of human intentions, or from the contrasts between intentions and results, or from the clash between wills and empirical (not mystical) forces, or from the irresistible effects of processes launched by men who are unaware of the ultimate consequences of their sorcery. Such contradictions, contests, and recurrences may well have been planned by God or Nature, but the working out of the plan can be accounted for in nonmystical terms—or at least we must try.

Precisely because of this conviction about man's part in the design, such an approach refuses to divorce the "why" from the "how" of human affairs. The laws of motion or behavior that we may seek or find are grounded in, and grow from, the realities and complexities of human nature as it unfolds in history. Any approach that focuses on the "how" exclusively, forgetting that men are political beings—i.e., beings in quest of ends—literally turns them into objects and drains all that is man's own contribution to history from the study of man in history. Thus, the final postulate beneath this approach is that "sociological determinism" is not of the same order as that which rules inanimate objects; its laws are more conditional and limited; their nature is altogether descriptive (like laws of physics), explanatory (in the sense of causal analysis), and comprehensive (in the Weberian sense of psychological understanding). Tolstoy starts with the assumption of a pattern. We begin with a concept that may well reveal there is no pattern.

III

Let us look first at the problems of *direction* and *meaning*. Without deciding whether men are free, or how free they are, do we find that the record of wars forms any pattern? Does any sense emerge from it?

Historians and social scientists have tried hard to discover patterns. When one looks for curves and lines, for recurrences and cycles, one tends to find them! And yet, the findings have not been impressive.[5] First, the various workers have not labored in the same vineyard: some have looked at civilizations, others at nations; some have dealt with large-scale violence, others with crises of all kinds

[5] See Raymond Aron, *Paix et Guerre entre les Nations*, chap. 11.

and sizes. Moreover, not a single one of their terms of reference is beyond dispute: in Toynbee's case, the concept of civilization obscures the fact that some of the worst violence in the record of mankind has erupted between rival or hostile units within the same civilization; even if it be true that every time of troubles is followed by the rise of a universal empire, it makes a difference whether the time is long or short, and whether the empire emerges from within or has been imposed from without. It may well be, as Kant prophesied, that men are being dragged to peace through ever-worsening wars, but the record of the wars shows neither a straight line from primitive warfare to modern total war (if our means of annihilation have become more sophisticated, it is also true that the number of civilizations or units annihilated by our cruder forebears is not exactly unimpressive) nor recurrent cycles of limited and unlimited wars. There may be *partial* orders—certain types of international configurations that can be shown to result in certain types of wars—but there is no discernible over-all order that dictates the succession of the partial ones. The search for a *sens,* meaning a direction, leads to a blind alley if applied to the whole of history. This does not mean that directions cannot be found in parts of the record—especially since the advent of industrial society, but here we do not yet know to what kind of a turning or terminal point the road leads.

So we must turn to the difficult problem of meaning. The obvious question is: meaning for whom? There is a primary distinction between the social scientist who observes and reflects on the record, but is, so to speak, *outside,* detached from it, and the historical actor caught *in* it. Also, there are different perspectives for different kinds of actors. One is the perspective of the private individual—the cog in the machine Tolstoy described. One is that of the society as a whole—the agglomeration of men living a common history, shaken by war's tempest. One is that of the leader who supposedly makes the decisions. The social scientist confronted with the problem of the meaning of war must ask his questions at all three levels, and each time he must distinguish between the meaning of war for the actor and the meaning for himself, when (retrospectively) he reflects upon the record from the angle the actor had occupied. It might be asked whether the social scientist can do all this. The answer is that he must. A comprehensive social science cannot avoid taking into account the meaning the action had for the actors. A social scientist who seeks to understand cannot but be a humanist concerned with man's fate, a historian concerned with the evolution of societies, and a specialist of international relations studying the behavior of competing units.

From the angle of the individual, the social scientist can hardly fail to see history as a graveyard of men, buried after having killed and been killed for an incredible number of causes. Retrospectively, it is hard to find a meaning here—and easy to lament with so many poets the absurdity of the whole story. Has there been a single cause for which men died that did not collapse despite their sacrifices or that did not oppress men despite their aspirations? Was there a single cause that was worthy of the sufferings it inflicted? It is easy, on the grand scale, to sympathize with the pacifist's sermon or to acquiesce in Brechtian cynicism. If one is a philosopher of progress who sees in the gradual mastery of man over his environment and in the unfolding of his freedom the true meaning of history, he must admit that this meaning was not easily revealed to the individuals who made that history; the disproportion between the brief span of man's life and the rewards in freedom's progress is obvious, and so are the countless tours and detours on a road that was anything but straight, anything but continually ascending. Consequently, Camus' precept—do not sacrifice man today to an uncertain tomorrow—has a certain force. Even if the end of the adventure were peace and freedom for all, the story would have been long and bloody enough to make of this final meaning a rather belated consolation. For the individual who died in dubious battle in, say, 413 B.C., the ultimate meaning of man's sufferings will be revealed too late—especially since we do not know what the end of the adventure will be, and since we do know that it might be annihilation.

On the other hand, while the social scientist *qua* humanist finds the meaning of the record both clouded and grim, the men whose acts and deaths composed this record did not, on the whole, find their conduct meaningless. It is our retrospective knowledge of the sequence of events that makes their behavior appear absurd; but the actors—perhaps misled, perhaps for foolish reasons—did not behave as if they were pawns of fate or hostages of a blind and bloodthirsty destiny. The pacifist (and the Brechtian) are "lucid" because they stand outside. But the meaning men have given to what seems senseless to the outsider is precisely what the outsider cannot grasp: it is the assertion of solidarity with one's fellow men, of one's own community, and the conviction, which is acted on, that there is no such solidarity without sacrifice. In this light, as

Philip Rieff has seen,[6] war is not only the sudden outlet of barbaric impulses repressed by society and state in ordinary times, but the outcome of man's identification with his society and state; what is denounced as regression or repression by the psychologist (standing outside) is experienced by the citizen as the price to be paid for the moral and psychological gains he owes to society, for the preservation of a community in which alone he feels able to fulfill himself. The state may well be the Pied Piper of death, but pied pipers succeed only because of the bonds of affection and loyalty that tie their followers to them. Therefore, whoever stands outside and denounces is in an ambiguous position: he places an absolute moral standard—respect for life, for instance—above his own group. With the benefit of hindsight, we always tend to celebrate Antigone; only her purity, it seems, can redeem the crimes committed on behalf of communities or factions that come and go. And yet we should be careful, for if we praise her too highly, we condemn not only Creon but all those who thought that Creon's cause was worthy of support. A certain moral blindness accompanies the assertion of solidarity that carries men to wars, but denial of solidarity on behalf of peace or life has a certain moral arrogance.

Thus, at the level of the individual, two conclusions emerge. The meaning of his acts is *ambiguous*, because of the contrast between the sense he had intended them to have and the results, which so often deride the hopes and debunk the faith that animated him. Also, the meaning of his acts is *tragic*, because they show that once the feeling of community reaches a certain degree of intensity—the degree of heat that sets off the explosion, war—this feeling demands two kinds of atrocities: it expresses itself at the expense of other communities (solidarity with one's group is affirmed at the expense of mankind), and it requires the sacrifice of its champions.

The dose of tragedy has considerably increased in this century. Modern total war, which distinguishes itself from past general wars both in the material means at the disposal of the combatants and in the involvement of whole populations not merely as potential *victims* (as often before in history) but as emotionally and actively mobilized *participants*, assures that the rival assertions of solidarity will inflict on mankind sufferings far more hideous than in many past centuries, and that the loyalty of the citizen to his community will be inseparable from a heavy load of guilt. In modern total war, where murder without risks, slaughter in anonymity,

[6] *Freud: The Mind of the Moralist* (New York, 1961) p. 273.

and the denial of the humanity of the foe prevail, the sacrifices of conscience which national loyalty demands have reached a new high. The range of crimes that the notion of just war is supposed to cover and legitimize is such that the justification itself stands exposed. Should total war be succeeded by nuclear war on a large scale, tragedy would be accompanied not merely by ambiguity, but by *absurdity* pure and simple. The meaning war had for the individual in the days when annihilation was only one possible outcome of the hazards of battle would disappear if total destruction were certain; and the meaning war had even when the annihilation of the community through battle was certain—a meaning found in the hope that the future would somehow redress and vindicate the horrors of the present—would disappear if the future itself became uncertain. War would have meaning only for those who saw in the joys and sorrows of this life a mere prelude to immortality after death—i.e., for those who find in this earth no autonomous meaning at all. The prospect of nuclear war throws light on Hobbes' philosophy. The meaning of war, and death in war, for generations of individuals, was found in the principle of community. If communities act so as to condemn themselves to certain obliteration, what except the force of habit and the constraints of force keeps the individual tied to his polity? The solidarity in nuclear death of men from conflicting communities would *ipso facto* dissolve national solidarity.

Let us move on to the next level: that of societies. Here, ambiguity marks both the judgment of the detached historian who surveys the record, and the experiences of the various societies that have come and gone through history. The historian sees war as a capricious but unextinguished fire whose flames both consume and weld. On the one hand, the record of chaos is almost overwhelming: whole civilizations have been annihilated by conquest. (Here again, there is contrast between intentions and behavior, or between behavior and results. The most pacific societies, whose social philosophies and organization shun war, are not always the most moderate when war comes; they are capable of fighting with utmost ruthlessness in order, so they think, to wipe war from history. Military societies, such as Sparta, are not always the more destructive ones.) And yet, chaos is not the final word: there is meaning in the madness. If history shows any (partial) directions at all, it is war that burns open a way. The meaning of war is to be found in its *historical* functions. Through war, the basic types of polities have appeared and disappeared, regimes have been established and destroyed, techniques and ideas have spread, the balance of power has been maintained and has broken down within the international system, world politics has moved from one system to the other. In other words, war has often brought the answers to the fundamental problems of politics. In carrying out those tasks, war has acted as the twin of revolution and as both the client and foe of commerce or technology; war has developed new tools for peacetime industry and trade, and technology has in turn provided war with new means.

The ambiguity experienced by societies that have gone through the trials of war are of a different kind. It results not from a contradiction between meaningless chaos and meaningful historical functions, but from the equivocal way in which the *social* functions of war—that is, the functions societies expect war to perform for them—are actually carried out, from the possible discrepancy between hope and outcome.[7] Sometimes wars stabilize and integrate a society; sometimes they disrupt it, paving the way either for upheavals at the center or for secessions or mergers. Sometimes, wars bring gains—through the defeat of the enemy—or help to avoid losses; sometimes wars bring gains to the enemy and losses or frustrations to oneself. Sometimes, the social function of war is to bring about the extermination of a hated foe; sometimes, hatred leads to one's own extermination. Also, the social and the historical functions of war often operate in contradiction: a war that stabilizes a society may also delay a necessary diffusion of ideas or techniques; a war that performs the latter may do so only by inflicting grievous losses on or by disintegrating a society.

Once more, tragedy is inseparable from ambiguity. In the past, it lay in the fact that the benefits of change—the spread of civilization, the destruction of frozen or obsolete patterns of culture—had to come through violence and the splintering of civilization. It lay also in the contrasts between expectations and results. Today, the tragedy lies first of all in the autonomous growth of the means of war. The total wars of this century have already taught us three sinister lessons: the prevalence of dislocation over integration; the predominance of the function of extermination over the functions of agonistic and instrumental wars; the militarization of peacetime life in preparation for war. That is, they have brought us the reversal of the situation Hegel deemed usual—a relaxation of social ties in peacetime and a return to integration in war. If we cross the line

[7] See Hans Speier, *The Social Order and the Risks of War* (Cambridge, Mass., 1964).

from total war to nuclear war, tragedy will triumph and meaning collapse. War, the great force of change, would then transform change into end. Tragedy today lies also in the contrast between the fact that those new means have deprived large-scale war of much of its historical function, and the fact that the social functions of war have not disappeared. The great historical changes listed above take place presently either without violence, through the domestic acts and efforts of the units, or through revolutionary violence, in which war is an adjunct. In other words, domestic processes of change have largely displaced inter-state war. But agonistic war, whose function is the integration of a unit, has rarely been felt to be more functional than in a world full of inchoate nations; if wars for profit have largely ceased to pay, there remain many other goals for which war may be thought instrumental; even a war of extermination can be deemed functional if one can hope, by striking first, to get rid of a hated and threatening foe while avoiding punishment. Thus, we live in a world in which only total nuclear war appears clearly dysfunctional to the observer as well as to societies but in which other kinds of wars are still perceived as functional by various societies. Moreover, war is being "internalized" through the permanent preparation of deterrence as well as through the substitution of revolutionary wars for classical war. In the final analysis, a limited war deemed socially functional, and war "internalized" by contemporary history can always become precisely the kind of war that has no other function but the destruction of meaning: nuclear war.

Let us reach the third and last level: the behavior of the competing units. Here, the problem is posed in terms the reverse of those we saw at the level of the individual. For the social scientist, there seems to be clear meaning. He studies the contests of units in a state of nature, but it is a state of nature profoundly different in one respect from that of the philosophers. In the latter, violence was either absent (Rousseau) or, more usually, the result of the absence of civil society (Hobbes, Locke, Montesquieu, Kant); i.e., violence was asocial. In the international state of nature (as in Rousseau's *de facto* society), violence is the direct consequence of civil society. It is both asocial in that it marks the absence of a general society of mankind, and social insofar as it is one of the instruments available to the units, one of the elements of their calculations and policies. For the specialist in international relations, the meaning of war is inseparable from that of the international competition itself. War has meaning because the competition itself has one—it has its own logic (which, as Clausewitz recognized, is also the logic of war), that of a clash of ambitions expressed in antagonistic policies. Thus, war derives its meaning both from the nature of the Policy that entailed it—the kinds of *visions* pursued by the statesmen, the types of *objectives* set by them in accordance with their visions, the kinds of courses of action (or *policies*) selected in order to reach the objectives, the elements of *power* available—and from the nature of the international system.

For the leaders of the units in an international system, the experience is much more ambiguous. On the one hand, they find war an available and useful tool in a game that has its rules and its institutions. Literally, they have never had the choice that detached observers (philosophers or moralists, psychologists or plain men of good will) sometimes assume they enjoyed—the choice between conflict and joint subordination to a common higher goal. The choice they experience is between satisfaction of their respective goals and frustration; between self-assertion and subservience. Thus, the ultimate frame of reference for action and justification remains the separate polity, and war becomes a meaningful "option"—especially since there are procedures and mechanisms of restraint or moderation that can make what is useful to one actor bearable to all. But, on the other hand, the very indeterminacy of the international competition makes this regulated and patterned state of nature not so different after all from the state of nature described by the philosophers: each participant lives in insecurity, makes his decisions on the basis of judgments that are gambles rather than predictions, and perpetuates through his own actions the vicious circle of risks and uncertainty. To the participant, the system is at the same time a "given," a challenge, and a mystery; the shaping of his own policy is an alchemical procedure that tries to take into account not only the system outside, but the capabilities, the political and social pattern of power, and the political culture within—not in order to "balance" them all but in order to reach goals. It thus resembles a shot in the dark, more than a keeping of accounts. The meaning will become clear only after the participant is through playing the game; whether he was right to play the way he did, whether he did well by exercising or renouncing the option of war, whether he improved his nation's lot or not, or even whether the long-term effects of a temporary improvement were good or bad is rarely clear at once. Thus, meaning for the actor remains doubly ambiguous—in part because of the gap between expectations and achievements in the leader's own time span, in part because the game is not over.

Tragedy, once more, goes hand in hand with ambiguity. In the past, the rules and institutions of the international competition served only to perpetuate the divisions of mankind from which the competition sprang—as if Sisyphus had found a way of introducing the maximum of variety and suspense into his athletic activity, while carefully preserving its harrowing nature. In this century, social scientists and participants alike have noticed that the costs of the game have risen, that efforts to make it more tolerable have failed, and that the new means of war have loaded the actor's balance of calculability and uncertainty toward the latter. Total war has carried tragedy to its highest historical peak. What is this total war, if not "absolute war" that represents both the essence of war (according to Clausewitz) and the spectacular denial of his assertion that war has its own grammar but not its own logic? What is total war, if not the self-destruction of the rules and institutions of the game, a technological Frankenstein that subordinates political calculations to military necessities, a vampire that injects public passions into the body politic until political calculations disappear altogether, a minotaur that obliges leaders to make choices that exceed the possibilities of ethical calculations? Today, political leaders live and act on the brink of the kind of total war that would compound tragedy with absurdity. Political and moral calculations would be flushed out completely once a certain level of intensity is reached. Statesmanship would lose its meaning in large-scale nuclear war: no political goals could be achieved; nor would moral action, which supposes not only restraints on the ends but also restraints on the means of action, remain possible. The statesman's life at the brink of nuclear war is life in tragedy and on the verge of absurdity; his continuing reliance on force, justified by the need to survive, makes sense only if deterrence works and would destroy the actor as well as the game if the gamble should fail. If war becomes the master of those who once saw it as a tool, the meaning of the game is lost. For the first time, the basic postulate of the game—that there will be a victor or a survivor to go on playing—is threatened. Either the leader will make of the state of nature a thoroughly asocial scene of total carnage, or else war will have to be tamed, and the scene will become far more social than before.

Thus, our conclusion is the same at all levels: the meaning of war is both ambiguous and tragic, and mankind has entered a phase where tragedy may blot out meaning. There will be meaning only if the tragic element in war is somehow reduced, if war is limited far below the scope it has already reached in this century. The question to which this assertion leads is as obvious as the assertion itself: are individuals, societies, leaders really able to master their fate? What are man's powers to act? We are back at the problem of freedom versus necessity.

IV

We are concerned here with man's freedom in his relations with others, with his capacity to act on others. Two different aspects of this freedom are of interest. One is a negative element: the degree of *indeterminacy*. A man is free if the different pressures that weigh on him, coming either from within his own personality or from the environment, are not so powerful as to annihilate his margin of choice, to dictate his behavior, to permit him the plea "I had no alternative." Indeterminacy is only a prerequisite of freedom; it is not to be mistaken for the exercise of freedom. However, not any such exercise can be seen as evidence of man's ability to shape events. For a second element, of positive character, must be taken into account: the *capacity to act effectively*, i.e., to choose among alternatives in such a way as to influence others. Indeterminacy requires that the causal network not be compelling for us; the capacity to act effectively requires that we be sufficiently in control of that network to be able to affect others. Man-in-history cannot be called free if the necessity that closes off his choice is a determinism of any kind, or if fortune (the interplay of forces beyond his control) deprives his acts of effects. The citizen of *The Social Contract* is free, both because he finds his law in himself alone and because this law of his (higher) self is the operative law of the community; in a corrupt state, the citizen who would follow the same law would have no real impact on public events and cannot be called a free citizen. (Indeed, his conscience will be torn between his inner law and the law of the corrupt polity.) He will be free only insofar as he restricts the circle of his acts and involvements to the area in which he can be effective; this is what *Émile* demonstrates.

If one accepts this distinction, then the problem of freedom in history becomes a matter not of point of view but of degree. And the detailed investigation of the degree of freedom becomes one of the chief, if not the chief, functions of the social sciences. Consequently, any generalization is bound to be misleading, even if it is limited to one sector of reality. Here, we are concerned with man's freedom in the realm of war. Two generalizations can be presented, with due awareness of their flaws.

The first one concerns the difference in the margin of freedom enjoyed by effective units in international relations—i.e., the political leaders—on the one hand, and that enjoyed by the individuals within those units on the other. On the whole, the margin is greater for the former. The exact amount of freedom at the leaders' disposal varies enormously, of course, depending on a broad range of concrete circumstances such as the geographical position of the unit in the system, the nature of the constellation of outside forces, the level and quality of consensus and support within, the amount of power available, etc. Sometimes, those data conspire to produce a situation that is almost entirely determined, in which all the vital decisions are made elsewhere; thus, Poland at the time of the partitions, or Denmark or Belgium in 1940. And yet, complete determinism is rare: the Poles, the Danes, or the Belgians could do nothing about avoiding invasion, but they could still choose between giving in without a fight and fighting the invader despite the outcome. Even within a narrow margin of indeterminacy, there remain possibilities for choice.

Here we must look at the second element. Is this choice capable of influencing events at all? In a situation of almost complete determinism, there may still be a significant capacity to act effectively, precisely because the game is played over long periods of time. Poland, closed in, has no freedom to prevent partition. But the choice between submission and resistance, while not affecting the immediate outcome, may affect a more distant future: submission may spare the inhabitants, resistance may facilitate revenge and compensations if fortune changes. When the margin of indeterminacy shrinks, the statesman's duty to find a way of affecting the future—and his definition of the way—become primordial.

Conversely, there may be situations of considerable indeterminacy, in which the forces outside and inside are complex enough to leave the statesman a great number of possibilities of maneuver; yet whatever course he chooses, he may find himself unable to leave a deep mark on events, to make events conform to his desires, or to make others follow his directions. This may happen either because of accidents, because others are even more skillful in using the same underlying forces so as to thwart his designs, or because trends that were not compelling enough *at the time* to rule out a certain choice are nevertheless *in the long run* irresistible enough to deprive this choice of any efficiency. Thus, Metternich was free to take measures to repress various nationalisms, but ultimately nationalism annihilated a good part of his work. Precisely because of the fundamental indeterminacy of the game, the statesman's most frequent problem is not so much the constraint that precedes and commands his decision, but the caprices of the contest that deprive him of control of the consequences of his decision. The very indeterminacy that leaves him with his options may deprive his choice of success.

The leader's freedom of action is to a large extent a function of his skill. The skillful leader is one who exploits the uncertainties that remain after all the constraints defining his situation have been measured, and either imposes on the uncertainties the consequences of his own choice, or at least exploits in his favor those probabilities that emerge amidst them. The bad leader is one who unleashes events beyond all reasonable hopes of control or who loses control over events that were within reasonable possibilities of control—i.e., a Mussolini or a Daladier—and thus needlessly sacrifices the capacity to act effectively. The drama of a Napoleon or a Hitler is not that their heady assertions of will and power were mere delusions, as Tolstoy stated, but that after a period of real and considerable freedom in which they manipulated constraints and dominated events, their *hubris* made them lose their mastery over the scene, thus creating constraints that reduced to nothing both their final margin of indeterminacy and their capacity to affect others.

If we look at the case of individuals, we find that both elements of freedom are reduced even more, although, of course, the degree varies. Even in a modern democratic state, the range of indeterminacy for the citizen is narrow. The state is organized so that only occasionally is the citizen called on to express himself—i.e., to act on matters of public concern. Society is organized so that it lets its members make choices much more easily along the lines of their professional specialization—*qua* workers, farmers, lawyers, teachers, etc.—than as citizens; paradoxically, it is when the state is in crisis that they tend to regain some freedom of choice as citizens and that politics regains its primacy.

If the constraints of society and the compelling apparatus of the state manage almost everywhere and always to reduce the freedom of choice of the citizen almost to naught, the capacity to act effectively is also limited. The citizens of various states are not primary actors on the international stage; they can influence inter-state events only insofar as they can control events within their own societies, insofar as they have an impact on their own leaders. Freedom for the citizens depends ultimately on the degree of democracy of their state. But democracy, a necessary condition, is not a sufficient one; one can influence events only if one has some mastery over them, and the trouble is that the public's expertise in international affairs is small. As a result, either its wishes will be disregarded by leaders who want to remain in control, or it will leave full responsibility to the leaders, more or less enthusiastically, or else, when the leaders let themselves be guided, the result will likely be the nation's loss of control, with disastrous results for all. For even when the desiderata of one's public govern one's own actions, they are without impact on, and all too easily exploitable by, other players in the game.

Another generalization would distinguish between time of peace and time of war. For both the state and the individual, the circle of freedom narrows during war. The state's area of indeterminacy shrinks because the resort to war entails a fully coercive use of power—the one use that requires the mobilization of most of the state's material assets. A war thus introduces both an almost tangible limit to what the state can hope to accomplish (although, of course, a skillful leadership can find ways of stretching the limits) and an almost categorical imperative (the subordination of most, if not all, of its other objectives to the one goal or set of goals for which the war is fought). Thus in wartime, the area of indeterminacy tends to be defined by the state's power. But the capacity to act effectively, while heavily dependent on such power, remains separate; what reduces it here is the hazard of battles. The paradox of war is that states often resort to arms because they see in it the only effective way of shaping events according to their ambitions or needs, and yet this very resort submits them to uncertainties far greater than those of the peacetime contest of wills. They are like men anxious for gain, tired of the slow, fluctuating ways of making an honest living, who decide to gamble in order to get rich fast. It is not surprising both that statesmen should find more advantages in brinkmanship—in wielding the threat of war after having put themselves in advantageous positions—than in the actual execution of the threat, unless the advantages are so clear as to reduce the uncertainties to the utmost.

For the individual, the difference between peace and war is not just the difference between more and less liberty, but the contrast between some and none. The mobilized citizen is under a constraint that few are strong enough to resist; those who do are barely capable of influencing events. The soldier's capacity to affect events reveals another paradox: whereas he loses practically all freedom to shape his own fate *qua* individual, he retains a certain capacity to affect his nation-state—not *qua* individual, but as a spare part in the machine of the state, as an instrument of the nation's policy. The advent of war means a divorce between one's private personality, temporarily repressed or suppressed, and one's vicarious public personality as the servant of a community on behalf of which one commits acts that one would never conceive of as a private man.

If these statements are correct as generalizations, then certain lessons emerge, which bring together what we have said about freedom and about meaning. For the state, the temporary decline of freedom brought on by war appears tolerable either when a gain is expected thereby or when the alternatives appear worse—i.e., in a situation of acute constraints or one in which influencing the immediate course of events appears impossible but in which war has at least the symbolic merit of indicating one's commitment to certain values or possessions. For the individual, the temporary loss of freedom is accepted not merely because there is usually no alternative, but also because of solidarity with the community, because of the process of identification with the nation that war sets in motion. The decline or loss of freedom are justified by the meaning—however ambiguous—that war possesses.

But this raises again the problem of total nuclear war. Along with meaning, nuclear war would annihilate what is left of freedom; it is clear that past a certain threshold, no state could in any way control events. The total wars of this century extended to all individuals the deprivation of freedom once reserved to those who were actually mobilized, and they curtailed the capacity of effective action not only for the vanquished but for most of the victors too. The victors of World War II could still justify this submission to the hazards and horrors of "hyperbolic war" in the terms mentioned above—the gains made by the Soviet Union, the losses avoided by the Western Allies that chose to fight Hitler. But those arguments collapse when gains are no longer to be expected, or when the alternative to such losses is annihilation. As for the individual, the price of group solidarity now means not merely the loss of freedom and the possibility of death, but the possibility of death for all.[8] It is not surprising if statesmen and strategists, un-

[8] See Hans Morgenthau, "Death in the Nuclear Age," *Commentary* (September, 1961), pp. 231–34.

sure of the self-atrophy of war in a world that is seething with conflicts, desperately try to find ways of preserving a modicum of control, so as to assure both a margin of freedom at least to the statesmen, and a minimum of meaning to the rulers and the ruled. Far from deserving the scathing invectives of perfectionists and utopians, always prompt to assume that nations (and nationals) have far more control over the game than is actually the case, such efforts deserve the highest praise. And yet, the very uncertainty that makes war still possible also decreases the chances of control once it comes. Those exercises in abstract limitation which assume that moderation, flexibility, rational calculation will still be conceivable below a very high threshold of violence have simply ignored the lessons of past total wars. The preservation of meaning and (some) freedom requires efforts to control war, if war comes; but the very difficulties of control in a world such as this require that those efforts aim (in addition to deterrence) at keeping the level of violence much lower than it has been in the recent past.

V

The uses and the limits of social science in helping us to understand issues such as the meaning of war and the freedom of the actors are familiar and obvious. In many ways, Tolstoy's attack was justified. Social science, however hard it tries to appear not to do so, does rely on causal analysis: even a "systems" science entirely expressed in a few mathematical formulas describing interactions would still be based on causal postulates, not necessarily sounder for being implicit. The dilemma remains the same: single-cause analysis is invalid, multiple causation is valid but too complex for scientific treatment, since it is not possible to follow in all their meanderings the interrelations among a large number of factors. Consequently, the best social science can do, in dealing with a problem such as war, is to accomplish a double, and doubly modest, task. On the one hand, it can show (and certainly it should never conceal) the limits of our knowledge. On the other hand, it can provide tools for the analysis of concrete situations. For instance, it can provide concepts for the study of both international systems and foreign policy; but, before any generalization can be made about the interaction of these two—one of the key problems in international relations—there must be many more case-by-case analyses. In the meantime, our generalizations can be no more than still untested hypotheses.

Even after such analyses have multiplied, and our concepts and schemes have been sharpened, we should not expect to be able to answer definitely why a certain war, why certain types of wars, happened when they did. As A. J. P. Taylor has shown in a brilliant passage of his most perverse book,[9] the social scientist's definition of the hierarchy of causes cannot but be largely subjective, precisely because there are so many causes at work and because one's ranking depends in part on the framework of one's study (is it of the immediate origins, does it go far back in time?), in part on the specific questions one tries to answer. Consequently, many different readings of the same reality are possible. Even if all historians agreed on the facts, they would still disagree on the respective weight of these facts; in the act of "imaginative reconstruction" that any causal analysis performs, assessments of motivation and causal efficiency vary considerably. What social science can do is show how the logic of human drives, ideas, impersonal forces, state calculations and reactions, leaders' personalities in a certain milieu —how all these made the resort to war as instrument, outlet, or outcome likely. More it cannot do, because reality itself does not lend itself to greater certainty. Social reality, to use Aron's distinction,[10] contains a part of necessity (such as, to borrow his own example, the development of industrialization), and this explains why reality is not so thoroughly unstructured that any reading of the record has surface plausibility. It also contains a part of human action, which can give to those irresistible processes any number of delays or accelerations, distortions or embellishments. The part of necessity gives us a minimum of certainty and predictability—but only a minimum, because its certainties are of a very general long-term order and the predictions we need most are those that are concerned with the field of human action, i.e., with the realm of uncertainty. The field of human action will always contain a heavy dose of mystery: both because interactions (especially in crises) have a chemistry of their own that would remain elusive even if we knew much more about the decisions made by the various players, and because those decisions themselves (especially under pressure, and especially when they are collective) always preserve a margin of contingency. The task of social science cannot be to dispel entirely a mystery that is part of human thought and life; it can

[9] *The Origins of the Second World War* (Greenwich, Conn., 1963), p. 102.
[10] *The Dawn of Universal History* (New York, 1961).

surround the mystery, but it must stop when the story it tells is probable or plausible.

Those who are disappointed with such modest accomplishments are often philosophers of history, avowed—like Tolstoy—or in disguise, like many contemporary heirs of a Comtean *scientisme* that tries to reduce the sum total of human activity to a set of laws. The trouble with social reality is that it obstinately refuses to support any such philosophy or science. There are trends, to be sure, but any interpretation of reality that retains only those trends, and decrees that they constitute *the* meaning of history is an arbitrary one that gives a privileged position to one portion of the truth on the basis of philosophical predilections. But if the record frustrates the philosophers of history, it need not discourage the philosophers. Although social science invariably shows that utopias cannot be achieved, that attempts to bring the city of heaven to earth lead to the strangest aberrations, that courses of action advocated *in abstracto* entail in reality risks, costs, and bad (or unintended) results inseparable from their benefits, it shows something else too: the very uncertainties of social reality that so often thwart our ambitions indicate also that there *is* room for action; the very ambiguities that mark the meaning of our conduct also signify that we can try to give it meaning, and even the basic forces that belong to the realm of necessity—industrialization, nuclear weapons—provide mankind with opportunities, not merely with risks and losses.

Moreover, although the gap between "is" and "ought" remains as obvious as ever, we seem to have reached a point in history where the "is" does dictate, if not an "ought," at least an "ought not." The conclusion we reach from a study of the record is that there will be no more record unless total nuclear war is avoided. The "counsels of wisdom" that follow from social science are twins of the philosophers' imperatives: peace, or at least the avoidance of all-out war, is the prerequisite for freedom and the prerequisite for a continuation of history; it is the condition without which men will have no chance to give their history any meaning at all. Social science tells us no more than that; it does not tell us with any degree of certainty what the safest way of avoiding nuclear war is, or what the chances for peace are if other forms of war persist and proliferate, or whether all-out nuclear war could still be prevented once a "controlled" nuclear war started. Nor does it tell us that the imperative of peace will be heeded.

And so, the tension between ambiguous history and the dictates of conscience, between facts that show the costs and clashes of values in society, and values that clamor for fulfillment in history, goes on. In the nuclear age, Sisyphus is caught between the threat of annihilation, which would retrospectively make his long contest with the gods meaningless, and the uncertainty that continues to mark his attempts to prevent the rock from crushing him at last. Mankind is caught between awareness of the meaninglessness of all-out nuclear war, the tragic ambiguities that would continue if politics-as-usual led to war-as-usual, and hope in the germ of a conviction that the avoidance of large-scale war is an imperative for each and all. International law, which bans the use of force as an instrument of policy, is obviously well ahead of the facts. But if the conviction grows, it may not be foolish to hope that the facts may slowly (no doubt deviously) move in the direction of the law; that is also the direction of the philosophers' most pressing imperative. It is certainly not foolish to work toward this end.

Politics has been the ambiguous art of conflict as well as of cooperation. Domestic politics has subordinated the former to the latter, and although the deprecators of violence forget too easily that many of mankind's achievements have been obtained through violence, it becomes impossible to justify or sanctify violence when the balance of gains and losses clearly leans to disaster. A world without large-scale violence may well not be a world of justice; as long as rival units with a common history but no common cause remain the highest possessors of power, even a world without major wars will still, for all its advances in the direction of society, be one of conflict, profoundly different from most domestic polities. But given our state of suspense between the probability of continuing injustice and hostility in a world without major war, given the difficulty of even reaching such a stage—when the proliferation of nuclear weapons continues and there is no sure way of limiting their spread—given the quasi-certainty of annihilation, if the future resembles the not so distant past, our duty is to use whatever freedom we have so as to avoid that annihilation, overcome the clear and present peril, and reach at last a world without major war. Prometheus will be rid of the vultures only if he returns the fire to the gods.